Hedy Lamarr

Screen Classics

Screen Classics is a series of critical biographies, film histories, and analytical studies focusing on neglected filmmakers and important screen artists and subjects, from the era of silent cinema to the golden age of Hollywood to the international generation of today. Books in the Screen Classics series are intended for scholars and general readers alike. The contributing authors are established figures in their respective fields. This series also serves the purpose of advancing scholarship on film personalities and themes with ties to Kentucky.

SERIES EDITOR
Patrick McGilligan

BOOKS IN THE SERIES

Von Sternberg
John Baxter

The Marxist and the Movies: A Biography of Paul Jarrico
Larry Ceplair

Warren Oates: A Wild Life
Susan Compo

Being Hal Ashby: Life of a Hollywood Rebel
Nick Dawson

Some Like It Wilder: The Life and Controversial Films of Billy Wilder
Gene D. Phillips

Claude Rains: An Actor's Voice
David J. Skal with Jessica Rains

Buzz: The Life and Art of Busby Berkeley
Jeffrey Spivak

Hedy Lamarr

The Most Beautiful Woman in Film

Ruth Barton

THE UNIVERSITY PRESS OF KENTUCKY

Scholarly publisher for the Commonwealth,
serving Bellarmine University, Berea College, Centre
College of Kentucky, Eastern Kentucky University,
The Filson Historical Society, Georgetown College,
Kentucky Historical Society, Kentucky State University,
Morehead State University, Murray State University,
Northern Kentucky University, Transylvania University,
University of Kentucky, University of Louisville,
and Western Kentucky University.
All rights reserved.

Editorial and Sales Offices: The University Press of Kentucky
663 South Limestone Street, Lexington, Kentucky 40508-4008
www.kentuckypress.com

14 13 12 11 10   5 4 3 2 1

Library of Congress Cataloging-in-Publication Data

Barton, Ruth.
    Hedy Lamarr : the most beautiful woman in film / Ruth Barton.
        p. cm.—(Screen classics)
    Includes bibliographical references and index.
    ISBN 978-0-8131-2604-3 (hardcover : alk. paper)   1. Lamarr, Hedy,
1913–2000.   2. Actors—United States—Biography.   I. Title.
    PN2287.L24B37 2010
    791.430'28092—dc22
    [B]

                                                    2010013914

This book is printed on acid-free recycled paper meeting
the requirements of the American National Standard
for Permanence in Paper for Printed Library Materials.

Manufactured in the United States of America.

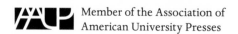

Member of the Association of
American University Presses

For Willie, Conal, Eoin, and Paddy

Contents

Illustrations follow page 94

Acknowledgments

Without the persistent advice and encouragement of Patrick McGilligan, this book would never have been finished. I would also like to thank the University Press of Kentucky—Leila Salisbury and Anne Dean Watkins and my anonymous readers—for their many and helpful comments along the way. I am particularly grateful to Chris Horak, without whose advice this would have been a lesser book; I haven't acknowledged his interventions on every occasion but they are threaded through everything I have written. Like everyone who has ever conducted archival research, I am indebted to the expertise of librarians. For their generous assistance, I wish to thank Ned Comstock at USC Special Collections and the staff at the Columbia University Archives, Margaret Herrick Library, Kiesler Stiftung Wien, New York Public Library, the UCLA and USC archives, and the Wien Bibliothek. Most of all, I would like to thank Rick Berg at USC for his enthusiasm, comments, and DVDs.

Many others also helped with answers to personal queries and assistance with research. Special thanks to Charles Amirkhanian; Marie-Theres Arnbom; Susanne Bach; Thomas Balhausen; Marlis Schmidt and Peter Spiegel, Austrian Film Archive Vienna; Matthew Bernstein; Christian Cargnelli; Kathleen Choo, Seminole County Library; Cordula Döhrer and Gerrit Thies, Deutsche Kinemathek; Martha Eggerth and Marjan Kiepura; Scott Eyman; Tag Gallagher; Jeanpaul Goergen; Stefan Grissemann; Anton Haslinger; Col. David Hughes; Gertrude Kittel; Jiří Horníček, The National Film Archive in Prague; Noah Isenberg; Marie Karney; Fabienne Liptay; Diana Long, City of Altamonte Springs Library; Puppe Mandl; Terry McDonald, Trinity College Dublin Library; Barbara Obermaier; Tatjana Okresek; Mauro Piccinini; Ursula Prutsch; Richard Reilly; Rainer Rigele; Christian Rogowski; Florian Seebohm; Elyse Singer; Peter Paul Sint; Chuck Stansel; Richard Thorpe; Michael

Tilson Thomas; Aris Venetikidis for Photoshop assistance; Anthony Weller; and Michael Wilson.

Research in the Cecil B. DeMille archives was carried out by McKenna Kirkpatrick. I am very grateful to him for his assistance.

Shortly after starting work on this project, I moved from University College Dublin to Trinity College Dublin (TCD). I would like to thank D. G. Fisher, Conn Holohan, Paula Quigley, and Kevin Rockett for their collegiality, and the research program at TCD for the financial assistance that enabled me to conduct the research for this book.

Most of all I would like to thank my family—my parents-in-law, John and Clare, my mother, Anne Barton, and my husband and three sons. This book is dedicated to them, with love.

Introduction: Waxworks

ON A SEPTEMBER DAY in 1973, Richard Dow, a caretaker at the Hollywood Wax Museum, started his workday as usual. "I walked down the dark corridors to the back of the museum, and I reached behind a black curtain to turn on a sequence of spotlights," he told reporters afterward. It was then that he saw the demolished figure of Madame Tussaud. "The more lights I switched on, the more damage I saw. I walked down one corridor and I tripped over the head of a mad scientist." Now feeling more than a little uneasy, Dow started to take stock of the damage. All in all, thirteen statues had been destroyed. These included: Jean Harlow, Vivien Leigh, Susan Hayward, Tyrone Power, Sony Bono, a couple of U.S. presidents, and Hedy Lamarr. "Now we'll have to keep a security man on after hours," mused Spoony Singh, the museum owner. "We used to have a watchman. We went through a string of them. But they complain of having to be there all alone with those wax figures. After a while some of them claimed they could see the figures moving."[1] The break-in led the museum to take stock of its silent luminaries; sadly Hedy Lamarr did not make the cut. She was melted down and later replaced by Angelina Jolie as Lara Croft.

If that break-in had occurred two or three decades later, the outcome for the Viennese actress, whose reputation derived from a brief, naked run through a wooded copse, followed by a swim, filmed by a long-forgotten Czech director for a 1930s European art film, might have been otherwise. When Hedy Lamarr arrived in America, her reputation preceded her. Few people had seen *Ecstasy*, the film that had made her famous. Fewer would later remember the plot of *Ecstasy* or their last glimpse (depending on which version they saw) of the character played by Hedwig Kiesler, as the eighteen-year-old was then called, on the station platform in the early hours of the morning, gently kissing her sleeping lover, folding her coat under his head, and walking away from him.

1

If art preempted life in the most curious manner in these early years of the soon-to-be renamed Hedy Lamarr, so too would there never be a shortage of stories and anecdotes to accompany her later progress through Hollywood. In the 1930s and through the war years, magazines competed to put her photograph on their covers, and gossip columnists revelled in her every move. Simultaneously, and with one voice, film critics agreed that Hedy Lamarr could not act. What did it matter, when she had been proclaimed the most beautiful woman in the world?

Her last film appearance was in 1958. Subsequently, she became best-known for a salacious autobiography (*Ecstasy and Me: My Life as a Woman*), published in 1966, and for a string of legal cases, most infamously involving shoplifting. She lived out her final years as a virtual recluse, her sight seriously impaired and her once-beautiful face destroyed by plastic surgery.

Since her death in 2000, and even somewhat before that, Hedy Lamarr's reputation has grown. To quite a large extent, this has been because of her increasing fame as an inventor; her design, with the American avant-garde composer George Antheil, for a long-range torpedo-guidance system forms the basis of our modern mobile telephone technology and also played a major part in the Cuban missile crisis. Several retrospectives of her Hollywood films have been staged, both in her hometown of Vienna and on American television. Documentaries have been produced, exploring her career, her personality, and her legacy. She is the subject of numerous Internet sites and entries.

Can waxworks come alive? Why the comeback? What is now so intriguing about the pampered only child of a well-off Viennese banker and his pianist wife, and her (mis)fortunes in exile? In part, this intrigue is due to our fascination with the stories of émigrés who fled fascist Europe for America. Although she is only one of many Europeans who found refuge in Hollywood, Hedy is one of the few high-profile women to have done so on her terms, rather than as the wife or daughter of a more famous man or as the protégée of an established director. Her continued insistence on doing things on her own terms was equally remarkable, even if it contributed toward making her the difficult individual she was.

The pages of this book are littered with anecdotes concerning the pranks her directors and costars played on her, particularly during the filming of love sequences. Without giving too much away in advance, they involve variously pins, bananas, batons, and suggestive comments, as well as picking her up by the ass and throwing her off the set. Maybe such behavior is still acceptable; certainly it was when Hedy was undergoing what passed for screen-acting training—most of the perpetrators of these pranks claimed they were prompted by a desire to see her express emotion. Cecil B. DeMille spoke of the challenge of breaking through her "impassive air," and with her beauty came a coldness that many men found threatening.[2]

In small ways, and often inadequately, Hedy took her revenge. She also married six times, which hardly makes her a feminist icon, nor do many of her other activities or her statements about sex and marriage— she told Zsa Zsa Gabor that "If a man sends me flowers, I always look to see if a diamond bracelet is hidden among the blossoms. If there isn't one, I don't see the point of flowers."[3] In role after role she played strong women who knew what they wanted—most often sexual satisfaction, professional satisfaction, and wealth. If she got her man, it was not because she was the cute-as-apple-pie good girl whom the entire neighborhood loved and the community respected; the opposite rather. Hedy made a career out of playing bad women, characters who threatened the veneer of respectability established by the community; in Hollywood, these were usually foreigners. In her case, they were often exotic natives, of which the most famous is her half-Arab Tondelayo in the 1942 version of *White Cargo*. Her roles came to an end in the complacent 1950s, when home and hearth were the order of the day and foreigners were dismissed as communists.

Most people assumed that she couldn't be beautiful *and* clever or independent or self-aware. Only a few of her fellow workers realized how much more lay below the glacial surface. One of these, as will be detailed, was King Vidor. Another was that equally displaced, unhappy, and eventually unhinged European in Hollywood, George Sanders:

> When I first met Hedy Lamarr, about twenty years ago, she was so beautiful that everybody would stop talking when she came into a room. Wherever she went she was the cynosure of all eyes. I don't think anyone concerned himself very much about whether or not there was anything behind her beauty, he was too busy gaping at her. Of her conversation I can remember nothing: when she spoke one did not listen, one just watched her mouth moving and marvelled at the exquisite shapes made by her lips. She was, in consequence, rather frequently misunderstood.[4]

Since then, attitudes have changed. They haven't altered beyond recognition and many of the prejudices that Hollywood harbored against Hedy Lamarr are still experienced by young women with ambition. Yet, today's world welcomes the combination of brains and beauty and is, perhaps, a little more understanding of what a previous generation of women had to become in order to succeed in any professional capacity.

Or maybe that's wishful thinking. The 2008 fictionalized biography *What Almost Happened to Hedy Lamarr: 1940–1967*, written by the actress's alleged friend, Devra Z. Hill, with contributions by Jody Babydol Gibson, tells of a Hollywood actress named Hedy Lamarr whose career is apparently best summarized by detailed accounts of her sexual romps and power-hungry manipulations. Her hold, for instance, on the weary studio boss, Beldin (presumably modeled on the already larger-than-life, Louis B. Mayer), who gave her her Hollywood break, is facilitated by the photographs she took of an incident in which he inadvertently throttled an aspiring actress with his over-zealous fellatio requirements. That the book is written as a soft-porn narrative ought to be no surprise given Jody Babydol Gibson's notoriety as the Hollywood brothel keeper whose tell-all publication, *Secrets of a Hollywood Super Madam,* named a string of high-profile celebrities as clients of her lucrative global escort agency. Hill herself, whose résumé includes masters' and doctoral degrees from unaccredited universities and a career as a self-help nutritionist, claims that the star asked her to write her biography. After Hedy's arrest for shoplifting, Hill developed scruples and decided not to continue. Few scruples are evident in this publication, which has sold itself on its suggestion that Hedy was Hitler's mistress, although in fact Hitler is never mentioned in the book and the suggestion is particularly obnoxious. So much for friendship.

While there's no point in being prudish when writing about Hedy Lamarr, there's little to be added in this respect to her own *Ecstasy and Me,* outside of what Devra Hill and Jody Babydol Gibson have cooked up. This disputed autobiography has become the official narrative of her life and most writers on her borrow from it generously. It is a run-through of the story of her life and career, heavily laced with spicy details of lesbian affairs, lovers (both named and unnamed), and the maneuverings of Hollywood's power brokers, most notably Louis B. Mayer. It concludes with transcripts from her sessions with a psychoanalyst. Later, Hedy pronounced that none of this was true and sued the ghostwriters. Yet, if much of *Ecstasy and Me* is fatuous 1960s pseudo-analysis, equally, much of it is, as will be detailed, factual. The account also omits certain key details, to which this text will return.

Mention the name Hedy Lamarr to a passing stranger and they are likely to whoop, "It's not Hedy, it's Hedley. Hedley Lamarr!" If they follow this up with loud flatulence effects, it is only in case you have missed their reference to Mel Brooks's *Blazing Saddles*, a cheery deconstruction of the classic Western, one of whose central characters is the unscrupulous attorney general, Hedley Lamarr (Harvey Korman). Already in 1974 when Brooks made his comedy, few people could name a Hedy Lamarr film. By the time of her death in 2000, she was another ghost of the 1940s, a name that conjured up the glamour of Hollywood stardom and its perennial whiff of decadence. She responded to Brooks's jokes with a lawsuit; by then, that was the way she communicated with the world outside whatever small apartment she currently inhabited.

My own interest in writing this biography was to explore the consequences of leading a life that was based on an image, and how that life became increasingly fictionalized. I'm interested in how Hedy's image, often literally (in the form of a portrait or painting), threatened to overwhelm her reality and how she fought to hold her own in a system that she both despised and needed.

I am curious, too, why Hedy Lamarr has been so neglected by post-1960s feminist historians who have reclaimed equally difficult figures such as Joan Crawford or Bette Davis or Marilyn Monroe. One of the few of these to pay attention to Hedy (as I hesitate to call her) was Jeanine Basinger. In her book, *A Woman's View: How Hollywood Spoke to Women, 1930–1960*, she divides the women of that era into three types: "fantasies," whose appeal was primarily to men; "real women," women who seemed real and recognizable to women in the audience; and "exaggerated women," a mixture of the real and the unreal, larger than life characters, such as those played by Bette Davis, whose exaggerated predicaments were understood and enjoyed most of all by women. Within these parameters, Hedy Lamarr falls into the first category, which Basinger also terms "dream images."[5] This unreality is the key to understanding her film performances; if she was wooden, she was also unreadable, lending an ambiguous quality to the parts she played. This in turn disrupted

Hollywood's commitment to narrative clarity and its privileging of plot. Writing of Greta Garbo, an actress to whom Hedy was often compared in her early years, Roland Barthes proposes that "her face was not to have any reality except that of its perfection, which was intellectual more than formal."[6] Hedy too was defined by her face which, like Garbo's, was most discussed as an archetype of beauty. Of her own contribution to the acting profession, she is reputed to have commented that "Any girl can be glamorous. All you have to do is stand still and look stupid." She never looked stupid, and, indeed, she may never have said this.

The first significant account of Hedy Lamarr's life and career, outside *Ecstasy and Me*, was Christopher Young's *The Films of Hedy Lamarr*, published in 1978. It replicates much of the material from the so-called autobiography. Young, who was a devoted fan, interviewed Hedy for his book and she seems to have provided him with much the same information that she gave (or did not give) to her ghostwriters. It is now out of print.

Since then Diane Negra has analyzed Hedy Lamarr's career as a metaphor for American interventionism and analyzed how the narrative of her escape from her first husband, munitions baron Fritz Mandl, and her embrace of American values came to symbolize America's rescue of a decadent but powerless old Europe.[7] Peter Körte has applied his imaginative and more Europe-centered approach to the star, writing *Hedy Lamarr: Die Stumme Sirene* (2000), which is less a biography and more a series of musings on the potency of her image.

The other sympathetic commentator on Hedy Kiesler, subsequently Lamarr, is Jan-Christopher Horak, who has argued for the importance of the star's strong prewar female characters, her "independent, sexually aggressive women of questionable morality," who always appeared morally ambiguous to middle-class eyes because they foregrounded rather than glossed over the exchange of sex for money.[8]

My decision to write about Hedy Lamarr started with a series of coincidences that drew me to her life story. They began with a now-forgotten Irish film star, called Constance Smith, whose life I researched for a book, *Acting Irish in Hollywood* (2006), on Irish film stars in Hollywood. Connie, as she was known, made her film breakthrough in 1946 after winning a Hedy Lamarr look-alike contest organized by an Irish film magazine. Trading on her looks and frequently let down by her lack of acting skills, Connie made it to England and on to Hollywood, where she was placed under contract to 20th Century Fox. Little educated, with no family support and few compatriots to keep an eye on her, Connie at first floundered and then fell from grace, her career determined by latent alcoholism and a long-term relationship with the equally unreliable, but considerably more famous, British documentarist, Paul Rotha. Connie's story ran parallel to that of Hedy in many ways; they even shared a director, Jean Negulesco. But unlike the Austrian, the Irish actress never learned how to better the system, and her life ended in utter destitution. Hedy was rumored to have died destitute too, though she didn't. Stories like Constance Smith's are seldom told, since failure is so invisible. But many, many of the exiles and émigrés who traveled to Hollywood in search of riches ended up having more in common with Connie than Hedy.

Both women moved on to more marriages and more lovers, but through their stories we can take pathways through history that connect us to other pasts and lives lived so differently to our own that is it hard to imagine that less than a hundred years have lapsed since the birth of Hedwig Kiesler in Vienna. In other ways, she still seems a most modern figure: smart, ambitious, outspoken, and more than a little ahead of her time.

I also want to locate Hedy Lamarr within a history of European exiles to Hollywood and to compensate for her omission in the many histories of these exiles. As in so many other ways, she didn't fit the classic image of the European actor in Hollywood, though her sense of in-betweenness was something that she commented on, over and again, particularly in later life.

After writing this book, I remain compelled by Hedy Lamarr's complexity, her short career, its long aftermath, and her resonance for our contemporary lives. It is too easy to assume that she was simply a victim of male predators and rapacious studio moguls—even if, from time to time, she said she was. When I was considering how to deal with the endless tales of sexual misdemeanors that followed her through life and pursued her beyond the grave, one helpful colleague suggested I attach an appendix listing her lovers (alphabetical order? longevity? merit?) to this volume. In the end, some found their way into this story, others didn't.

We cannot divide Hedy Lamarr's on-screen roles from her offscreen myth. I think she could, mostly, but played a game with Hollywood where she pretended that she could not. What draws me now to this

Viennese actress is the question of how her star image became so bright and then so tarnished and then, once again, began to glimmer and beckon film historians, academics, and the public to its light. Waxwork sculptures do not come to life, but we can reanimate the spirits that inspired them with our interest. I hope that I can go some way toward achieving that.

IF YOU LIKED:

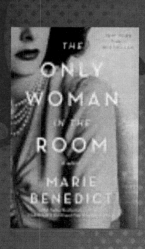

YOU WILL LOVE THESE BOOKS!

RIVERHEAD
FREE LIBRARY

330 Court Street, Riverhead, NY, 11901

CHECK OUT THESE GREAT BOOKS!

Resistance Women
Jennifer Chiaverini
CHIAVERINI

The Huntress
Kate Quinn
QUINN

Mistress of the Ritz
Melanie Benjamin
BENJAMIN

Hedy's Folly: The Life and Breakthrough Inventions of Hedy Lamarr, the Most Beautiful Woman in the World
Richard Rhodes
B LAMARR

1

A Childhood in Döbling

HEDY LAMARR was born Hedwig Kiesler on 9 November 1914, in Vienna. Later, she added two middle names, Eva Maria, to her given name. Her father, Emil, from Lemberg (Lwów) in the West Ukraine, was manager of the Creditanstalt Bankverien.[1] Her mother was born Gertrude (Trude) Lichtwitz, to a sophisticated family in Budapest. Both her parents were Jewish and Hedy too was registered at birth as Jewish. The Kieslers lived on Osterleitengasse in Döbling in Vienna's fashionable 19th District. Later Hedy moved with her family to Peter-Jordan-Straße, also in Döbling. There she lived on the top two floors of a house owned by a well-to-do tea merchant named Pekarek.

Döbling, at the end of World War I, was an overwhelmingly Jewish area, and by the outbreak of World War II, had a population of around four thousand Jewish inhabitants and its own synagogue. Bounded by the Wienerwald (Vienna Woods), the architecture reflected the tastes of its settled, middle-class citizenry. Ludwig van Beethoven composed part of the *Eroica* Symphony in Döbling, and in the 1890s it was the summer home to the Strauss family. The actress Paula Wessely also hailed from the area, as did the scriptwriter Walter Reisch, both of whom would later work with Hedy.

The Lichtwitz side of Hedy's family was well-connected and cultured; the Kieslers were less so, but Emil, who was sixteen years older than Trude, had brought to the marriage the benefits of a good job and solid prospects. Trude was just twenty when Hedy was born and elected to give up her ambitions to be a concert pianist when she had her first daughter and only child.

With Trude's family background and Emil's salary, the Kieslers fitted in comfortably in Döbling. On the one hand, there was little to distinguish them from other well-connected non-Jewish families; on the other, with their dominance of the arts in particular, but also of banking and commerce, these families often intermarried and many worked and socialized together. These were the families, who, in fin de siècle Vienna, filled the theaters and concert halls, patronized the leading writers, musicians, and painters of the day, and accumulated the important art collections. These activities guaranteed them an entrée into political circles, where artistic expression was more highly valued than ideological debate. In Vienna in particular, as Michael Rogin has argued, "the Hapsburg monarchy sustained itself by show. In keeping with the theatrical quality of political life in the empire, the Viennese theatre was more important than the parliament."[2] Thus, Jewish artistic success became a guarantee of influence that extended far beyond the upper circle.

Along with their cultural standing came a commitment to education and a sense of public duty to help those less privileged than themselves. Much of the Vienna so admired today was built with Jewish money; among those whose names were associated with its culture of design was Hedy's cousin Frederick Kiesler. Born in 1890 in Czernowitz, then part of the Austro-Hungarian empire, Kiesler made his name as an avant-garde theater designer, later qualifying as an architect in America. Standing less than five feet tall, he was an inspired writer and often described as a visionary designer; while Hedy was a child, Frederick was making his name with his concept of the "Space Stage" (a form of theater design influenced by the layout of a circus ring). By curious coincidence, it was Kiesler who arranged for the world premiere of the surrealist film *Ballet Mécanique,* directed by Dudley Murphy and Fernand Léger, in Vienna in September 1924, when Hedy was just ten years old. The composer of the film's music was George Antheil, whose life was to become so intertwined with Hedy's in Hollywood. In 1926, Frederick Kiesler and his wife moved from Vienna to New York, where they spent the rest of their lives. One of his first jobs in New York was to design the Film Guild Cinema on 52 West 8th Street for the avant-garde programmer Symon Gould. The cinema's program was mostly drawn from Soviet and European arthouse films and one might guess that his little cousin's scandalous *Ecstasy* was part of its 1930s repertoire.[3] Later, Kiesler became best known for his Shrine of the Book, a wing of the Israel Museum in Jerusalem, the repository for the Dead Sea Scrolls.

Hedy was a child of the First World War, an event with sweeping repercussions for the Jews of Vienna. The collapse of the Hapsburg monarchy and the inauguration of the First Republic saw the Viennese Jews, along with the old aristocracy, stripped of their wealth and influence. After the war, fuel shortages and a drastic lowering of living standards left Vienna more susceptible to the city's omnipresent anti-Semitism, and from the 1920s, the Viennese Jews were gradually becoming aware of a new, hostile atmosphere that infiltrated all aspects of society. No doubt the Kieslers felt the shock too, yet life for the young Hedy (pronounced "Hady") was still protected and very traditional.

The move to Peter-Jordan-Straße brought the Kiesler family into the heart of Döbling's Cottage District. The term, borrowed from English, is misleading. These were substantial homes, designed and built in the period after 1872 when the architect Heinrich von Ferstel set up the Viennese Cottage Society. Their ambition was to create several streets of one- and two-family houses. No new houses would be built that deprived the existing cottage dwellers of a view, light, and the pleasure of fresh air. Each design could be different, but all had to conform to the overall ideal—solid, comfortable, airy houses built around enclosed family gardens. In time, the whole area became referred to as simply the Cottage. Leo Lania, the left-wing journalist and writer, described it as

> the cradle of Austrian literature, the cradle of the Viennese operetta. In the salons of its little villas, through whose windows the eye could sweep unhindered across gentle hills and the wooded approaches of the Kahlenberg as far as the green ribbon of the Danube, began and ended all those "affairs" of Viennese society which furnished Arthur Schnitzler, Hugo von Hofmannsthal and Hermann Bahr with their chief themes. This was the birthplace of the "sweet Viennese girl," the "Merry Widow," psychoanalysis, atonal music, and modern painting. From Sigmund Freud to Gustav Mahler, from Arnold Schoenberg to Gustav Klimt—all the men who represented pre-war Viennese art, music, literature, intellectual life, and built its international fame, revolved around the Cottage, even if a few of them did not live there.[4]

The house at 12 Peter-Jordan-Straße had high ceilings and an ornate wooden veranda that led onto a well-planted garden. Couches draped with rugs and casual tables filled the rooms; floral curtains hung from the windows, shielding the furniture from the bright sunlight of the Viennese summer. The walls were covered with family portraits, the striped wallpaper reflecting the overall tone of an English country house. One of the rooms was dominated by Trude Kiesler's grand piano and there Hedy too learned to play. The family dachshund was, as Hedy entered her teenage years, running to fat.

Even though Hedy never mentioned her Jewish origins in her autobiography or referred to them in interviews, she certainly moved within an artistic environment dominated by talented Jewish individuals. From Trude, Hedy inherited her taste for theater and the arts, and her cultural education came from her mother's side of the family. Her schooling, too, was enlightened; she attended the Döblinger Mädchenmittelschule, now the GRG XIX (a local girls' secondary school). The school, then housed in a private home in the Kriendlgasse, catered to the neighborhood's wealthy Jewish families. Two of its first pupils, in 1905, had been Sophie and Anna Freud, the daughters of Sigmund Freud. Later, Anna Freud taught there, only leaving in 1920.

In the summer there was swimming in the river and family outings to the lakes surrounding Vienna. In all seasons, they hiked in the mountains, and her father liked to row. Throughout her life, Hedy was to retain her love of water and of swimming; later in America, she dreamed of the fresh air of the Wienerwald and the freedom of the outdoors.

She later said that being an only child spurred her to become an actress. She used the space below her father's desk as her first stage, performing fairy tales for an invisible audience. As a small child, she liked to dress up in her mother's clothes and her father's suits and hats. When she came home from the cinema, she would act out all the parts she had just seen. "Grandfather was perhaps the only one who ever encouraged me," she remembered with some acerbity. "He could play the piano and to his music I danced. It was awkward my dancing. But he said he thought it was beautiful. The rest of the family gave me little encouragement."[5]

References to her parents as unloving abound in Hedy's interviews, yet at the same time, she always looked back on her early years in Döbling with intense nostalgia, as a time of security in what was to become a life ruled by uncertainty.

• • •

HEDY LAMARR

Gertrude Kiesler was a small, dark-haired woman whose personality may have run on the cold side. Hedy believed that her mother had really wanted a boy and this was why she would never tell her that she was attractive or let her look in a mirror. Frau Kiesler's version of this story tallies in detail but varies in motivation. She wanted, she said, to ensure that her daughter did not come to rely on her beauty but would instead develop other skills, and not be spoiled: "When she was dressed for a party, and looked very lovely, I would say 'You look very well.' When she did something clever I would tell her 'You did all right.' But I underemphasized praise and flattery, hoping in this way, to balance the scales for her."[6] One shouldn't be too surprised by the comments of Hedy's mother; they reflect common theories of parenting in her day. Later, Hedy would respond to her own children's needs in a disconcertingly similar manner.

In any case, Frau Kiesler did not always manage to control her unruly daughter, even less so how other people reacted to her. A besotted schoolteacher, when told to allow her no special favors, replied that, "When she walks towards me, and looks at me, I can do nothing."[7]

When she was twelve, Hedy's grandmother, Rosa Lichtwitz, died. Taking advantage of her mother's temporary distraction, she entered a beauty contest. With the winnings, she bought her first fur coat. We may imagine what Trude Kiesler's response to this frivolity was.

Still it was Frau Kiesler who was responsible for introducing Hedy to the wonders of the stage. "One day," Hedy remembered, "mother promised me a nice present if I were good. The present was a visit, my first, to the theatre. I saw a stage play for the first time. I was thrilled and speechless. I don't remember the play, its title or anything about it. But I never forgot the general impression. School held but one interest from then on. I took part in school plays and festivals. My first big part came in *Hansel and Gretel*." The first film she saw that had the same effect on her was Fritz Lang's *Metropolis,* released when she was thirteen.[8]

Along with theater, Hedy developed an early interest in young men, one too that was to accompany her throughout life. Her first true love was a boy who has survived in the telling only as Hans. When she was not quite sixteen, he gave her her first kiss in the Vienna Woods; he was, she remembered, the director of a chain of shoe factories.[9] In another interview, many years later, she said he was twenty-five years old and already seeing a girlfriend of hers. One day, when she was supposed to be at a piano lesson, she ran off to the cemetery to try to resolve her loyalties to her friend or to Hans. When she returned home, she found that everyone had become hysterical looking for her. Eventually, she and her girlfriend sat down and said, "This can't go on"; they instructed Hans to choose between them. He chose Hedy: "I was in heaven. We had secret meetings, it was all so exciting and romantic. Once, though, my father caught me coming home late—it must have been nine-thirty. He scared me and then I think he hit me, in my face."[10]

Another friend of Hedy's from her Döbling days was Franz Antel, later to become a film director. All the young men in the area fell in love with Hedy, he remembered, but she only had eyes for the rising Austrian actor, Wolf Albach-Retty (later to become the father of Romy Schneider), who was eight years her senior and kept her for himself. He was a good-looking young man and liked to flirt with the other teenagers. Hedy too was beautiful, with a strong personality, and they made a striking young couple.[11]

Hedy's early childhood may have been protected but it was not without adventure and trauma—according to *Ecstasy and Me,* her early experiences included attracting the attention of a flasher, being raped, and becoming the focus of attention of, first, a lesbian cook and then a lesbian family friend. She herself had a teenage lesbian experience while at finishing school in Switzerland.[12]

Perhaps more reliably, her mother recalled later that

> steadfast as she is within, she is also a chameleon. She changes with the people she is with. Superficially, she changes, and for the time. As when she had her first beau, at home in Vienna. She must then have been twelve. This was a very learned boy, an intellectual. Suddenly Hedy was the best in the school! She was not a bad pupil, our Hedl, but she was not the best. All at once, she was the best! All at once, her nose was all the time in a book, a big heavy book! I only wish it could have lasted longer, that one![13]

A later beau was a very intense Russian boy, filled with the new idealism of his native land. When Hedy was told to apologize to her father for a misdemeanor, she announced that, "I will say the words, but—[my] thoughts are free." Frau Kiesler blamed the Russian.[14]

Despite the temporary influence of the intellectual boyfriend, Hedy was easily distracted from her studies. When she was in Switzerland, she realized that she was in danger of missing a beauty contest in Vienna. She persuaded a friend to cable the school in her parents' names and request that she be allowed to return home.

She said later that although she had always wanted to be an actress, she took up designing and went to design classes to occupy the "waiting time" before acting.[15] Ironically, designing and inventing would eventually become as much a part of her legacy as acting. That, however, was far in the future. For the time being, she learned her European languages, how to cook and sew, and with her neighbor's child, Hancy Weiler, dreamed of fame on the stage.

According to Christopher Young's account of her life, around this time Hedy met Franz von Hochstetten on an Alpine hiking trip and they became engaged.[16] Becoming engaged seems to have been a particularly delightful pleasure for the young Hedy, and one probably doesn't need to linger too long on the unfortunate von Hochstetten, for whom a worse fate was in store.

2

The Most Beautiful Girl in the World

HEDY NOW SIGNED UP for acting classes with Professor Arndt in Vienna.[1] According to *Ecstasy and Me* and several interviews that she gave, Hedy forged a handwritten note to the school from her mother and slipped off one day to Austria's largest film studio, Sascha Film Studios, where she talked herself into a job as a script clerk. While there she overheard the assistant director say he would be interviewing actresses the next day to play a secretary. Hedy seized the opportunity: "Between scenes I went to the make-up table of one of the actresses and put on lipstick, eyebrow pencil and powder. I combed out my hair which I always have liked to wear long and free and went back on to the set. Going to the assistant director, I said boldly, 'I want to play the part of the secretary.' "[2] According to *Ecstasy and Me,* her boldness landed her a small part in her first film: Alexis Granowsky's *Storm in a Water Glass* (*Die Blumenfrau von Lindenau/Sturm im Wasserglas*). That assertion, however, was mistaken, as *Storm* was directed by Georg Jacoby in 1931, and Hedy's first film was actually Jacoby's *Gold on the Street* (*Geld auf der Strasse*), which was released by Sascha Film in 1930.

The prolific Jacoby was well regarded as a director of light comedies and admired for his effortless way of manipulating small details to produce films of great charm. He had started his career just before the First World War, working on sex-education and epic films, nearly sinking his reputation on a version of *Quo Vadis* (1923) with Emil Jannings in the role of Nero that was ill-cast and ran massively over budget. With a new war now seemingly unavoidable, and the economic depression in full grip, audiences were happy to hand over their cash in return for an hour or two of screen comedy. Jacoby's tendency to play moments of chaos to the hilt made him one of their favorites, particularly because he crisscrossed between comedic and musical sequences. Although his comedies seemed innocuous, they allowed audiences to enjoy a gentle critique of the way things were without any danger of serious political engagement.

Although the Viennese film industry could not compete with its prolific neighbor in Berlin, it still turned out a respectable twenty or so films per year in the early days of sound. These films, more than anything else, contributed to the enduring myth of Vienna as the city of "waltzes and lieder, of exquisite emotional sacrifice and dashing but heartless young officers, of Franz-Joseph court intrigues, evenings with 'Heurigen' at the Prater amusement gardens, not forgetting the epitome of seductive naivety, the 'Wiener Mädl' [Viennese young woman]."[3] Production centered around the Sascha Film Studio, founded in 1910 by Count Alexander Joseph "Sascha" Kolowrat-Krakowsky and relocated from Bohemia to Vienna in 1912. The Sievering Studio, where Hedy acted in her first film, was located in the 19th District, conveniently close to her home. As a classic *wiener mädl*, Hedy inherited a reputation that she would effortlessly exploit: that of the famed innocent-but-seductive Viennese beauty.

Gold on the Street is most notable for being Sascha Film's first sound production, an achievement that was facilitated by funding from the German Tobis Film (subsequently Sascha-Tobis Film). Sascha-Tobis would make its name and secure its income with a flurry of light comedies, of which *Gold* was the first. *Gold's* story takes place on the day Dodo (Lydia Pollman), the daughter of a banker, is set to marry Max Kesselberg (Hugo Thimig), her solid but dull fiancé. All are ready for the wedding to start, save Dodo, who is elsewhere, pleading with the famous tenor Dallibor (Karl Ziegler) to run away with her. When that plan fails, she takes up with the globetrotter Peter Paul Lutz (Georg Alexander), who conveniently comes into a fortune and is able to prevent the wedding and run off with Dodo. Hedy's role was too minor to warrant a screen credit or a mention in the press.

In her second film, *Storm (Die Blumenfrau von Lindenau)*, Hedy played a small part as "Burdach's secretary." The making of the film was a big event in Vienna, particularly since its 13 March 1931 opening was planned to coincide with the unveiling of the Sascha-Filmpalast.[4]

The story was an adaptation of Bruno Frank's well-known comedy *Sturm im Wasserglas,* with the title changed so that audiences wouldn't mistake it for an art film. It takes place on the day the small town of Lindenau is preparing to elect a new mayor. The front-runner is Town Councilor Thoss (Paul Otto), who has campaigned as a friend of the people. All appears to be favoring Thoss, that is, until the Flower Lady intervenes. She is outraged because her dog, a mongrel named Toni, was impounded after she failed to pay for its license. With the townsfolk on her side, an idealistic journalist, Burdach (Harald Paulsen), highlights the councilor's duplicity. This wins Burdach the heart of Thoss's young wife, who leaves her husband for the journalist and all falls happily into place in the end. The film's modest critique of the pomposity of officialdom and its assumption that the townsfolk would unthinkingly support anyone from their class went down well with certain reviewers. Audiences, too, reportedly laughed and applauded throughout the Berlin premiere, which was attended by the director and Toni. The only drawback was technical— some of the dialogue was lost when viewers laughed for too long; the trade press recommended that filmmakers bear this in mind when making further sound comedies.[5]

The star of that film was nominally the German beauty Renate Müller, who would later die in mysterious circumstances after becoming embroiled with leading Nazi figures. Much of the critical praise, however, went to the veteran Viennese comedienne Hansi Niese, who played the Flower Lady and whose performance, it was predicted, would win her a new generation of fans in Germany. With her small role, Hedy ought not to have expected a mention, nor did she receive one in most of the reviews. Still, the critic of *Lichtbildbühne* was sufficiently taken with the secretary at the newspaper, whose eyes were "as pretty as a picture," to devote a line in his review to the unknown, and still unnamed, performer.[6]

While reviews of *Storm* were appearing in the press, Hedy was branching out. Her formal schooling, as far as she was concerned, was over. The March edition of *Die Bühne* carried a photograph of Hedy taken by the up-and-coming Viennese photographer Trude Fleischmann. The accompanying text describes Hedy as a young "society woman, who has just finished her schooling and is looking for a career in film."[7] Who inserted this notice? One suspects that Hedy sweet-talked someone with influence into promoting her in what was then one of Vienna's most popular theater and society magazines. But more important for her career and her burgeoning reputation as a local beauty with acting ambitions, Hedy met Max Reinhardt.

The great Viennese-born director had always had an ambivalent relationship with his native city, moving back and forth between it and Berlin. In 1923, he began running the Theater in der Josefstadt and (thanks to the generous pockets of his patron, the war and inflation profiteer Camillo Castiglioni) restored it with "real gold and red brocade and velvet, with Venetian chandeliers and ceiling frescos by old masters and an asbestos curtain displaying the oversized reproduction of a Canaletto view of Vienna."[8]

Reinhardt arrived in Vienna in April 1931 to hold auditions for his forthcoming production of Edouard Bourdet's comedy *The Weaker Sex*. Meanwhile, he was pitching a last-ditch battle to prevent his acting school, the Reinhardt Seminar, from folding. A man for whom there was never enough time, Reinhardt shuttled between the two sets of demands, arranging private financing for the acting school and auditioning a queue of aspiring actors whose hearts' desire was to work for Herr Professor. Playing for Reinhardt, as everyone knew, could make an actor's name, and unfilled parts were few as many of the leading roles had been taken by cast members from the Berlin production. To no one's surprise, Reinhardt regular Paula Wessely was soon named, but in early May he unexpectedly announced that the role of the First American would go to the hitherto unknown Hedy Kiesler. The part was small but "nett" (nice).[9] Overjoyed as Hedy must have been, there was more good news to come.

Another minor cast member was the future Pulitzer Prize–winning author and journalist George Weller. According to Weller, it was during the rehearsal of a café scene with Hedy that Herr Professor turned to a group of reporters who were hanging around the set and said, "Hedy Kiesler is the most beautiful girl in the world." Word soon swept through the acting community. By October 1931, the trade paper *Lichtbildbühne* was quoting Reinhardt on the extraordinary beauty of Hedy Kiesler, a description soon to be echoed by Louis B. Mayer. Praise such as this was not awarded lightly; all Hedy Kiesler had to do now was learn how to act.

Reinhardt apparently instructed Weller to teach Hedy some appropriate American songs. Hedy's idol, Weller soon discovered, was the American tennis player Helen Wills; otherwise, her familiarity with

American culture was limited to renditions of "Yes Sir, That's My Baby" (she sang the title only for all lines regardless of length), "Yes! We Have No Bananas" (she hummed the melody), and "Sonny Boy" (she sang all the words and knew the melody). These and other exercises in Americanization took place in a small room backstage.[10]

The Weaker Sex ran at the Theater in der Josefstadt from 8 May to 8 June 1931 and received enthusiastic reviews, with critics opining that this was now as much or even more a Max Reinhardt play than the original by Edouard Bourdet. Hedy attracted no critical notices but it was a thrilling start, particularly in a city that valued its theaters infinitely more than its film productions and valued Max Reinhardt most of all.

Playing in the Theater in der Josefstadt also offered Hedy the opportunity to spend time with its sometime-manager, Otto Preminger, and his friend Sam Spiegel. According to Franz Antel (Hedy's childhood neighbor), Antel made the introductions. In his memoir, Antel recalls when, as a young man moving up in the 1930s film business, he learned that Sam Spiegel was in town. Knowing that Spiegel had a taste for pretty young women, Antel introduced first himself, and then a number of handpicked Viennese beauties. Of these, the most stunning was Hedy Kiesler, a school friend of his friend Melly Frankfurter. Spiegel was instantly smitten and asked her out to dinner and dancing and, Antel discreetly murmurs, whatever usually follows. Spiegel owned a large Ford coupé and competed with Preminger for the young woman's attentions. The rising producer would take her out to the Döblinger Bad and the Femina.[11]

Working with Reinhardt was to open doors for the rising star as it did for so many other aspiring young actors of her generation. Being a Reinhardt actor was an effective calling card and anyone who could claim an association, particularly those who later emigrated to Hollywood, did. In August 1931, Hedy packed her bags and left for Berlin.

She was not alone in making this journey; many others in the Austrian film industry also followed the promise of money and opportunity to the capital of German-language filmmaking. The transition from silent cinema to talkies was under way, and the conventional German accent was considered too harsh by many. Audiences were reportedly roaring with laughter as previously silent stars opened their mouths and produced streams of sibilants and double consonants. The softer intonations of Southern Germany and Austria were more agreeable, and demand for actors from these regions grew, especially for the romantic roles. Hedy was also literally not alone; she traveled with Alfred (Fred) Döderlein, who was also en route from Vienna to Berlin and with whom she was having a brief affair.

Berlin was a magnet for the artistic community of the day. One of its adopted sons was Christopher Isherwood, whose account of the capital's decadence was immortalized onstage and then film with *Cabaret,* an adaptation of his *Berlin Stories.* Another vivid chronicler was Otto Friedrich. In *Before the Deluge,* he depicts Berlin in the decades between world wars as its population first saw the economy crumble beneath inflation and unemployment and then soar on the back of financial speculation; political instability was the order of the day, and militarism the first resort of the ruling classes. This was a city where hunger and artistic brilliance were bedfellows and all shades of sexual expression were on parade. The twenties were not the Golden Years for everyone, Friedrich reminds us, yet the names of the people, places, and events most associated with the Berlin of that time have retained a magical ring: "Marlene Dietrich, Greta Garbo, Josephine Baker, the grandiose productions of Max Reinhardt's 'Theatre of the 5,000,' three opera companies running simultaneously under Bruno Walter, Otto Klemperer, and Erich Kleiber, the opening night of *Wozzeck* and *The Threepenny Opera.*"[12] Albert Einstein moved to Berlin, as did W. H. Auden and Isherwood; Vladimir Nabokov gave tennis lessons to the wealthy as their children raced their new motorcars along the recently constructed speedway. "Berlin's nightclubs were the most uninhibited in Europe; its booted and umbrella-waving street-walkers the most bizarre," Friedrich continues. "Above all, Berlin in the 1920s represented a state of mind, a sense of freedom and exhilaration. And because it was so utterly destroyed after a flowering of less than fifteen years, it has become a kind of mythical city, a lost paradise."[13] No wonder, then, that Hedy should be drawn to this pulsating Center City.

By most accounts, Hedy moved to Berlin to study under Max Reinhardt; however, the Deutsches Theater archive has no record of her attendance in either Reinhardt's courses or in his Berlin productions. Certainly, she would have kept up with Reinhardt in Berlin; in fact,

Hedy went to work with another great theater name of the day, Alexis Granowsky.

Through Granowsky, Hedy would encounter a circle of Russian émigrés whose political leanings were far to the left. Leo Lania describes Granowsky as "one of the most remarkable men I have ever met: a character out of a Russian novel."[14] He had been born to a well-to-do Jewish family in Riga and lived a life of privilege before the First World War, studying and traveling in Europe and mastering several languages. The Russian Revolution "made him a beggar," according to Lania, "but poverty impressed him as little as wealth." A close friend of Chagall and Mayakovsky and Maxim Gorky and his wife, in Russia Granowsky had been at the center of a coterie of Jewish and Soviet intellectuals. His Jewish Academic Theatre of Moscow (GOSET) became the sensation of Moscow and "the Bolsheviks overwhelmed him with honours, which in those years of civil war often had to take the place of bread, or even coal to heat his theatre. . . . The Soviet Government even let him keep his valuable library and his rare collection of erotic prints."[15] After a performance at GOSET, this group of intellectuals would retire to the Gorkys' Moscow apartment and argue about art, politics, and theater through the night.

Granowsky's first film, *Jewish Happiness,* was produced for Sovkino in 1925, but it was in theater that he flourished. When Freud saw his stage production of *Night in the Old Market* in Vienna, he said he was "deeply moved."[16] By the 1930s, however, the advent of a more hard-line approach to the arts in the Soviet Union forced Granowsky to flee the country. "He thought himself a Western European—by culture and upbringing. But he was a Russian. This contradiction was his ruin."[17] After a few productions at the Reinhardt Theatre in Berlin, Granowsky turned to filmmaking, making his German debut with *The Trunks of Mr. O. F. (Die Koffer Des Herrn O. F.)*.

Lania, himself a Russian Jew, journalist, and writer, who had been brought up in Vienna and had long been a Communist, wrote the script for Granowsky. He too was working with Reinhardt at the time, though he had previously scripted the film version of Brecht's *The Threepenny Opera (Dreigroschenoper)* for the famed Austrian film director, Georg Wilhelm Pabst, and collaborated with the left-wing theater director, Erwin Piscator, on his "political theater." Lania remembers the part of Helene in

The Trunks going to a "young girl just out of dramatic school. She was inexperienced, shy and very pretty. Her name was Hedy Kiesler."[18] Granowsky shot his film between 15 September and 17 October 1931 and it premiered in Berlin on 2 December 1931.

Once again, Hedy was acting in a comedy, this time as the pretty young daughter of the mayor of Ostend (Alfred Abel). Another of the film's rising stars was Peter Lorre. The film is subtitled *A Fairytale for Grown-Ups* and the story starts with the unexpected appearance at a modest hotel of thirteen suitcases bearing the initials O. F. The town's motto is apparently "Better two steps back than one step forward." A small-time local journalist named Mr. Stix, played by Lorre, starts a rumor that the cases belong to the millionaire Mr. Flott, and that he has come to invest in Ostend. In anticipation of Mr. Flott's arrival, the townspeople shake off their apathy and set about modernizing Ostend. Mr. O. F. does not arrive, and Ostend continues to develop until it becomes a metropolis. Only then is the error revealed. The suitcases were destined for Ostende, not Ostend.

Hedy's part was small, but more significant than her Vienna roles. She is generally seen in long or medium shots with a just a few close-ups of her face, which is still rounded and more charming than classically beautiful. Indeed, her overall demeanor exemplifies the ideal of small-town wholesomeness. She plays a strong character who is well able to scold those who displease her, but whose natural environment is the domestic space. In a sequence near the film's end, her character is explicitly contrasted with that of the imported cabaret singer Viola Volant (Margo Lion). Helen and her mother are waiting for the mayor to return for dinner. A phone call to his office finds him claiming that he has to work late. In fact, a cut to the other side of the room reveals that he is enjoying the company of Viola Volant, who is sitting and smoking a cigarette in a pose that reveals a considerable amount of leg. Hedy/Helene's virtuous domesticity is again emphasized in the next scene where she phones her fiancé, Baumeister Stark (Harald Paulsen), to discover that he too is allegedly working late. Sufficient scolding results in him scurrying round and the twosome are shortly married, thus concluding one of Granowsky's several parodies of bourgeois life.

Critics were divided over the production, in particular its fairy-tale qualities and Granowsky's decision to film in a nonrealist manner (the narrative was interrupted throughout with songs written by Erich Kästner). Some attributed the production's aesthetic to the influence of Reinhardt's theater, while others saw in the cinematography reminders of the Soviet cinema. Still others questioned the need to spell out the meaning of the satire.[19] This prompted the question of *The Trunks'* political message, which Lania said was intended as a critique of capitalism.[20] Given the recent collapse of Germany's industrial base and the country's subsequent revitalization through credit and speculation, capitalism was certainly ripe for satire.

For *The Trunks'* admirers, Granowsky's production was a breakthrough in an otherwise arid filmmaking environment; it was, *Der Film* commented, "a commentary on its time," its strength being its reliance on symbols and images rather than on its realist qualities.[21] Less politicized commentators refused to see anything more in this left-wing production than a good-natured comedy about small-town attitudes.

In February 1932, the film was cut by almost half and re-released in April with a new title, *Building and Marrying (Bauen und Heiraten)*. According to the trade press, the filmmakers had heeded their critics and made substantial edits to tighten the structure and plot.[22] In fact, the reasons were more sinister. When the film was re-released, it was without opening credits. The credits had listed several Jewish performers along with Erich Kästner's songs, all of which offended the censors. Also stripped was its portrayal of the decadence into which Ostend swiftly slipped. None of the sequences featuring Hedy was excised, which suggests the censors did not know she was Jewish.

Writers on Granowsky tend to dismiss his films, seeing them as little more than cash cows pulling down the end of an illustrious theater career, but *The Trunks* was a major release. When the film's message was not being debated, critical attention focused on its technical aspects and their contribution to the development of sound film. Its star to be watched was perceptively noted as Peter Lorre (Aribert Mog, later to star with Hedy in *Ecstasy*, also played a small role). Lorre's performance imbues the film with its sense of decadence; his insinuating, unctuous persona is compelling. What is perhaps most interesting for the purpose of this book, however, is the underlying assumption that Hedy Kiesler was a name familiar to audiences. Only *Variety* sounded a sour note: after commenting that Granowsky's film was "original in its idea and outstanding for photography" as well as "intentionally intellectual," the reporter noted that "among the players is the young Viennese actress, Hedi [sic] Kiesler, introduced over here with much propaganda. She does not carry out the advance heralding."[23]

Granowksy was inundated with offers of more film work after the release of The Trunks, but he had meanwhile married a wealthy German woman and moved to Paris to found his own company. "His first picture, Le Roi Pausolle [actually Les Aventures du Roi Pausole or The Adventures of King Pausole], a musical revue, was the most expensive picture made in Europe up to that time. And his private life was as sumptuous as his films. The waiters at exclusive Paris bars hadn't seen such tips since the legendary champagne bouts of the Russian grand dukes in Montmartre." But, "All the luxury and success did not make Granovsky happy or deaden his longing for Russia. He refused to admit it. The close air of the dictatorship made it impossible for him to work, he said, but in the free atmosphere of Paris and London he could not breathe."[24] His wife left him and he died in 1938, a poor man.

The Trunks opened belatedly in Vienna on 4 June 1932. The critics were delighted; several compared it favorably to We Don't Need Money or Fun and Finance (Man Braucht Kein Geld), Hedy's next film. Indeed, it seemed that appreciating Granowsky's film suggested that Viennese society possessed a more cultured outlook than Berlin: "We have heard that in Berlin it was pretty unanimously dismissed. But we savages are better people and for us Granowsky's grotesqueries were a delightful surprise."[25] Although Hedy remained mostly unheralded, one critic offered that Hedy Kiesler was supposed to look pretty and she did, and another mentioned her as part of the excellent cast.[26]

Hedy stayed in Berlin to work with producer Arnold Pressburger on his new film We Don't Need Money, which was shot quickly in November 1931. A founder of Allianz-Tonfilm, Pressburger hired Carol Boese to direct his latest project. Boese had none of Granovsky's political credentials; the high point of his career was his codirection (with Paul Wegener) of the expressionist classic Der Golem (1920). Otherwise, Boese is best remembered for his routine comedies. Adapted from a play of the same name by Ferdinand Alternkirch, We Don't Need Money revisited the themes of wealth accumulation and distribution familiar to audiences of The Trunks. The story centers on the activities of a shopkeeper named Brandt in the small town of Groditzkirchen. When some speculative investments in oil drilling go wrong, he and the local bank official, Schmidt

(Heinz Rühmann), devise a plan to save face. Brandt announces that his millionaire uncle from Chicago, Thomas Hoffman (Hans Moser), is due to arrive shortly. But when Hoffman arrives with seven huge suitcases, he has just one $10 gold piece in his pocket. "No one must find out," Schmidt insists. Schmidt ensures that Hoffman stays at the best hotel in town, but there he keeps the unfortunate visitor a virtual prisoner. With the myth of investment now personified, the bank official and the shopkeeper can obtain limitless credit and the two exploit this nonexistent capital until Brandt becomes wealthy and Groditzkirchen becomes an industrial city of extraordinary influence. The swindle also enables Schmidt to court Brandt's beautiful daughter Käthe, played by Hedy.

In *We Don't Need Money*, Hedy is again presented as a sweet young woman, without the slightest hint of the glamorous beauty she would project in her Hollywood years. The script required her to perform with an ensemble, which she did with reasonable competence, although she expressed herself mostly by rolling her eyes. Her vocal delivery, however, was hampered by a tendency to become shrill in long, heated speeches. Even in this early part, her character is no pushover and when Schmidt kisses her, she slaps him across the face. As was true throughout her career, the young Hedy Kiesler appears happiest when her character has ticked off a would-be lover and put him firmly in his place. She is also considerably taller than Rühmann, which only adds to the comic effect. In one scene, she appears rather startlingly in a bathing suit turning somersaults in her bedroom, an activity that emphasized her almost androgynous figure.

The film was an enormous success, which was attributed to the strong original script written by Karl Noti and Hans Wilhelm and led to its comparison with *The Trunks*; both films, it was said, were not just genre films but also expressed strong personal visions. *We Don't Need Money*, however, was credited as "livelier, funnier and less complicated" than Granowsky's production.[27] The film managed, a *Lichtbildbühne* critic suggested, to stay topical without reminding audiences of the miseries of life. Not normally noted for his light touch, director Carl Boese had acquitted himself well.

Hedy Kiesler, the *Lichtbildbühne* critic added, looked good enough to eat ("zum Anbeißen hübsch") and showed talent.[28] This focus on the rising talent's looks over her acting skills foretold reviews to come. German *Variety* was in agreement: Hedy Kiesler was "enviably young and slim."[29]

The *Kinematograph* critic was more circumspect: "Hedy Kiesler really has nothing to do other than show off a couple of pretty costumes. She will have to content herself with being part of the general praise for the film."[30] *Der Film* was even less encouraging, noting that Hedy's acting had "no dramatic appeal."[31] Thunderous applause greeted the final credits at the premiere in Berlin's Capitol cinema on 5 February 1932, and the film enjoyed a long run in both Vienna and Berlin. It also opened in the Hindenberg Theatre in New York in November 1932, where it played in a German version. The *New York Times* was as enthusiastic as the German press had been and welcomed the performance of the young Hedy Kiesler, "a charming Austrian girl."[32]

In Vienna, the film premiered on 22 December 1931, in time for the holiday season. On opening night, the audience laughed long and loud and the closing titles were met by rounds of applause. Here was a film, most reviewers agreed, that treated the current economic crisis with wit and intelligence. The appearance of Hedy Kiesler, now inevitably referred to as Max Reinhardt's protégée, had been widely anticipated in advance. She looked charming, the *Wiener Allgemeine Zeitung* noted, "but her acting is a little self-conscious."[33] Meanwhile, Viennese authorities realized that posters adorning the city walls declared, "We don't need money." In a moment of humorlessness, they ordered them to be removed.

In Berlin, Hedy stayed with Joe and Mia May, whose lives were to become peculiarly entwined with hers. Joe May was born Julius Otto Mandl in Vienna in 1880, which made him a cousin of the equally wealthy Fritz Mandl, Hedy's future husband. Unlike Fritz, however, Julius frittered away his share of the family fortune before turning to filmmaking, an occupation that permitted him to exercise the autocratic character traits that he also shared with Fritz. In April 1902, Julius Mandl married the actress Mia May and took her surname, calling himself Joe May. In the same year, their daughter, Eva Maria, was born. As will be seen in the next chapter, Hedy would later suggest that Eva Maria committed suicide because of her cousin Fritz Mandl's attentions.

Joe May was at the peak of his career when Hedy met him, with a reputation as a director that put him on a par commercially, if less so artistically, with the big names of UFA studios, such as Fritz Lang and F. W. Murnau. Later again, Hedy would be one of a number of people to help Joe when he fell on hard times. On this occasion, however, she only stayed with the Mays for a few months and by the time *We Don't Need Money* premiered in February 1932, she had left Berlin. Hedy planned to return, although she never would. The next year, Hitler's rise to power saw a mass exodus of the Austrian-Jewish film community back to Vienna, where they enjoyed a temporary haven before the *Anschluß* (annexation of Austria) in 1938. However, in 1932, Hedy left Berlin because she had been cast in a new film to be shot by the renowned Czech director Gustav Machaty. Its title was *Extase* or *Ecstasy*.

3

Ecstasy

By the time he began filming *Ecstasy*, Gustav Machaty enjoyed a reputation as a director of art films. His most celebrated work was an erotic masterpiece, *Seduction (Erotikon)*, made in 1929. The film concerned the sexual encounter between the daughter of a station master and a stranger and opens with scenes from their night of love, which marked the film as highly explicit without being pornographic. Immersed in Czech modernism, the Jewish Machaty had reputedly worked in Hollywood as an apprentice to D. W. Griffith and Eric von Stroheim, though this may be a self-penned myth. He was definitely back in Czechoslovakia by 1926, when he made *The Kreutzer Sonata* and *Seduction*. He followed this in 1931 with his first sound film, *From Saturday to Sunday (Ze Soboty Na Nedeli)*, which was also the first Czech sound film. Scored by the Czech avant-garde jazz composer Jaroslav Jerek, the film still feels like a silent era production. Structured again around a young woman's awakening desire, the story follows a prim secretary who is offered money for sex while out with her friend at an up-market nightclub. Outraged, she slaps her escort and flounces out into the rain. In a sequence that anticipates *Ecstasy*, she is soaked in a downpour and accepts a passing stranger's offer to come and dry off in his apartment. There follows an intensely erotic sequence, after which a series of misunderstandings leads the couple to part and finally be reunited.[1]

Machaty met Hedy in Berlin in 1931. He liked casting unknown or nonprofessional actors and struck by Hedy's looks, he chose her for the part of the young woman Eva in *Ecstasy*. Shooting on *Ecstasy* began in July 1932, although the film had been in preparation long before that. While she was waiting for Machaty to begin, Hedy returned to the Viennese stage. In February 1932 she replaced Marta Lille in the role of Sybil (originally played by Karin Evans) in the Komödie Theatre in

Noel Coward's *Private Lives* for the last few weeks of its run. Sybil is one of the four main characters in Coward's comedy of manners; it was another good part for the young actress. Hedy Kiesler's star was quickly rising.

To shoot *Ecstasy*, the cast and crew traveled to Czechoslovakia. The bathing scenes were shot near Jevany, close to Prague. Otherwise, the outdoor scenes were shot in the Carpathians, in and around Dobšiná (site of the famed Dobšinská Ice Cave). They lived in this "godforsaken place," according to Hedy, "like the most simple of people from the Steppes. And because the sun only shines brightly there for a few hours, and in the morning and afternoon a thick mist falls over everything, we had to be careful to use every minute we could. At lunchtime, we huddled in the small camera van to grab a quick bite of food."[2] The café sequence was shot on the elegant Barrandov Terraces on the outskirts of Prague, a location that would have been easily recognizable to locals, as it was a popular day trip from the city. The film was shot in three language versions—German, Czech, and French. For the French version, Aribert Mog was replaced by Pierre Nay and Leopold Kramer by Andre Nox. The Czech actor Zwonimir Rogoz played the father in all three versions. Hedy, too, played Eva in all three versions; "she learnt Czech in a few weeks," Aribert Mog told a reporter.[3] In fact, as Joseph Garncarz has demonstrated, Hedy was post-synched by a Czech speaker having first of all delivered her lines in Czech to camera.[4] Not only could she play her role in multiple languages, she also endeared herself to her director by translating for him on set.

Ecstasy continued the celebration of awakening female sexuality that had made *Seduction* such a conversation piece. The story focused on a young woman, Eva (Hedy Kiesler), who marries a much older man, Emil (Zvonimir Rogoz). He turns out to be impotent and she leaves him. During a nude swim in a lake, her horse bolts, taking her clothes with it. She is rescued by a young engineer, Adam (played by Aribert Mog), working with a gang of laborers. They fall in love. Her humiliated husband shoots himself and she leaves Adam. The film ends at this point in certain versions; in others, an added scene sees Eva nursing a child, while in another shot Adam is at work, apparently dreaming of his lost love.

HEDY LAMARR

The camera delights in caressing Hedy's face and framing her body in one erotic pose after another. In the film's early sequences, as long as she is trapped in her marriage to Emil, she is presented as a precious object, part of the opulent furnishings of that wealthy man's life. Only when she frees herself of the city's glamour, by literally tearing off her clothes and throwing herself in the water, is Eva able to return to the Garden of Eden and find her Adam. Machaty did not require that Hedy act, she simply had to let herself be filmed. He saw to it that through framing and diffuse lighting, this slightly plump teenager was transformed into an object of post-pubescent desire. Gone was the small-town daughter of the house that her audiences knew from her Weimar films; this Hedy Kiesler was defined by her languid movements and natural sexuality.

Shot just three years after D. H. Lawrence's *Lady Chatterley's Lover* had been the subject of an obscenity trial, Machaty revisits much of the territory that made Lawrence's novel so controversial. Here, again, is the story of a young well-bred woman caught in an impotent marriage and finding sexual release in the freedom of the outdoors with a younger, more earthy lover. In his essay on the film, written shortly after its release in Europe, Henry Miller teased out the connections between the two. Each time he saw *Ecstasy,* and that was four or five times, he noticed that the audience responded in the same way: "cheers and applause mingled with groans and catcalls." The hostility, he was convinced, "has nothing to do with the alleged immorality of the film. The audience is not shocked but indignant." This indignation he ascribed to the film's pacing, which delivered none of the conventional pleasures of narrative drive but rather forced the spectator "whether he will or no, to swim in the very essence of Machaty's creation . . . Beneath the public's hostility is the grudging admission of the presence of a superior force, a disturbing force." Since Miller locates this force in the solar plexus, we needn't doubt his point; what is disturbing about this film is its sexual energy, an energy that moves beyond the boundaries of the screen and, in Miller's description, into the auditorium. Machaty's Adam and Eva are creations of the instinct rather than the intellect: "Their meeting is that of pure bodies, their union is poetic, sensual, mystical. They do not question themselves—they obey their instincts . . . In *Extase* the drama is one of life and death, life impersonated by the two lovers, death by the husband.

The latter represents society as it is, while the lovers represent the life force blindly struggling to assert itself." So in the final sequences of the French version, as the lover is left sleeping on the bench and the train pulls out of the station bearing away his mistress, the audience was most disturbed—"Is there perhaps the flicker of a suspicion in their addled pates that life is passing them by? I notice that the resentment is largely confined to the male members of the audience. Could one read into that a Freudian story of bankruptcy?"[5]

Miller was dismissive of the undertones of Soviet filmmaking that he picked up in *Ecstasy*, but they influence its aesthetic as much as Lawrence. The engineer, by virtue of his profession alone, is highly reminiscent of the idealized virile hero so beloved by Soviet filmmakers. Similarly, the repeated shots of the husband's monocle and his perfectly shined shoes seem like a direct steal from Eisenstein.

What is most striking about the film's politics is its refusal to punish Eva for her sexuality, either for abandoning her husband or having an affair with the engineer. Whichever ending we see, she remains in control, a figure of nature and an object of desire, but equally a strong, independent young woman, who cedes authority neither to her father, nor her husband, nor her lover. If her association with water and horses are representational clichés, the film's narrative, such as it is, never seeks to contain her or limit her freedom of choice.

Aesthetically, Machaty's film is strikingly beautiful. It could have easily been a silent era production, and it comes as a surprise when the characters talk to each other (the entire film contains fifteen lines of dialogue).

The two key scenes that garnered the film such publicity, and a misleading reputation for pornography, were the nude swimming sequence and a close-up of Hedy's face as she simulates orgasm. All this was filmed, according to Hedy, without her being aware of the consequences of what she was doing: "The director shouted 'If we do not do this scene, the picture will be ruined, and we will collect our losses from you!' . . . 'I won't. I won't take off my clothes!' I was thinking of my parents . . . not to mention the crew we were shooting with, and the public, later on. Impossible!"[6]

She did take off her clothes: "I remember it was windy but warm, and the breeze was refreshing on my body as I undressed gingerly behind the broadest tree I could find . . . One deep breath, and I ran zigzagging from tree to tree and into the lake. My only thought was 'I hope they get the splash.'" Evidently not; Machaty was behind the microphone, urging the young actress to do one more take: "I wanted to refuse, but there was no turning back now. Shivering, I scooted back to the first tree. Mysteriously, somebody had put a terrycloth robe there. I dried off, and waited for the damned gun. It had jammed! After a moment, the megaphone voice shouted, 'Go!' Again I zigzagged, probably breaking all speed records, again I swam a bit, and then stuck my head up."[7] This time the take was good.

Hedy also insisted that she had not known what a zoom lens could accomplish or that the script contained nude scenes.[8] Subsequent comments by the production crew suggest that she knowingly agreed to do the nude scenes: "As the star of the picture, she knew she would have to appear naked in some scenes. She never made any fuss about it during the production."[9] That a nude performance was expected of the film's star was confirmed by Lupita Kohner. According to her, her future husband and then producer, Paul Kohner, had proposed her for the part of Eva. Lupita Tovar (as she still was) was already working in Hollywood but traveled to Berlin to meet Machaty, anticipating the role would be hers. However, when Kohner saw the script, which made it clear that nudity was expected, he insisted Lupita not take the role.[10]

Hedy's next test was the lovemaking scene. Machaty was looking for a sequence that would suggest beyond doubt that the expression on her face indicated to the audience that she had reached orgasm: "I was told to lie down with my hands above my head while Aribert Mog whispered in my ear, and then kissed me in the most uninhibited fashion. I was not sure what my reactions would be, so when Aribert slipped down and out of camera, I just closed my eyes." Machaty was not impressed. Mumbling about the stupidity of youth, he looked around until he found a safety pin on the table: "You will lie here," he said, "I will be underneath, out of camera range. When I prick you a little on your backside, you will bring your elbows together and you will *react!*"[11] Numerous pinpricks later, a howl of agony from Hedy gave Machaty the shot he was looking for. If the nude bathing had not been enough, here was a scene that made the film censors of the world draw a collective breath.

The descriptions of the shoot from *Ecstasy and Me* were written (by Hedy, we may assume) many years after the event and in the knowledge of the effect the film had on her reputation, being both her making and her undoing. At the time, however, she prevaricated over her participation in Machaty's picture. She told one interviewer that this film would finally allow her to demonstrate her acting skills on screen, and that she was lucky to be in the hands of such a talented director as Machaty.[12] Elsewhere she said her part offered good opportunities and was from quite a different mold than her previous two films. In the same interview it was also reported that "officially" she and Aribert Mog were "unofficially engaged."[13] A few days before the premiere, however, she gave an interview to the *Wiener Allgemeine Zeitung,* where she clarified her feelings about her role. She was just, the paper explained, recovering from a bout of flu that had kept her from working for several weeks. Going back over her casting in the film, she insisted that Machaty had been clear that there were nude sequences in the film, but these were very brief and she would be covered by leaves and flowers. When shooting started in the Carpathians, she found herself to be the only woman on set. When the nude scene was announced, she refused to participate but Machaty produced her contract and insisted. "What else could I have done all alone in the godforsaken Carpathians?" she demanded. Hedy first saw the finished film in Prague and wasn't too upset by what she saw, since no one knew her there. In Vienna, however, the situation was extremely embarrassing as all her friends and acquaintances would see her performance. Now she wanted Machaty to remove the sequences but he refused.

She also claimed a body double had been used for some of the sequences (indeed, it seems that a body double was deployed in certain of the scenes, although not in the swimming shot). Perhaps most surprisingly Hedy announced that she was shortly going to Berlin and then would return to Vienna before leaving for America with her mother, where she had a contract with Paramount and would soon be appearing in Hollywood films.[14]

In another interview she said that she was never paid for the role and had taken it, "because I was in love with somebody." This "somebody" was presumably Aribert Mog. Even more salaciously, a further rumor claimed there was a version of the film where the two really made love.[15]

This is after all the story of Adam and Eve, with the emphasis on the pleasure rather than the punishment that temptation brings. Hedy's nudity is associated with the outdoors and freedom, sentiments that might have recommended it in Germany, where naturism was enjoying a boom and where Machaty hoped the film would reach a wide audience.

"In the 1920s," according to Chad Ross,

> organizations and publications—often working in tandem—that advocated nudism proliferated at a fantastic rate. As befits the first great age of mass culture, during the Weimar Republic nudism became a mass cultural phenomenon in which millions of Germans participated, whether as members of nudist leagues or more simply (and far more likely) as weekend beachgoers. Furthermore, nudist ideologues and proponents made use of the latest technology of the day—photographs, cinema—to further their movement.[16]

The difference, of course, was that German nudism (and its equally popular Austrian counterpart) was inspired by a moral outlook that equated the naked body, male or female, with a healthy, wholesome lifestyle. Machaty's ambition was to dispense with the conventions of bourgeois decorum; the heavy-handed Freudian symbolism that saw Eva's first encounter with Adam marked by wildly galloping horses was just one detail in a creation that would test the limits of the art film across Europe.

Hedy's parents must indeed have been horrified. Across their hometown, posters announced that *Ecstasy* was the "Talking point of Vienna" and promoted the film with the slogan "An erotic play of uninhibited natural drives." The film's premiere was held on 18 February 1933 and it opened in four of the city's biggest cinemas. In a two-week period *Ecstasy* attracted audiences, so the publicity posters claimed, of 71,000. Viennese cinemagoers were able to see the uncut version of the film, though it may have been altered after its release.[17] The reactions of the Viennese film critics were mixed. In the *Neue Freie Presse,* the reviewer noted that it was Hedy Kiesler's beauty and the expressiveness of her fine, spirited face that was the artistic achievement of Machaty's film. Otherwise, the writer continued, the film was confusing and a failed experiment in form, but striking in the beauty of its images. The nudity, he said, was tasteful, and nothing people had not already seen in pictures of lake and river bathing. The *Wiener Zeitung* reviewer Edwin Rollett also found fault with Machaty's ambitious attempt at a new kind of cinema and considered Eva's motives hard to understand. It seemed to Rollett that the film started three times and each time came to a halt. Yet again, however, Rollett was full of praise for Hedy Kiesler, who was not only beautiful but, as the many close-ups demonstrated, intense and expressive. The *Wiener Allgemeine Zeitung*'s critic wrote lyrically of Hedy Kiesler's beauty. The *Neue Zeitung* was less appreciative of the film's finer qualities. "It shouldn't be called 'Ecstasy,'" its critic stormed, "it should be called 'Scandalous'! . . . Nudity in cinema is never aesthetic." Even worse, Machaty's effort was boring and its narrative, mindless. It could only have passed the censors, the writer continued, warming to the theme, because they fell asleep during the screening, a dereliction of duty that might otherwise have saved the public the disappointment of seeing the film.[18]

If the Viennese film critics were divided over the artistic merits of *Ecstasy*, for the citizens of Vienna, the issue was a little different. At the seven o'clock screening on the film's opening night at the Ufa-Tonkino, some audience members hissed and booed; four people were forcibly removed by security staff. This evidently prompted the rest of the audience to join in, filling the auditorium with catcalls, hissing, and shouting. Some left of their own free will during the screening; others remained to the end and started demanding that management be called. Cries of "We want our money back. It's a scandal!" were heard. As cinemagoers for the next showing began attempting to take their seats, the police were called to restore order.[19] Similar public outcries accompanied other screenings elsewhere; much of the public's unhappiness was not about the film's erotic content, but its misleading advertising, which had, according to Rollet, "awoken in them unjustifiable expectations of obscenity."[20] This kind of response, over frustrated expectations, would be echoed by filmgoers from Paris to New York.

Audiences in Germany, where the film was first banned and then released under the title *Symphony of Love* (*Symphonie der Liebe*), also greeted the screening with laughter and whistles from certain seats and with reproaches for this behavior from others. The German version was heavily censored and contained two scenes shot especially for it. One scene made it clear that Eva was already divorced from her husband when she met her lover, a second added a happy ending, with the lovers united. Later,

Machaty claimed that the film had been banned because Hedy Kiesler was Jewish, though there is no evidence to support this. More spicy rumors spread after the war: that a copy of the film had been found in Goebbels's private safe; that it was Göring's favorite film and he also had a private copy.[21]

Ecstasy in America

Ecstasy was distributed in the United States by Eureka Productions, which also traded under the name Jewel Productions. In January 1935, the Customs Bureau of the U.S. Treasury Department denied entry to a print of the film. The case came to court, and the judge, District Judge John C. Knox, ruled in favor of the plaintiff, declaring, "I think that this is the only verdict that properly could be returned . . . this picture, in my judgment, had no purpose to serve and was intended to serve no purpose other than to bring about a glorification of sexual intercourse between human beings and between animals and to arouse lustful feelings in those who might see it. It is suggestive of sexuality throughout."[22]

Despite a swift appeal lodged by Samuel Cummins, general manager of Eureka Productions, a zealous U.S. marshal burned the film. No pushover, Cummins simply ordered another print and won on appeal. Cummins's interest in film distribution was not limited to controversial Czech pictures: In 1934, he imported a film made by Cornelius Vanderbilt Jr. from Germany, which Cummins renamed *Hitler's Reign of Terror;* the film introduced many Americans to the realities of Nazi dictatorship. Cummins also produced *War Is a Racket* that year, which aimed to discredit arms dealers. He ran a sharp business distributing exploitation films and was familiar with the art cinema circuit where such releases were often shown.

With the new print of *Ecstasy,* he did, however, exercise some sleight of hand. This version contained a scene of a typewriter moving along its carriage while a voice-over read that the girl's divorce had been granted and she was now free to remarry (a close-up of the typed letter ends with the line "I hope that your next marriage will be a happy one"); a new ending showed Eva standing with a baby in her arms while Adam gazed wistfully at the hill where he first glimpsed her.

Cummins's new 1935 print went into immediate circulation in independent picture houses and in states where it was not banned outright. He had thirty-six prints in circulation and audiences saw different versions depending on the local censorship regulations. Critical responses varied widely among those who saw the film on the independent circuit. Most knew of the film's reputation from press coverage of its European release, and it was also widely believed the Nazis banned the film because Hedy Kiesler was Jewish. The story of Fritz Mandl's attempts to buy up all existing prints of the film (detailed in the next chapter) was also familiar to many, as was the rumor that he pressured his old friend Mussolini to award the top prize at the Venice Film Festival to *Man of Aran* instead of *Ecstasy*.

Informed critics also knew that the film they were reviewing contained the inserted sequence in which we are informed that Eva has obtained a divorce from her husband. They most likely were cheated of the view of Hedy Kiesler's naked breasts and the orgasm sequence but were treated to a new soundtrack composed by William Colligan and Henry Gershwin, rather than the original by Giuseppe Becce. As Vinzenz Hediger has discussed, Machaty likely anticipated censorship problems and shot several versions of *Ecstasy* to accommodate local censorship requirements; most writers agree that the preferred version is the 2005 reconstruction by Prague's state archive, Narodni Filmarchiv.[23]

The Legion of Decency's response to Machaty's film was typical of the moral perspective taken on Hedy's role: "[The love] affair, accompanied by heavy-handed symbolism, is portrayed solely on an animal plane. 'Bestiality' would be a far more descriptive title than 'Ecstasy.'"[24] Other critics deemed it an art film with appeal to that specific audience. For a few, *Ecstasy* was considered art of the highest order:

Someone has well defined great art by stating that it will yield only in part to dissection and analysis. Always there remains an elusive residue of the unexplainable. For this reason we are at a loss for words with which to convey the qualities of *Ecstasy*. It is a pictorial poem, a symphony in moods and movement expressed in the most evanescent overtones of sight and sound. It lives with a harmony and a rhythm which are the rising and falling rhythms of nature, and it overwhelms us with the ecstasies and the inappealable tragedies which they bring. No picture which we have seen has so completely realized the cinema as an independent art form.[25]

In a subsequent editorial in *The Hollywood Spectator,* editor Welford Beann returned to the film and its triumph as an art film, praising in particular its spare use of dialogue: "*Ecstasy* was made by people who know what motion pictures are. Ours are made by people who lack such knowledge, or perhaps by people who are not allowed by the higher-ups to apply such knowledge to their screen creations."[26]

Those reviewing the film as a work of art managed to turn a blind eye to Cummins's and the independent cinemas' marketing campaigns for *Ecstasy,* which promoted the product as the "sensational uncensored European version" and decorated their lobbies with sensual images of the naked Hedwig Kiesler. Cummins released the film in certain districts to coincide with the opening of other films starring Hedy (now Lamarr); thus, *Ecstasy* received a November 1940 release in New York to coincide with the first night of *Comrade X* (King Vidor, 1940) and Cummins re-released it in New York in 1950 to take advantage of the publicity for Cecil B. DeMille's *Samson and Delilah,* in which Hedy played the starring role.

Viewing the new print in May 1937, Joseph Breen, the sober head of the Production Code Administration (PCA), whose job it was to enforce morality on Hollywood, pronounced that "the picture is definitely and specifically in violation of the Production Code. This violation is suggested by the basic story and by a number of the details, in that it is a story of illicit love and frustrated sex, treated in detail and without sufficient compensating moral values." The PCA ensured that Hollywood cinema conformed to the standard of morality set forth in its Production Code, and Breen was charged with guiding filmmakers toward acceptable treatments of taboo subjects, such as sex, particularly premarital or miscegenation.[27] Filmmakers either heeded Breen's advice or risked having no outlets that would show their film. Cummins appealed Breen's decision, pointing out that, among other issues, the film was already being shown at independent production houses and if anything people were disappointed that it was so mild.[28]

PCA vice president Francis Harmon urged Breen to remain steadfast. *Ecstasy* violated the Production Code on several counts, primarily in its refusal to take a moral stand on the actions of its protagonists, its depiction of nudity, and its proposal that adultery was attractive. Warming to his theme, Harmon wrote that

> this girl, married unfortunately to an impotent husband, could have secured an annulment under civil law or the canonical law of various religious bodies. She had adequate grounds for a divorce. Yet her craving for sexual satisfaction is so pronounced that she dashes through a terrific storm to commit adultery with a man who had caught her fancy, as uninhibited by legal or moral considerations as her father's mare which ran away with her clothes at the neigh and scent of a stallion. Nor does the picture have sufficient compensating moral values to correct this distorted attitude toward the sacred union between a man and a woman, licensed by the state and approved by religion, upon which our entire social structure rests.[29]

As always, the most pressing anxiety weighing on the administrators of the Production Code was that susceptible individuals (i.e., women and members of the working class) would be led into the moral abyss by watching this kind of fare. *Ecstasy,* they concluded, was designed to wake lustful desires in those who viewed it. Doubtless, they were less worried by the reaction of audiences who had benefited from the kind of education that they relied on to guide their decisions.

When PCA board members viewed the contentious film in Columbia's projection room, they were quite immune to its artistic merits; indeed Harmon remarked that his colleagues were so bored during the first few reels, it was hard to persuade them to stay. Only during the scene in the engineer's cabin did they begin to sit up and take notice.

Once again, Joseph Breen declared that *Ecstasy* was not suitable fare for the American public, and editing would not make it so.

Proposals to remake the film immediately began circulating Hollywood, most particularly in the PCA offices. In 1941, a Mr. Geza Herczif wrote a script intended as a remake of *Ecstasy,* with the same title. Herczif was an associate of Martin Licht, director of Wyngate Company.[30] The script was rejected by the PCA. Wyngate, however, leased *Ecstasy* from Eureka and, despite the PCA, it gained a limited showing from October 1941 through September 1942. As a result, it once again became the subject of a court case, this time over the American rights to the soundtrack (anyone today watching the film on DVD or in an English-language version will not hear the original soundtrack, most of which was replaced, most notably with Tchaikovsky's "None But the Lonely Heart").

By July 1945, Machaty himself proposed a remake. The new version would feature a voice-over from Eva, affirming that she was divorced from her first husband and would marry Adam. Set in Prague, it was to star Hedy Lamarr and Aribert Mog with Zwonimir Rogoz as Frederick and Leopold Kramer as the Father; Joy Williams was to narrate.

However, the script, titled *My Ecstasy,* contained both the nude sequence and the orgasm scene. The PCA informed Machaty that the film could not be titled *Ecstasy* or anything similar and they approved a new title, *Rhapsody of Love.* Machaty also had to remove the offending scenes before the film received the PCA's Certificate of Approval in February 1949. Machaty's producer was the Pix Distributing Corporation in New York City, which was headed by Harry Rybnick. Pix changed the title to *My Life.*

Released in January 1950, the film played in New York City's Rialto Theatre. However, the Rialto advertised it as the complete version of the original *Ecstasy* and adorned its foyer with stills from the original alongside news reports of its sensational nature. The PCA sent two employees, Gordon S. White and Arthur deBra, to see what the Rialto was showing. They reported back that the film was being advertised as "HEDY LAMARR in *MY ECSTASY*" and that it carried a Production Code Seal but that this was a completely different film from the one the PCA approved. Furthermore, it included "close-up detail of the Heroine presumably in the act of her surrender."[31]

PCA chief Joseph Breen was far from happy: "This seems to me to be a pretty clear cut-and-dried case of bad faith, and I hope you will keep me advised as to the developments. It is really shocking!"[32]

On 2 February 1950, the two agents, now accompanied by a Miss Young, returned to the Rialto to see how things were shaping up. Not only did they find the same picture playing, the only change was that the PCA's seal had been removed. The New York State Censor Board issued a general alert for any versions of the offending picture and the *Ecstasy* print went underground. In January 1951, the illicit print again appeared at the Times Theatre at 42nd Street and Eighth Avenue.

The film also played in Germany in 1950, where it was again promoted on the promise of sexual explicitness and Hedy Lamarr's nude scenes. This version had a new ending, shot with a stand-in for Hedy, where the young couple, it hints, live happily ever after in South America. In Frankfurt, screenings of the film were accompanied by protests that took the form of defacing the posters bearing the star's naked image. The protestors were divided into two camps: a Catholic youth organization that was opposed to the film's eroticism, particularly as promoted in its publicity, and filmgoers who were disappointed by its lack of erotic qualities.[33] Again, the suggestion that the film had been banned in the 1930s because its star was Jewish was revived by the Jewish press.

In America, the film continued to emerge and vanish equally swiftly, and, as so often was to be the case, to disappoint audiences by its unpornographic take on sexuality. Exhibitors began to intervene and Pauline Kael reported hearing of "versions in which someone had decided to prolong the ecstasy by printing the climactic scenes over and over."[34]

In 1933, however, all this was yet to come and the film's beguiling star was still named Hedy Kiesler and only nineteen years old. She was, as far as most people were concerned, an exquisite Viennese *mädl*, whose acting abilities were as yet untested by a major dramatic role. Her reputation was the creation of men who were considerably older and worldlier than she. She would soon meet one more such man, her first husband, Fritz Mandl.

4

Fritz Mandl

THE SUCCESS and notoriety of *Ecstasy* opened doors for the young star; although for the moment those were to be stage doors. Interviewed during the shooting of *Ecstasy*, Hedy was firm: she did not want a Hollywood career. "I don't want to become a slave to cinema," Hedy said. "I want to film when I feel like it, and to take a break when I don't. I'll probably go back to Berlin."[1] Any mention of a contract with Paramount and a trip to Hollywood with her mother vanished as unexpectedly as they had appeared. What she did not then know was that she had left Berlin and the Weimar film industry for good.

As the German film industry increasingly fell under Nazi control, a brief window of opportunity opened for studios in Vienna. Over the long winter of 1932, nothing had been filmed. By summer, the Filmhof Café was filled with the same faces that had so recently gathered in Berlin's Romanische Café. Six companies were filming simultaneously in The Sascha Film Studios, and anyone from the opera world willing to work in a light operetta, set in Vienna, and featuring sweet young Viennese girls, could name their price.

According to Christopher Young's account of Hedy's life and her autobiography, during this period her fiancé, Franz von Hochstetten, pleaded with her to marry him and when she refused, he committed suicide. Soon afterward, Hedy met Count Blucher von Wahlstatt and they announced their engagement. This too ended quickly. If true, the engagement must have ended around December 1932. It's difficult to pinpoint where and how the many rumors surrounding Hedy started, particularly when you find them repeated in *Ecstasy and Me*. From a young age, she seems to have reveled in the company of adoring men, many of them older. She also seems to have held little regard for the bonds of marriage, but beginning in her teens, evidently enjoyed the idea of marrying. As she grew older, she slipped in and out of a fantasy world, emerging from it only to utter often garbled pronouncements. For the moment, however, she stood squarely in reality; yet she was determined, sure of her talent, and of the power she had over people. She did not hesitate to use that power to her advantage.

In early 1933, Hedy was actively looking for more roles. That year, the popular Viennese actor Willi Forst was preparing to direct his first film, *Unfinished Symphony (Leise flehen meine Lieder)*, which was about the love affair between Franz Schubert and Countess Esterhazy. Walter Reisch was working on the script and their first choice for the plum role of the Hungarian Countess Esterhazy was the young Hedy Kiesler. Also on board was the renowned costume designer Gerdago, known as the Edith Head of Austrian Film. Hans Jaray was confirmed to play Schubert, and Luise Ullrich, who had starred in Max Ophüls' *Liebelei,* was cast as the innocent object of Schubert's attentions.[2] There was one problem, however: Forst and Reisch joined forces to tell the producer, "Pretty is not enough. She has to sing Schubert songs. She was not trained for singing and she cannot sing Schubert songs. We have to take Martha Eggerth."[3] Eggerth had a minor film career but was better known for her beautiful singing voice. Hedy was replaced.

The film was shot from March through May 1933 and Hedy dropped into the studio one day to visit the filmmakers. She was very sorry, Eggerth remembered, not to have played in the film.[4] *Symphony* was a monumental success across Europe and catapulted Eggerth into stardom overnight; her career in musicals lasted until the war, when she and her husband, Jan Kiepura, fled to America. Both resumed their careers in America, with their main triumphs now on Broadway.

If Hedy was disappointed not to play in *Symphony,* another opportunity shortly came her way. In autumn of 1932, the forthcoming production of *Sissy* in the Theater an der Wien was all the talk in Viennese theatrical circles. *Sissy* was based on the courtship between the young Emperor Franz Josef and Elizabeth (nicknamed Sissy), the favorite daughter of Bavaria's Duke Max, and had been composed by the violinist Franz Kreisler.

He badly needed the income—a recent $10,000 win at the tables in Monte Carlo barely saved him from selling his collection of rare books and manuscripts. Relying on sentimental songs he knew would strike a chord with his audience, Kreisler recycled his well-worn violin tunes from earlier operettas and added in two new numbers: "Wine Is My Weakness" and "With Eyes Like Thine, 'Tis Sin to Weep."

To play the title role was the dream of any young star, and it was no surprise when Paula Wessely was chosen to play the latest incarnation of Sissy. The operetta premiered on 23 December 1932 in time for the Christmas season, with Paula Wessely as Sissy and Hans Jaray as Franz Joseph. Reviewers and audiences were enchanted and management of the chronically impoverished theater anticipated a long and lucrative run. In early January, it was announced that Rose Stradner would take over the role of Sissy from Paula Wessely, who would soon move on to a new role elsewhere.[5]

In early 1933, for a short period Hedy was the understudy for Paula; unexpectedly the *Wiener Allgemeine Zeitung* reported that Hedy had been announced as the successor to Paula Wessely for the role of the Countess Elisabeth in *Sissy*.[6] Rose Stradner had since been contracted to take over the part of Fanny in the comedy *Fanny* playing at the Raimund Theater; only when she had completed this contract could she play Sissy.

An announcement was placed in the *Wiener Allgemeine Zeitung* on 20 January confirming that Hedy Kiesler would replace Paula Wessely. Once again her portrait appeared in *Die Bühne,* this time in profile with a cigarette delicately placed on her lips and photographed by Edith Glogau.

In the end, Paula Wessely played Sissy until March 1933, when she was replaced by Rose Stradner. The director, Hubert Marischka, also pressed her to reschedule her holiday so she could stay on in the role. Then, before she began her second month as Sissy, the director abruptly informed Rose Stradner that her contract would be terminated and Hedy Kiesler would now play Sissy. Rose Stradner was outraged and demanded compensation for breach of contract. On 23 March, Hedy nonetheless replaced her. Hedy's performance was greeted with enthusiasm:

> She looks wonderful, tender and really attractive. And she performs with real charm too: simply without affectation, talking and singing with the high voice of a child in which from time to time the echo of

a Wessely accent is detectable. In short, a delightful Sissy, without the stardom and pomp of a sophisticate, but with easy, childlike tones.[7]

Playing Sissy confirmed Hedy as a rising star in Vienna's film and theater world; the role was the most cherished part to which any young performer could aspire. It was also curiously portentous—the real-life Sissy (Elizabeth of Bavaria) had enjoyed a charmed childhood before an accidental meeting with Franz Joseph I led to her capturing the heart of the older man. He insisted on marrying her, and so she became, at age sixteen, Empress of Austria. Beautiful and rebellious, she soon found her position meant she could no longer behave as she wished; it also put her on a collision course with her mother-in-law, who controlled the up-bringing of her grandchildren, ensuring that Sissy seldom saw them. The young empress took to traveling the world, seemingly in search of a cure for her many illnesses, often in the company of lovers. Much later, her only son, Crown Prince Rudolf, was to die with his lover in the May-erling tragedy, and she herself was assassinated at the age of sixty. The tale of the beautiful royal captive has always charmed the Viennese, and in 1955 it made a star of Romy Schneider who, when she was even younger than Hedy, debuted in a trilogy of enormously popular Sissy films directed by Ernst Marischka.

If her casting as Sissy made the young Hedy Kiesler's reputation, it also had another, more sinister outcome. Through her newfound fame, she met her notorious first husband, Fritz Mandl, Joe May's cousin.

The Mandl family was Jewish and originally came from Hungary. Like the Kieslers, they were wealthy and socially well connected. Ferdinand Mandl converted to Catholicism to marry Fritz's mother, a family maid, Maria Mohr, from Graz. Fritz was born in 1900, though it took ten years for his father to convert and marry Maria. Fritz Mandl was therefore raised as a Catholic and beneath a shadow cast by his birth; the latter possibly prompting his lifetime spent seeking the acceptance of high society.[8] Mandl was to become one of the most successful businessmen of his generation, known variously as "Austria's Munitions King" and the "Merchant of Death." The Mandl family munitions business flourished during the First World War, with those employed in their factory, the

Hirtenberger Patronenfabrik, rising from five hundred to two thousand before World War I and climbing to more than four thousand during the war. The factory went bankrupt after the defeat of the Hapsburg Empire, and Alexander Mandl lost control of the business. In the late 1920s, Fritz Mandl negotiated a shrewd loan from a bank that enabled him to return the factory to family ownership. Mandl's own political interests were to the far right, though this did not prevent him from equipping both sides in the Spanish Civil War. Democracy, he once said, "is a luxury that might be borne, perhaps in prosperous periods."[9]

A man of medium height, Mandl was an impeccable dresser, with an eye for fine clothes and good food. The Mandl family had a long-standing interest in film production. Joe May, as previously noted, was Fritz's cousin. Leo Mandl, Joe May's nephew, was the director of Messter-Film GmbH and the director-general of Sascha Film in Vienna; in December 1922 Leo Mandl took over the operation of May Film. Fritz Mandl enjoyed rubbing shoulders with those in the film and theater world, and being seen in the company of beautiful women. He particularly had an eye for actresses.

He was notorious for his treatment of women. His first wife was the performer Hella Strauss, who later sued him for $80,000 in back alimony. Next, he had an affair with Eva May, Mia and Joe May's daughter. She had started acting at age sixteen, had married three times, each time to a film director (Martin Liebenau [Erik Lund], Lothar Mendes, and Manfred Noa), and starred in a string of German films. Her chaotic personal life led to a break with her father, and she was evidently desperately unstable. Hedy claims Eva committed suicide as a result of her relationship with Mandl; however, although Eva commited suicide in 1924, shooting herself with a revolver as she had done so often onscreen, this was not her first attempt.[10] What Hedy did not mention was that Eva May was also Fritz Mandl's second cousin. Long after his marriage with Hedy had ended and he was living in Argentina, Mandl offered his third wife a divorce settlement of just 800 pesos a month to support her and their children. His fourth wife charged him with assault.

Fritz Mandl was capable of both extraordinary generosity and perverse immorality; for instance, Mandl rescued Hugo Marton, his private banker, from a prison camp after the Anschluß; later Mandl had an affair with Marton's wife. He gave handsomely to the Red Cross, bribed numerous officials, and looked after his staff well. As Marie-Theres Arnbom has written, to this day Mandl is remembered in Hirtenberg for paying his workers a rate well above the national average. For the Austrian working class at large, however, he was the personification of fascism, the fat cat capitalist who armed the Heimwehr to keep down the workers.[11] His attempts to disavow his Jewish heritage were not taken at face value; commenting on his background, his politics, and his insistence that he had been educated with the Piarist Fathers, one journalist wrote of this "man of small to medium height, son of good Jewish parents," that his activities only proved that "when a Jew is stupid, then he really is stupid."[12]

As befitting a man with social ambitions, and one with considerable wealth, acquiring a trophy bride was imperative. Throughout 1933, Mandl diligently pursued Hedy. One night after Hedy's appearance as the lead in *Sissy,* Mandl showed up backstage and presented her with his card. Next, according to Hedy, he appealed to her parents for their support in his marriage plans. Wealthy and influential as the Kieslers were, they seem to have been won over by Mandl. So too was Hedy—in May 1933, the couple announced their engagement. It was also announced that the future Mrs. Mandl would end her career. "I am so happy about my engagement," she told the press, "that I am unable to be sad about my departure from the stage. It has been made so easy for me to give up my lifelong ambitions to be successful in the theater. I was a little sad to say good-bye to all this but I am really optimistic about the future and am really happy."[13] On 16 May, she gave her last performance as Sissy and the next day left for Paris. It was presumed she would return at the end of June for her wedding.

On 10 August 1933, the couple married in Vienna's baroque Karlskirche. Sometime prior, Hedy had converted to Roman Catholicism and Fritz Mandl to the Reform Church. The wedding party lunched at the Grand Hotel and the couple departed for Venice that evening, to honeymoon at the Excelsior Hotel on the Lido. "We spent many golden, glamorous weeks at the Lido," Hedy recalled a few years later, "dining, dancing, swimming, gliding along the Venetian canals in our own gondola, watching the Lido crowd disport itself."[14] Mr. and Mrs. Mandl were only two among many famous names vacationing in Venice that summer, but Fritz Mandl ensured that he and his young bride kept their distance from the celebrity set; and so they moved on, through Europe's most elegant resorts, to Capri, Lake Como, Biarritz, Cannes, Nice, and Paris, with Mandl always jealously guarding Hedy from others' attentions.

Once back in Vienna, in early January 1934, Mandl installed his wife in the Mandl mansion, a ten-room apartment at 15 Schwarzenbergplatz near Vienna's famed Ring Boulevard. With marriage came a massive estate that included the renowned Mandl hunting castle, the Villa Fegenberg, near Schwartau. Hedy now had maids, jewels, and wanted for nothing. She had every luxury, she later commented, except freedom.[15] She began to wear black and to dress more conservatively to rein in her personality. Still she was guaranteed to attract attention wherever she went.

Shortly after their marriage, Mandl apparently arranged for a private screening of his wife's latest film. Furious with what he saw, he ordered every print and negative of Ecstasy bought and destroyed, an edict that simply sent more prints into circulation and increased the film's notoriety. Indeed, it seems that Machaty was more than happy to sell his prints to Mandl, knowing that enough existed to make the eradication of Ecstasy impossible.[16] Although this story was widely circulated and repeated throughout Hedy's life, Mandl later stated that it was all just a publicity stunt dreamed up to promote the film.[17] It does seem odd that he arranged for the film to be destroyed well after it had completed its Viennese run, and there are no reports in the trade press of his alleged campaign. True or false, the myth enhanced Ecstasy's currency as forbidden fruit, as may have been intended.

With work out of the question for now, Hedy soon became bored. Mandl may not have literally locked her inside his castle, as she and others later claimed, but by moving his young bride into the Villa Fegenberg where she had only staff for company week after week, he effectively kept her away from temptation. Horse riding passed the time as did swimming in a pool fed by natural springs, but there was little else to do other than wear the expensive clothes Mandl chose for her. Her husband would appear late at night and on weekends with his guests. One day, she later told Farley Granger, "she decided to entertain herself by taking all sixteen toilet seats from the house out on to the lawn that swept down to the lake to paint them in the sun. As she was beginning the last one, she spotted a long line of black Mercedes limos in the distance coming up the long drive to the house. Her husband had not bothered to call her to warn her that he was bringing important guests for the weekend."[18] Berta Kaiser, then a fourteen-year-old kitchen maid at the Villa Fegenberg, remembered that Mandl himself would come to the kitchen to oversee the preparations for the evening's entertainment, never Hedy, who was too young to know about such matters. She was just there to be beautiful. Still, the staff was fond of her and awed by her looks and fine clothing. The couple, Berta Kaiser also noticed, slept in separate bedrooms.[19]

Soon Hedy realized that Mandl deliberately kept her short of cash and assured her that she could shop on credit when she wished. Determined to outwit him, she went shopping with a vengeance, buying up thousands of schillings worth of clothes, furs, evening gowns, and coats. According to Hedy,

> My program of buying went on for weeks and, during it, I became a new person. I was gayer, happier, and at the same time (imbued with this new secret purpose) more amenable to my husband's wishes . . . All of which led him, far from suspecting my true design, to do that which I had hoped he would do, namely give me an allowance of my own. "Hedy," he said, "your purchases are staggering even to a man of wealth. I will not have this go on. I shall therefore stop your credit and give you cash for your needs. This allowance is not comparable to your extravagance; but it must from now on, suffice."
>
> I had won![20]

In her autobiography, Hedy relates another incident that she claims occurred soon after she married Mandl. Finding herself unsupervised one afternoon, she slipped out of their mansion and into a crowd of shoppers. Soon she spotted Mandl behind her on an escalator. She rode to the bottom and hurried out a side exit, finding herself in a familiar part of town; nearby, she remembered, there was a notorious peephole club. Pushing enough money for the fee and a large tip in the surprised attendant's hand, she slipped into the club and headed upstairs to join the afternoon regulars in the booths. In front of her eyes, a formally dressed man and two nude women were forming a "sandwich" tableau on a round bed draped in red velvet. Behind her, Hedy heard Mandl's voice and guessed that his tip would be more generous than hers. She quickly exited the booth, and, like Alice, found herself on the other side of the glass, now transformed from voyeur to spectacle. Before Mandl could climb the stairs, a young man walked in and started to undress. Surprised that Hedy was not performing her part, he wondered if this was her first time, while musing that she looked familiar. As *Ecstasy* had been showing all around town, this could well have been so. Hedy began to undress and at that moment, Mandl banged on the door, demanding to know who the hell was in there. "What the hell do you care?" came the reply, "a broad and me." Unable to believe that this might be his wife, Mandl apparently departed, leaving Hedy to enjoy "the strangest love-making any girl ever had" and to be tipped afterward in gratification.[21]

Did this happen? Not surprisingly, no one has since stepped up to confirm or deny the story. The incident is only one of a number in the book that describe how its author finds herself in a position where a stranger takes advantage of her and where she comes to enjoy the experience. It's a scenario that, in various forms, underpins many a Hollywood narrative: the heroine stands up to a forceful man who breaks down her resistance by seducing her. Maybe this and the other incidents did occur, or maybe the ghostwriters invented them (though this seems a risky creative decision), or maybe in later life Hedy's sexual fantasies usurped the reality of life with Mandl in a city on the brink of war, in an environment where to be Jewish was to be increasingly fearful.

In Schwartau, Hedy presided over a dinner table that accommodated writers such as Ödön von Horváth, and Franz Werfel and his wife, Alma. According to Hedy's autobiography, they also counted Sigmund Freud among their circle. If these names reflected Mandl's cultural interests, some of Mandl's other guests were more sinister. Certainly, they included Mussolini, but, according to Hedy, another diner was Adolf Hitler.[22] It seems unlikely that Mandl would have entertained the German leader, even if Hitler were in Vienna at this time; later, Mandl actively moved against Hitler. Mussolini was another matter; he and Mandl shared many interests, not least a friendship with another well-known Austrian fascist, Count Ernst Rüdiger von Starhemberg. Von Starhemberg was the owner of thousands of acres of land and some thirteen castles across Austria; in the 1923 Putsch, he fought for Hitler, whom he counted at that time as a personal friend. By the time Von Starhemberg met Mandl, however, he had run through the family fortune and needed the munitions baron's financial support to stay at the forefront of the politics of the day.

Mandl and von Starhemberg made a formidable pair. The latter was socially well connected; Mandl brought money and ruthless business acumen to the partnership. Their vision was clear: when democracy became unworkable, Mandl told an interviewer in 1933, then you need a strong pair of clean hands. These were Count von Starhemberg's, he pronounced confidently, a man who had supported his political ideals with his own fortune.[23] These ideals were now invested in a private militia, the Heimwehr, and in February 1934 the twosome deployed the Heimwehr to crush the socialist revolution in Vienna. Equipping the Heimwehr and aligning himself with von Starhemberg were characteristically immoral moves on the part of Mandl, not least because a considerable proportion of the Heimwehr's membership was motivated by anti-Semitism. Von Starhemberg himself was, like Mandl, quite immune to the finer points of ideology, on occasion inciting a crowd with Nazi-inspired slogans and, when it was more convenient, reassuring the foreign press that the Heimwehr completely rejected Nazi racial theories.[24] Mussolini bought weapons from Mandl at top rates to help finance his and von Starhemberg's activities, and for a time, as part of his strategy to strengthen Austria against Hitler, the Italian leader threw in his lot with the two Austrians.

This then was the company the young Hedy Mandl found herself keeping. It was at one of von Starhemberg's balls that a conversation took place that suggests there were more sinister reasons for her marriage to Mandl. According to Jewish-German writer Heinz Liepmann, it is based on an encounter with Hedy that took place on the night of 22 November 1934. By this stage Dolfuß had been assassinated and von Starhemberg was vice-chancellor and minister of State Security. The guests at the ball included Prince Nicholas of Greece, Madame Schiaperelli, Franz Werfel and Alma, Prince Gustav of Denmark, actress Nora Gregor (now von Starhemberg's lover), and General Malleaux of the French General staff. But the figure that caught Liepmann's gaze was that of a young woman whose beauty, heightened by the simplicity of her gown and the size of her diamond pin, outshone this display of wealth. This was Frau Mandl, dancing in the arms of her much-older husband, Fritz. Soon after he entered the ballroom, Liepmann observed Mandl leave with Count von Starhemberg and sensed a shudder of foreboding run through the collection of guests. What were these two men planning? Seizing his chance,

Liepmann asked an acquaintance to introduce him to Hedy. "Let us sit down for a moment," she suggested. "Only then did I notice," Liepmann recalled, "that her soft alluring beauty was really intoxicating when enhanced by the vital charm of her eyes and her voice. She appeared sophisticated and naïve at the same time—great international hostess and sweet Viennese girl."[25] They talked about her father, whom Liepmann had known. He was a shrewd businessman, Liepmann remembered, tall, handsome, and always well dressed, with blue eyes and dark hair growing grey at the temples. Hedy sighed at the thought of "my poor old daddy," but she was soon swept off by another admirer for a waltz. How could the repellent Mandl have won himself such a beautiful young bride, Liepmann wondered aloud to his friend Ödön von Horvath.

According to von Horvath, the Kieslers had found themselves on the verge of bankruptcy after the death of Hedy's father. Hedy and her mother attempted to win back some of their lost fortune on the stock exchange and, in doing so, lost the rest. Hedy then took a job as a stenographer but was much too pretty to work in an office, "You know what I mean," von Horvath added suggestively. At last, through the intervention of an old family friend, Hedy was hired at Sascha Studios and it was there that Machaty discovered her. The accuracy of the report is questionable, given that Liepmann apparently believed Emil Kiesler had died a few years previously (Herr Kiesler died unexpectedly of a heart attack a year later in February 1935).

At this point, Horvath paused and both men listened as a detachment of Heimwehr militia passed by; a single light coming from above suggesting that Mandl and von Starhemberg were engaged in some menacing plot. "Why did she play in *Ecstasy* at all?" Liepmann wondered. Horvath shrugged. "I think she can hardly be blamed for it," he answered. "The film itself is a very ambitious and purely artistic work and I think that nobody, least of all Hedy, had the faintest idea that the great public would regard it as a 'naughty' film."

Sympathetic as he was to Hedy's suffering over the public reception of the film in the previous year, von Horvath suggested that she was foolish not to have kept a low profile after the scandal erupted. Instead, she took a part in Max Reinhardt's 1931 stage production of *The Weaker Sex*, cast most likely because of her notoriety as much as her acting.

Gripping Liepmann's arm, Horvath pointed to the figures of Mandl and von Starhemberg walking together arm in arm. Hedy left her dancing partner and walked over to Mandl. The band struck up a waltz and the munitions baron began to dance with his young wife. Liepmann watched him lean over and say something into her ear and observed how her eyes opened wide, apparently in horror. More political machinations were afoot.

There are perhaps too many inaccuracies in Liepmann's story to render it useful but certainly it is worth mulling over the similarities between the portrayal of the aging husband, unflattering as it was, in *Ecstasy* and Mandl's own stature and status. Nor should one dismiss the possibility that Hedy's very youthful marriage was sanctioned by her parents because of the financial security they felt it would bring her. Certainly, like Sissy, she may have felt trapped by the obnoxious Mandl and his wealth, age, and position.

In August 1934, *Ecstasy* was entered at the Second Venice Film Festival. The version enjoyed by festivalgoers was the one ending with Eva nursing her baby while Adam lost himself in work.[26] Because the festival still had no access to a suitable cinema, *Ecstasy* was screened, as were other entries, in the open air. As darkness fell, the audience took their seats in the garden of the Hotel Excelsior to watch Machaty's film. They were enchanted and saluted the ending with a standing ovation and calls of "Bravo!" It was the longest round of applause to greet any film at the festival. The next day on the Lido, all the talk was of *Ecstasy*. Should Eva have left her husband? Should they have stayed together to bring up their child? As Francesco Bono remarks, overnight the unknown Austrian Hedwig Kiesler was transformed into a diva. Dressed in the most elegant designs, she was seen around Venice with one arm linked to her husband (apparently now reconciled to his wife's scandalous performance) and the other arm linked to von Starhemberg, who was in town conducting business with Mussolini. One journalist was certain he spotted the young star throwing off her clothes and jumping naked into the sea.[27]

Needless to say, controversy also followed the screening of *Ecstasy*, with the influential Catholic press outraged by its content. Il Duce (Mussolini) demanded that a private screening of the work be held in his home at the Villa Torlonia. A print was flown to him in Rome where he is rumored to have gasped over Hedy's beauty, a signal that the film could continue to be shown. As Francesco Bono advises, these anecdotes should be taken with a pinch of salt; particularly in this case, as Hedy already knew Mussolini from his friendship with Mandl.[28] Whether the Pope actually banned the film is again a moot point; in any case, this screening turned out to be the only opportunity Italian audiences had to see *Ecstasy,* which received no further commercial release. The Mussolini Cup for Best Foreign Film that year went to a rather different offering, Robert Flaherty's *Man of Aran,* but Gustav Machaty won the Cup of the City of Venice as Best Director.

Tiring of life as a trophy bride, Hedy turned to her old mentor, Max Reinhardt. When Mandl, attending to business abroad, deposited her with some friends of his in St. Wolfgang, she persuaded them to drive her to Salzburg. There she met Reinhardt and they had a long talk. Reinhardt, however, could offer her nothing as long as Mandl was against her return to work.

In 1936, the Austrian Association of Cinema Producers declared a ban on hiring Jewish performers or talent. Mandl began moving his assets out of Austria in anticipation of a German takeover. Hedy made her own plans. During the time Mandl and Ernst Rüdiger von Starhemberg were business partners, Hedy was apparently having an affair with von Starhemberg's younger brother, Ferdinand, and on Friday, 13 November 1936, the twosome fled Mandl's mansion and boarded a train to Budapest. Hedy had heard there were theater opportunities there and planned to visit the home of a childhood friend. "When the train pulled into the Budapest station, there was my husband waiting. His face was a grey mask of fury."[29] Elsewhere, it was rumored that Hedy was seeing not Ferdinand but Ernst Rüdiger von Starhemberg himself.

Her next attempt to escape, according to her autobiography, involved the connivance of the English Colonel Righter. A hurried conversation persuaded the nervous military man to promise his help but in an underhanded double-cross, Mandl revealed to Hedy the recording equipment he installed to eavesdrop on her conversations; worse again, he told her that Righter was on his payroll.

By now it seemed the talk of Vienna was of Hedy and Mandl's marital problems. Her acting aspirations first sparked the flame, but Hedy's public appearances with Count Max Hardegg, the gossip of Viennese society for weeks, probably further aggravated their struggles.[30] Eventually, in early 1937, Hedy, disguised as one of her maids, whom she had hired for her look-alike qualities, fled Mandl:

Early that Thursday morning, I put three sleeping pills in Laura's coffee, packed her suitcase, left her some money, dressed in my maid's costume with the collar turned up and sneaked out the servants entrance.

I had the keys to Laura's battered car, and I reached the railway unchallenged . . . The platform was deserted when I bought my ticket and started a twelve-minute wait. Like a novice spy, I imagined the stationmaster was scrutinizing me. And there was a telephone by his elbow. Somehow I managed to turn my back on him, and my studied casualness until the train did arrive and I did board it were not wasted on me in a later motion picture with Paul Henreid (*The Conspirators*).[31]

Although this story stretches credibility, it may be true, at least to the extent that Hedy did escape Mandl, who was, by all accounts an intimidating, controlling husband. She escaped with just a few items of clothing and a bag of jewels. These jewels were her insurance, the kind that would withstand the economic consequences of war. They remained in their paper bag, by her side, in her home of the moment. All Mandl's wives, according to his daughter, Puppe, received jewels; and it was the only thing they could take away with them.[32] Occasionally, Hedy's jewels were stolen, or maybe "stolen"; only at the end of her life did they finally disappear, this time apparently for good.

Both in her own account of her 1937 escape and in the version she gave Christopher Young, Hedy said that soon after she left Mandl, her mother wired her with the news of her father's death, which intensified her heartbreak. This is a curious mistake, since, as was noted, Emil Kiesler died in early 1935.

According to Young, Hedy appealed to the Holy Rota in Rome for an annulment of her marriage to Mandl. Her request was denied, and she traveled to Nevada to obtain a divorce.[33] Hedy, however, claimed she obtained a divorce in Paris. It seems likely that Mandl had his marriage to Hedy annulled in 1938 on racial grounds.[34] They may even have discussed divorce before that; one rumor claimed they were planning to travel to Riga (the Reno of Europe) for a quick dissolution of their marriage.[35]

According to the Nuremberg Race Laws of 1935, a "full Jew" was a person with three Jewish grandparents. Those with less were designated as *"Mischlinge"* and fell into one of two categories: first degree equaled two Jewish grandparents; and second degree equaled one Jewish grand-parent. Mandl was only too aware that he was of "tainted" stock: "Because I only have two grandparents who are of pure Aryan stock, this question is of the utmost importance to me. Perhaps Cardinal [Innitzer] could also be of some help since he was always well disposed towards me and a good word from him in important places would be very influential."[36]

Motivated, like his good friend Cardinal Innitzer, by a desire to keep all parties happy, Mandl was less interested in conforming to Nazi decrees than in protecting his financial interests, in this case his salary from the Hirtenberger Patronenfabrik, which was now in full production, gearing up happily for war. An annulment from the marriage with Hedy, a full-blooded Jew, was—not to put too fine a point on it—worth RM 2,000 monthly to Mandl.[37]

In 1953, Mandl's third wife, Herta Schneider, charged Mandl with bigamy on the grounds that he never divorced Hedy. In pursuit of her share of Mandl's Argentinean assets (which she valued at £2,600,000), Schneider had filed for divorce, charging among other things that Mandl had dragged her around their luxury apartment by the hair. Mandl counter-claimed that they were never really married, as he had never properly divorced Hedy. According to his solicitors, Mandl had obtained a divorce from Hedy in Texas but the Vatican had refused to recognize it. He married Schneider in 1939, subsequently obtained a Mexican divorce from her, and then married Gloria Vinelli in Mexico City in 1951.[38]

The story of Hedy's escape from Mandl followed her throughout her life. Its overtones of privilege and melodrama set it apart from other accounts of Jewish exile from Nazi-occupied territories. Most of all, her story eliminated the uncomfortable fact of her Jewishness, an aspect of her identity that she never again mentioned. This may also account for her neglect in the many studies of Jewish émigrés to Hollywood, rendering her a more lightweight character in a narrative focused on persecution and its consequences. What should be remembered is that her Jewish identity would have surfaced had she stayed in Austria. It is nearly certain too, given the pattern of her life, that she would not have stayed with Mandl, whose political activities she loathed and who could not have controlled her in the way he wanted.

Mandl in turn fled Vienna as Hitler annexed the arms factories. With the suspicion that he might be Jewish hanging over him, the businessman escaped along with his father, his sister, and Herta Schneider to Argentina. Before he left, Mandl sealed a deal with the Nazis allowing him to keep his non-Austrian holdings. In return he allegedly carried Nazi funds belonging to Göring, Ribbentrop, and other high-ranking party members to invest in Argentina. As his former wife built her reputation in Hollywood, so he built his, financing Juan Perón's successful electoral campaign and developing a local arms program. It seems that he and Hedy kept in touch over the years, though nothing suggests that they ever again met face to face.

Many years later again, in 1979, Manuel Puig opened his science fiction novel *Pubis Angelical* with a woman dying in a Mexican hospital. As her life slips away, she becomes not herself but her two shadows, one a Viennese actress who marries a weapons maker prior to World War II and later moves to Hollywood; and the other, "W218," a sexual conscript in an alternative present. Puig makes his actress a tragic heroine. Locked in a fortress by her billionaire husband, whose fortune comes from making arms for the Nazis, she eventually escapes disguised as one of the doubles her jealous husband has planted around his island home. Nothing goes well in this story centered on the theme that men will inevitably betray women. Only the actress's alter ego, the sex slave, triumphs, and then only because she realizes that forcing men to change is futile—it is far better for women to believe in themselves than to become an object of male desire. There is no evidence that Hedy Mandl, by then Hedy Lamarr, ever read Puig's book. She might have found his conclusion simplistic.

5

The Most Beautiful Woman
in the World

SWITZERLAND WAS REGARDED by many German and Austrian refugees as a station on their way to France until 1938, when it introduced measures prohibiting Jews from crossing its borders. The better-heeled refugees, whose numbers now included Hedwig Kiesler, chose to spend the winter of 1936–1937 in St. Moritz before heading to Paris. The Swiss resort was a flurry of cocktails, parties, and gossip. As Erich Maria Remarque wrote in his diaries, some refugees began to sink under the boredom, for them drinking began in the early morning; others withdrew into themselves; fights broke out. Certain prominent Jewish dissidents were discomforted to find themselves rubbing shoulders with regular holidayers, whose political views differed sharply from their own. Among the filmmakers, the most prominent was Leni Riefenstahl, Hitler's favorite. Billy Wilder was also found in St. Moritz as were the Hollywood stars Eleanor Boardman and Kay Francis.[1] Remarque had fled to Switzerland in 1933. His best-known antiwar novel, *All Quiet on the Western Front,* had been made into a hugely successful Hollywood film, and he was friendly with many people that Hedy would later encounter there, notably Charles Boyer. Back in Germany, Remarque was persona non grata for the same reasons he was feted in Hollywood; the premiere of *All Quiet* in Berlin had prompted a display of Nazi flag waving, with Goebbels marching out of the cinema to chants of "Judenfilm! Judenfilm!" Nazi supporters set off stink bombs in the auditorium along with releasing hundreds of white mice. Bizarrely, the Nazis then invited Remarque to become Minister of Culture for Prussia. When he declined and went into exile, they responded by banning his books and decreeing that anyone who owned a copy of *All Quiet on the Western Front* must relinquish it to the authorities.

Remarque was extraordinarily good-looking, deeply romantic, and a serial womanizer. He was also bored in St. Moritz and enchanted by meeting Hedy. She embodied, as his biographer writes, "all the qualities that Remarque found attractive—a stunning beauty, an actress, sophisticated, louche, German-speaking." Soon they began an affair that lasted until the summer of 1937, when two events occurred in short succession: Hedy left for London and Remarque met the woman who was to become his greatest love, Marlene Dietrich.[2]

In London, Hedy was introduced to Louis B. Mayer. Mayer was there to sign up Greer Garson and, one version of the story goes, was unaware that Hedy Kiesler was the naked girl in *Ecstasy,* something his aides were afraid to tell him.[3] It seems unlikely, however, that Mayer was unaware of who Hedy was or that she did not tell him. Predictably, the most colorful version of the encounter is found in Hedy's autobiography. She remembers Mayer opening the meeting by acknowledging he had seen *Ecstasy:* "Never get away with that stuff in Hollywood. Never. A woman's ass is for her husband, not theatergoers. You're lovely, but I have the family point of view. I don't like what people would think about a girl who flits bare-assed around a screen." He then proceeded to give the young hopeful a lesson on how Hollywood morality worked. "We make clean pictures and we like our stars to lead clean lives," Mayer said. "Of course we don't control them. I don't like shenanigans, but I don't stop them. If you make love . . . fornicate . . . (he hesitated) . . . screw your leading man *in the dressing room,* that's your business. But in front of the camera, gentility. You hear, gentility."[4] Whether or not Hedy was accurate in her memory of this exchange, the tone of Mayer's words rings true.

In his biography of Mayer, Charles Higham describes a man who controlled, or tried to control, every aspect of the studio he ran in the most paternalistic, if ruthless, fashion: "Mayer believed that actors did not know what was good for themselves; he controlled them to the point of personally putting saccharine in their coffee to keep their weight down, telling them what they could eat for breakfast, lunch and dinner, whom they could marry, whether it was time to have a baby or not, how to obtain an abortionist if a picture was at stake; he was as stern and loving to them as he was to his own daughters."[5] Communist or fascist, gay or straight, prepared to sleep with him or not, all modes of belief or behavior were tolerated by Mayer as long as they were kept private. On the screen only perfection was allowed; Mayer's was not a realist aesthetic. More than that, it was an aesthetic that excluded ethnicity from its concept of beauty. Only gentiles could become stars at MGM, and if they were Jewish, they were to conceal it at all costs: if Hedy was to assimilate to American culture, specifically Hollywood culture, she must lose her Jewishness and she must also act American. It was this disjuncture—between her inherited identity, with its emphasis on artistry and the expression of intelligence, and her need to assume a new identity, including the particular associations that came with being an actress in America—that would shape her Hollywood career. For now, however, this was all before her.

Mayer had traveled to Europe to ensure the best of its fleeing artists made their way to MGM. Many of them were introduced to Mayer by agent Ad Schulberg, who actively helped her Jewish clients escape fascism. Mayer had another reason to prioritize any talent Schulberg sent his way, since they were having an affair.[6] In fact, he may well have already met Hedy as they both moved around Europe in the summer of 1937. Rumors that Mayer was interested in hiring Gustav Machaty and the Hungarian Ilona von Hajmassy, among a raft of other big film names, were now widely circulating in Vienna, and Machaty could easily have suggested Hedy's name to the mogul.

Hedy told Otto Preminger a different version of her London meeting: "A hotel suite full of cigar smoke and men in shirt sleeves playing cards. He [Mayer] was no longer interested in her. He told Bob Ritchie, one of his assistants, to offer her the standard seven-year contract with six month options, starting at a hundred and fifty dollars a week."[7]

Hedy refused and decided to risk another approach. Mayer was to travel back to Hollywood in early September on the *Normandie*. The French liner was the pride of the ocean, having just crossed the Atlantic in three days, twenty-three hours, and two minutes, a new record. Hedy decided that she too would be on board and, according to her own account, made swift arrangements to travel as governess to the child prodigy, violinist Grisha Goluboff, whom Bob Ritchie was also trying to promote.[8] In fact, in 1937, Goluboff was now eighteen years old and in little need of a governess. Born in California to Russian émigré parents, he had already made his name in America and Europe, giving his first recital when he was barely ten. In 1932, in the wake of a successful European tour, he was gifted a Pietro Giovanni Guarnerius by Baron von Schlippenbach, an influential patron of the arts in Berlin. When Hitler heard of this, he was enraged the violin had ended up in the hands of a Jewish child and, barely a day after his inauguration, cabled the German consulate in New York, demanding the precious instrument be returned. Soon after, Henry Ford, ironically a notorious anti-Semite himself, loaned Goluboff a Stradivarius. In 1936, Goluboff was invited to play in the Salzburg Festival by Max Reinhardt and stayed with him as his guest. It may be that he and Hedy met each other through Reinhardt at Salzburg, though soon afterward Goluboff decided to settle in Los Angeles, where he made his first film recording, a short orchestral piece for Paramount Pictures. He was next invited by Louis B. Mayer to play for him, with a view to signing a contract with MGM. His manager, Isadore Noble, however, was unsure how the studios would handle a musical prodigy and how this would affect his image. Bumping into Max Reinhardt in Los Angeles, Noble consulted with the director as to how to proceed; Reinhardt advised against signing and Noble agreed that, for the time being, it would be better to stay clear of Hollywood.[9]

When Goluboff met Hedy on the *Normandie*, therefore, he was already an established performer, who had made his first film recording. His family is clear that Hedy was not his mentor despite her claim otherwise: "I got Bob's little violinist a contract too!"[10] "It was Grisha who helped her, actually," his sister, Gladys, said. "From what I remember Grisha's manager and others say, she was rather an opportunist and used it to advance her own career."[11]

The ocean journey started inauspiciously when the gigantic liner lost a propeller just outside of Southampton and had to return to Le Havre for repairs, adding a day to the voyage. Mayer's guests, among them Walter Reisch, were already beginning to sense that this trip would test MGM's new family. One of its recent members was Sonja Henie, then better known as the Swedish skating champion; she blushed when anyone greeted her. Hedy, it was observed, was less reticent and wasted no opportunity to ensure that Mayer noticed her. Reisch, of course, knew Hedy; many of the other passengers were familiar with the reputation she had garnered from her role in *Ecstasy*.

Mayer was traveling with his second in command, Benny Thau, and his press representative, Howard Strickling. The ship finally set off across the Atlantic and immediately ran into a ferocious storm. Undeterred, the mogul proceeded with his business and summoned Reisch to his cabin. Ignoring the Austrian's seasickness, Mayer began to kick around a few story lines. Most important, he decided to invest a little more in the alluring Hedwig Kiesler; she would get the contract she sought.

Hedy's life was immediately transformed. The lower decks of the *Normandie* boasted a mini shopping mall of the world's most luxurious stores—Dior, Poiret, and Chanel. Mayer sent his new protegée off on a shopping expedition. Having stepped on board in a gray tailor-made suit with one pair of gloves, no suitcase, and not a dollar to her name, she landed in America with a complete designer wardrobe and a set of matching suitcases to carry it.[12] She also acquired a new name.

Choosing that name had provided Mayer and his guests with some delightful onboard entertainment. Kiesler sounded German and that, for obvious reasons, was out; Mandl also had political connotations that nobody wished to consider. "Every afternoon they held story conferences around the Ping-Pong table on the 'A' deck of the *Normandie* with Strickling, Thau, and all the others, trying to decide how to go about introducing the young beauty to the members of the New York Press who would infallibly arrive on the boat," Reisch remembered. In the end, it was Mayer who came up with Hedy's new last name. Recalling the late Barbara La Marr, he decided to rename Hedy Kiesler, Hedy Lamarr. Mayer, Reisch mused, wasn't superstitious, exclaiming jauntily, "We are going to replace death with life."[13] Hedy had no idea that she was to become the reincarnation of a woman whose activities had been the subject of constant scandal since she had posed nude at the age of sixteen. In other uncanny twists: Barbara La Marr had become pregnant in 1922; her baby boy was born and given up for adoption before she adopted him herself. The original La Marr married five times and ended her life tragically, dying as a consequence of failing health brought on by heroin addiction. Mayer could not have known that Hedy herself would move on to another five marriages or adopt a son who may have been her own, but he was able to ensure Barbara's reincarnation in other ways. Part of the publicity buildup for Barbara La Marr had been to dub her "The Most Beautiful Woman in the World." Mayer now bestowed this title on Hedy, along with her new name and wardrobe. Hedy boarded the ship as companion to a musical prodigy; she left it a star.

On the same trip, Mayer met the eminent Viennese lawyer Paul Koretz, who negotiated contracts for Luise Rainer and the newly named Hedy Lamarr. According to Scott Eyman, "Those troublesome women became a running joke between the two men, as Mayer would often chastise Koretz for 'putting these crazy women in my life.' "[14]

Hedy and Sonja Henie were not the only Europeans Mayer collected on his trip. Returning aboard the *Normandie* were British producer/director Victor Saville, who had several screen rights Mayer coveted; Rose Stradner, the other Sissy; Austrian tenor Joseph Schmidt; and two singers, the Hungarian Ilona von Hajmassy and the Polish Miliza Korjus. Greer Garson was on board too, as were an array of other well-known names, including Douglas Fairbanks Jr. and Cole Porter. They arrived in the United States on 30 September 1937. Howard Dietz, head of publicity, was on hand to ensure the press appreciated Hedy, and they certainly did. Her looks alone turned heads, and then there was her reputation from *Ecstasy*, by now a cause célèbre. Asked by the press to lift her ankle-length skirts and show a little flesh, Hedy refused. She still outshone the other members of Mayer's *Normandie* cast. Dietz and Strickling were content with their work and promptly moved their starlet west to Hollywood. On 4 October 1937, Hedy signed her first contract with MGM, or technically, their parent company, Lowe's. Her salary was to be $550 per week.

Once settled in MGM and attending daily English lessons, it seemed that there was no suitable role for the new arrival. Unsure what to do with an actress who spoke little English, whose country was easily mistaken for Germany, and whose reputation was, to say the least, raunchy, the studio prevaricated. A reputation for nudity soon became the least of Hedy's problems.

"Did you appear in the nude?" Dietz asked her.

"Yes."

"Did you look good?"

"Of course!"

"Then it's all right, no damage has been done."[15]

A more immediate difficulty for Hedy was that her nubile European figure was considered somewhat plump for Hollywood audiences. Her height, at five feet and seven inches tall, was just right—good for fashion but no threat to the shorter male stars. Her weight was the issue. A strict diet shed sixteen pounds and gradually transformed her into a svelte American; meanwhile, she was instructed to pose in slacks or dresses so that the camera would focus on her face rather than her body. Nothing, it seemed, could be done about her small breasts.

Still Hedy was excited about her move. She told the Austrian film magazine *Mein Film* that Louis B. Mayer was personally overseeing her introduction to Hollywood and that she was to fill the gap in his pantheon of stars left by the death of Jean Harlow.[16]

MGM also contracted Gustav Machaty and toyed with the idea of having him direct his discovery again, perhaps in a remake of *Within the Law*. But when screen tests revealed that Hedy photographed beautifully but had no idea how to act, Ruth Hussey was cast in the film. Mayer began to consider loaning out his new signing and letting another studio try her out. She was offered to Goldwyn for *The Adventures of Marco Polo* (Archie L. Mayo, 1937), but Sam Goldwyn chose Sigrid Gurie to star opposite Gary Cooper; nor was Paramount keen on her for the Ronald Colman vehicle *If I Were King* (Frank Lloyd, 1938). Hedy was not the only MGM actress that found herself with a contract but no roles. Most of her fellow travelers on the *Normandie* were soon equally idle, although Miliza Korjus was cast in *The Great Waltz* in 1938.

Greer Garson, Hedy Lamarr, and Ilona von Hajmassy (renamed Ilona Massey) christened themselves the "Neglected Imports" and spent their time together wondering if Louis B. Mayer would ever keep his promises.[17] Meanwhile, they were encouraged to attend parties, and soon Hedy was mixing with the Hollywood social set. Having grafted his Austrian discovery onto the name and identity of an illustrious silent star, Mayer's next fantasy was that Hedy Lamarr would become the new Greta Garbo. With that in mind, he had Hedy watch Garbo's old films day after day so that he might remake them with Hedy in the parts so recently occupied by the Swede. In the film colony, meanwhile, rumors circulated about the exact function of Mayer's "harem."[18]

As war in Europe became inevitable and news of the fate of the Jews who had remained there grew more disturbing, the first wave of emigrants, and those who had traveled voluntarily to California to pursue careers, realized they must act on behalf of those who had been left behind. Notable among these was the Hollywood agent Paul Kohner, now husband to Lupita Tovar. A native of Teplitz in what was then Bohemia and, after World War I, Czechoslovakia, Kohner came from a cultured, bourgeois Jewish family. His background was similar to Hedy's and so many of the other new emigrants. By the late 1930s, he had struck out on his own as an agent and when war broke out in 1939, he was contacted by a group of Jewish writers whom he had known in Berlin and Vienna who asked him to help them emigrate to America. Kohner appealed to individual studio heads and successfully negotiated contracts for several writers, which would allow them to gain exit papers; they would also receive a minimal salary from the studios. Of course, once these men (and they were all men) arrived in Hollywood, the irreconcilable differences between the two cultures became apparent. Kohner's brother, Frederick, later remembered the newcomers with their heavy suits, starched collars, and durable shoes: "Uprooted, bewildered, alienated, the refugees were rarely able to make satisfactory contact with their American colleagues. They never became part of any group—except their own. At lunch they sat together and spoke German. Evenings they met at someone's place, in a nondescript living room, and commiserated about the fate of Europe."[19]

Sunday was open house at the Kohners, and Lupita Kohner recalled Marlene Dietrich and Billy Wilder cooking scrambled eggs in their kitchen; she and Paul also kept up with Hedy through her Hollywood career, only losing touch with her in later life; "she didn't talk much, she was very quiet . . . you never knew what went [on] in her mind."[20] The Californians knew little and cared less about the old European culture that had formed these emigrants. Max Reinhardt's name was one of the few they respected or were familiar with. Mentioning it opened doors; many did.

For the women who accompanied their husbands, or who, like the Kohners' mother, arrived at the last minute, life in this modern, anonymous city was intolerable. Helene Kohner took to hitching lifts and riding around in buses, just to find people who would listen to her talk about "home." Paul Kohner set up the European film fund to help those emigrants that he could and made it his mission to find them work, but many sank into despair.

One of Kohner's clients was Gustav Machaty. In 1937, he married Maria May; work was slow and in March 1939, MGM let him go. He moved from occasional job to occasional job but was beset with money problems. The eventual release of Ecstasy in the United States earned him nothing as by now he had lost ownership of the rights. Maria May was forced to sell the jewelry she had brought with her from Europe; in 1942 Machaty learned that his mother had died in the Treblinka concentration camp. The hard times took their toll on their marriage and a divorce seemed imminent. Still they stayed together long enough for Machaty to direct his one minor Hollywood success, Jealousy (1945), starring Hedy's future husband, John Loder. From a story by Dalton Trumbo about the apparent suicide of the young wife of a failed writer, it eerily foretold what was to come in Machaty's own life. On 4 October 1951, Maria was found dead in her Los Angeles home; she had committed suicide with an overdose of sleeping tablets because, it was rumored, of a failed affair with Fritz Lang.[21] Machaty left America soon after. He spent much of the rest of his life trying to raise funds for a remake of Ecstasy.

Another client of Kohner's was Hedy's cousin by marriage and host from her Berlin days, Joe May. After the death of their daughter, Mia May permanently retired from the stage and screen, but Joe continued working until conditions prevailed against him. Together, he and Mia fled to Hollywood in 1934. By 1948, Joe May was in despair. He wrote to Paul Kohner that he had sold his wife's last small ring for $60; those who answered his letters could not help him, most did not reply. How was he to pay the $44 he still owed for the car that in Los Angeles was his lifeline and which he had refinanced to clear his other debts?[22] It was hard enough for May to humble himself privately to his friends and colleagues; publicly, when he did gain work in Hollywood, he was completely unable to adapt to becoming a small cog in an alien machine. He gained a reputation for being stubborn and difficult, and his scripts did not translate. The only solution to his problems that May could see was to exploit his Viennese heritage. In March 1949 he opened the Blue Danube Restaurant in West Los Angeles, his second attempt to replace filmmaking with catering (he had opened the Wiener Bar in Hollywood in 1937). His friends chipped in, offering financial help as well as the promise of patronage. The roll call of investors reveals the extent of the Austrian presence in Hollywood: Henry Koster, Otto Preminger, Walter Reisch, Robert Siodmak, Joe Mankiewcz, and Hedy all supported the Mays in their new venture, as did Billy Wilder, himself the recipient of Joe May's help when he first arrived in Hollywood. For a few brief weeks, The Blue Danube became the heart of the exile film colony and the original investors were joined at table by Ernst Lubitsch, Conradt Veidt, and other homesick émigrés. The venture only lasted long enough to take the shine off the kitchen instruments, and Joe and Mia spent the rest of their lives receiving help from Kohner's European Film Fund, rarely leaving their house. Joe May died in Hollywood on 29 April 1954.

The crucial distinction between the cultural life of the Viennese and other middle-European Jews and that of Hollywood was that the European Jews were part of a high-culture elite, associated with theater, classical music, and painting. Even when they did involve themselves in the kind of films that Joe May turned out in such large numbers in Berlin, or the kind of light comedies that gave Hedy her early experience, theirs was still an insular culture. In America, they found themselves in a society that defined itself through its embrace of populism, notably in cinema, radio, and dance hall entertainment. The founding, mainly Jewish, fathers of Hollywood had swiftly grasped this and with it the need to provide a model of entertainment that was meaningful to anyone anywhere on the globe. As the Machatys, the Mays, and so many other émigrés found, the divide between their old middle-European culture and the brash new environment of America was simply unbridgeable.

We need to measure Hedy's achievement against this background, particularly given that she traveled without the support of a Svengali director (as did, say, Marlene Dietrich) or a significant résumé. All that she could rely on were minor appearances in a few little-known German films and a reputation for nudity gained in an art film that no one had seen, although many felt they had. Being beautiful wasn't enough either; alone in Hollywood, speaking poor English, aged only twenty-three, Hedy had to be tough.

Bolstered by Mayer's interest in her career, yet with no roles in sight, the young arrival needed to ensure that she kept her name in the gossip columns by being spotted at celebrity events. Arriving on the arm of an established director or star guaranteed glamour shots in the next day's newspapers; without these, she was in danger of becoming just another lost emigrée on the MGM lot. Hedy set to work.

6

To the Casbah!

IN EARLY 1938, Hedy began seeing Reginald Gardiner, the suave English star, who, like her, was on the rise in Hollywood. She credits him with introducing her to Walter Wanger, who was preparing to shoot *Algiers* with her old friend from Switzerland, the French matinee idol Charles Boyer.[1] It was Wanger who transformed Hedy's career.

A cultured Hollywood maverick and the scion of a wealthy second-generation German-Jewish family, Wanger was at the height of his success when he signed up Hedy. He had sealed a distribution deal with United Artists that would see him produce such films as Fritz Lang's *You Only Live Once* (1937), John Ford's *Stagecoach* (1939), and Hitchcock's *Foreign Correspondent* (1940). Wanger was holding Charles Boyer to a two-picture contract and had finally persuaded Boyer to play Pépé Le Moko (Pepe Le Moko in the American version) in a shot-by-shot remake of the 1937 French film of the same title. This method, Wanger hoped, would substantially reduce production costs. Boyer was justifiably anxious about reprising a part famously performed by Jean Gabin and only consented with the understanding that he would have "director approval."[2] It was Boyer, therefore, who chose John Cromwell to direct. In the end, *Algiers* was not an exact remake of *Pépé Le Moko;* the original's heady sensuality and moral ambiguity were more than the Breen office would permit. "We have received and read the script for your proposed picture PEPE LE MOKO," Joseph Breen wrote to Walter Wanger. "In its present form, you will understand that it is not acceptable from the standpoint of the Production Code by reason of the definite suggestion that your two leading female characters are both kept women [. . .] The dialogue should be changed, so as to get away from the suggestion that Ines is Pepe's mistress."[3]

To tone down the film, Wanger hired James M. Cain to rewrite the opening twenty minutes. Next, Wanger's regular collaborator John Howard Lawson intensified the relationship between Pepe Le Moko and the European beauty Gaby to stress that his love for her sparked his desire to return to Paris. Lawson also changed the ending so that Pepe no longer committed suicide but was shot by the police.[4] Even with these changes, the film promised an exoticism that was guaranteed to play well with Depression-era American audiences: "ALGIERS. Where blazing desert meets the blue Mediterranean, and modern Europe jostles ancient Africa," the opening credits declare. "A stone's throw from the modern city, the native quarter, known as the *Casbah*, stands like a fortress above the sea. Its population includes many tribes and races, drifters and outcasts from all parts of the world—and criminals who find this a safe hiding place from the long arm of the law. Supreme on these heights rules one man—Pepe le Moko—long wanted by the French police."

The French authorities were instantly provoked and objected to Joseph Breen that it would misrepresent "the character and moral standing of all French people and customs in that locality." Wanger's response was pragmatic: "As remarkable as it may seem, I assure you the majority of Americans do not know where Algiers is."[5]

Before Hedy had been cast, producer David O. Selznick had proposed that his new discovery from Sweden, Ingrid Bergman, should take the part. After Hedy gained the role, a furious Sylvia Sidney refused to play the secondary character of Ines, a thankless part that makes her little more than a doormat for Pepe. Boyer himself was horrified at what he had signed up for, as Cromwell remembered:

> Boyer was the unhappiest man in southern California. He felt doomed to imitate a Jean Gabin performance, and never appreciated how different his own Pépé was from Gabin's. Boyer showed something like genius to make it different. It was a triumph of nuance. The shots are the same, the dialogue has the same meaning, but Boyer's Pépé and Gabin's Pépé are two different fellows, but in the same predicament.[6]

Further, there was a problem with the leading lady. "Hedy didn't make trouble, didn't have an ego problem," Cromwell recalled. "The problem was that she couldn't act, and we knew it before we started shooting or even rehearsing." Luckily for Hedy, Charles Boyer understood what it felt like to be cast adrift in Hollywood. He took her to one side and told her to follow his lead. He sought to keep that little spark of arrogance that he sensed in her and to use it to draw out her emotions.[7]

That he failed to do so was of little consequence. Hedy's performance in *Algiers* suggests that she had absorbed few Hollywood mannerisms. She still presented herself to the camera just as she had in *Ecstasy* and let it do its work. Dramatically speaking, her contribution was minimal, as indeed Mireille Balin's had been in the original. In each version of the film, Gaby is more important for what she represents—the Paris Pépé dreams of and the acquisition of wealth, here symbolized as pearls—than for anything she does. Indeed, Hedy's performance, although slightly less animated than Mireille Balin's, is a reasonable copy of the original. "I just did my job in the best way I knew how under particular circumstances," she said of *Algiers*.[8]

The Casbah, the narrator intones after the opening credits, is "the melting pot for all the sins of the world." Into this overheated world of lust and criminality walks Hedy's Gaby, impeccably attired in a black evening gown and pearls, her lipstick glistening on full, sensual lips, her eyebrows arched, skin white as marble. Pepe enters the room from another door; as his eyes fall on Gaby, the camera pauses on a close-up of her neck and pearls. The camera cuts to a close-up of Pepe's eyes and to an equally daring close-up (a shot taken directly from the original) of Hedy's mouth as she smiles, lips parting to reveal two perfect rows of teeth. This woman is not just expensive, but dangerous and desiring; she is also shortly to be married to the wealthy André, an overweight, perspiring, older man, not far removed from the husband in *Ecstasy*. Marriage, the film makes clear, is a contract in which love plays little part. "After all, you don't marry for fun," Gaby's friend Marie (Claudia Dell) reminds her (in a sequence not in the original). "I didn't." Later, after Gaby has met and dallied with Pepe Le Moko, she spells out her deal with André, who is now intent on preventing her from returning to the Casbah: "We've got to be honest. Why do you think I am marrying you? Look at yourself and then look at me. I've never lied to you. You knew I didn't love you when I promised to marry you . . . until we are married I do as I please. That's fair enough."

Both films pay lip service to the moral conventions of the day by having Gaby learn, incorrectly, that Pepe has been killed and thus consent to return to Paris, while Pepe dies on the docks watching the ship depart.

In the end, neither Wanger nor Boyer need to have worried about whether Hedy could act. The critics agreed with one voice that she could not. But, they gasped, she was beautiful.[9] *Time* magazine's review was typical of the media responses to Hedy's Hollywood début:

> Actor Charles Boyer's confident, romantic, tragic Pepe Le Moko, and Joseph Spurin-Calleia's unhurried, calculating Slimane are cine-memorable. So are Director John Cromwell's handling of this strangely fraternal, chaseless man hunt and such intense scenes as that in which an informer (Gene Lockhart), backing away in terror as his executioners advance, jars a mechanical piano into action, dies to a ragtime tune. But best of all is the smoldering, velvet-voiced, wanton-mouthed femme fatale of Algiers, black-haired, hazel-eyed Viennese Actress Hedy Kiesler (Hollywood name: Hedy Lamarr). Her coming may well presage a renewal of the sultry cinema of Garbo and Dietrich.[10]

What Wanger achieved (and where Louis B. Mayer would fail) was to harness the promise of sexual abandon to a veneer of European sophistication. In this he was helped by the newly restyled Hedy. Gone was the soft plumpness of her sixteen-year-old figure and the loose, natural, flowing hair. The actress had not only shed several pounds since arriving in America, she had adopted what would become her trademark look: gleaming, dark chestnut hair, parted in a straight center part and falling to her shoulders in a slight wave, her eyes gazing beneath perfectly symmetrical arched brows directly at the camera, as if to confront the viewer in the act of staring. Her other look was away from the camera, up and outward, beyond the frame, suggesting a refusal to engage with the voyeurs and those who might claim to possess her. One has the feeling, seeing those early Hollywood images, that Hedy is someone who is always withholding something of herself.

James Wong Howe, the esteemed Hollywood cameraman, won the first of sixteen Academy Award nominations for his photography on *Algiers,* and to Howe must go much of the credit for creating Hedy's ambiguous image, of making her at once alluring and unobtainable, sexual and remote. Wong took three days to shoot the moment that Gaby and Pépé meet. Until that point, he had shot Hedy in shadows, not fully revealing her face. Then, in the key meeting, he revealed her face, gleaming in the darkness, before pulling in to a close-up of her lips and eyes. Hedy was thrilled with the outcome, asking Wong to shoot her like this throughout;[11] Howe explained that he couldn't, because if he did, he would lose the effect. Instead, Howe lit Hedy from above, sculpting her face and highlighting her perfectly set cheekbones. Again and again, he isolated her cheekbones, her lips, and her eyes, creating an image that was as unreal as it was beautiful.

The studio also hired the prolific and respected stills photographer George Hurrell to shoot Hedy's publicity stills. He too photographed her looking into some impenetrable mid-distance, this time gazing down and out of the frame. In Hurrell's photos of Hedy, she appears rigid and constricted, much more so than was usual with his other subjects. "I didn't get much out of Hedy because she was so *static*. Stunning. But it was the nature of her, she was so phlegmatic, she didn't project anything. It was just a mood thing."[12]

Throughout 1938, Louis B. Mayer, now suddenly confident that he had another star to add to his heavenly collection, made sure that no American remained unaware of Hedy Lamarr's beauty. Posters bearing her image, her face shot in close-up, were pasted on billboards in every city across the country.

The Lamarr look was widely copied; Joan Crawford adopted it to overcome a career lull and appeared as a brunette with a middle part in *The Ice Follies of 1939* (Reinhold Schünzel, 1939), and many others followed suit. It was said that Vivien Leigh was selected for *Gone With the Wind* (Victor Fleming, 1939) as much for her resemblance to Hedy as to Scarlett O'Hara, though that may not be true. Snow White, having started out a blonde, was redesigned as a brunette. Turbans likewise took off as an indispensable fashion item, as did extravagant costume jewelry. Casbah fashions included a sultry pure silk print dress in blue and black designed by Nettie Rosenstein.

Hedy's predilection for placing a small jewel at the center of her part became the latest fad, as did being photographed with slightly open lips, a promise of sexual adventure if ever there was one. To her audiences, she was at once the epitome of European class and, equally important, filled with Oriental promise. Later, and much more crassly, Hollywood would re-present their star in "blackface," making her over to be a lissome native. For now, she was pure fantasy, a white woman with a promise of the exotic. In an opinion article, Gladys Hall wrote that if Hedy's primary appeal was to men, her glamour was a welcome gift to women, because it made them feel good about being feminine:

> We have gone through an arid spate of years during which women have become economically independent and as flat, erotically, as the flat-soled shoes we wear. For in the pursuit of our comparatively new-minted freedom we have gone in for men-tailored suits, equal standards, straight-from-the-shoulder talk, shiny noses, rubbing elbows with men in business offices, cocktail bars, splitting the checks, standing on our own feet and *standing* there. We have waived the courtesies and the gallantries and have accepted the "Hi, Toots" of too-casual Romeos. We have forgotten perfumes and laces and spangled fans and beauty spots and lovers who die for love for us and laces and jewels and veils and those immortal lilies who toil not, neither do they spin.[13]

If Hall was right to sense in Hedy's success the rediscovery of glamour, embodied equally by Dietrich and Garbo, she was less perceptive in her proposal that this signaled a return to the days of chivalry. Hedy's appeal was predicated much more on a fantasized decadence promised by *Algiers*' Casbah setting. She was forbidden fruit and any woman could aspire to that, if few were likely to achieve it.

The premiere of *Algiers* on 13 July 1938 was widely promoted as an international event; the global cast and its far-flung setting suddenly became an opportunity for Hollywood to declare itself part of world affairs. The *Los Angeles Times,* in another approving review, wrote that: "Patriotic longings of the French supply a more or less fundamental theme in 'Algiers.' "[14] This fusion of a vague patriotism with doomed romance amid mysterious settings proved just the formula for prewar audiences, who flocked to the film. In particular, they went wild over the scenes between the two exotic lovers. They even fondly mis-remembered Boyer begging Hedy to "Come wiz me to ze Casbah," a phrase that has gone down in movie history, even if neither ever uttered it.

When Hedda Hopper scurried round to the new star's Beverly Hills bungalow for an interview following the release of *Algiers,* she was guided around to the back garden by a woman she described as a motherly French woman, though this was more likely to be Hedy's maid and secretary, Ericka Manthey. Hollywood's ace columnist met Hedy sitting surrounded by flowering plants and miniatures of Snow White and the Seven Dwarfs. The interview ran through Hedy's life swiftly, rehashing, as was to happen until after her death, the details of Mandl's wealth, his imprisonment of her, and her escape from his Grimm's fairy-tale castle. Soon they were on to *Ecstasy* and Mandl's at-tempts to destroy all the prints.[15] Over and again, in this and other in-terviews, Hedy tried to distance herself from Machaty's film. She failed then, and would fail for the rest of her life, because *Ecstasy* already de-fined her.

In September 1938, now feeling assured of a Hollywood career, Hedy bought a house on North Camden Drive in Beverly Hills. With money to spend, she indulged her longtime interest in design. She decorated the house herself and built extra rooms. Then, she added a swimming pool and a pavilion in the garden where guests could change. Her social calendar blossomed. She and Reggie Gardiner met regularly with Wal-ter Wanger and his new lover, and later wife, Joan Bennett, whose ex-husband, Gene Markey, Hedy would subsequently marry.

Wanger followed *Algiers* with *Trade Winds* and cast Joan Bennett in it as the socialite, Kay Kerrigan. A twist in the story had Kay dye her hair from blonde to brunette as she tried to give the slip to a detective who was trailing her around the globe. Wanger decided to go one better and transform pretty English rose Joan into sultry Viennese Hedy. Donning a wig, Joan did indeed bear a strong likeness to Hedy and Wanger was most taken by the transformation. Not only was Bennett made over to look like the star of *Algiers,* Wanger had the crew light and photograph her just as they would Hedy. After *Trade Winds* was released, her new look became a major talking point and Joan Bennett had her hair permanently dyed to maintain the effect. It dramatically reinvigorated her career.[16]

Hedy and Reggie Gardiner were also friends with Basil Rathbone and his wife and were widely reported attending parties and premieres around town, one of which was *Faust,* directed by Max Reinhardt. Their circle also included the Zanucks, Joan Bennett's sister, Constance, and Douglas Fairbanks Jr.

According to various accounts, in the late 1930s Hedy was also having a secret affair with her old Viennese mentor Otto Preminger. Samuel Fuller, who worked unofficially on scripts with Preminger at the time, relates how the director instructed him to deliver a small package to his lover on the set of her latest film. Opening the little box with care, Fuller found an expensive bracelet and a card that said, "I will love you forever, your Otto." Fed up with his role as Cupid, Fuller snipped the bottom off the card and signed it "G": "I figured there was a Gary, a George, or a Groucho in Hollywood who might have been just as happy to send Lamarr that strand of ice as a memento of his affection. Even now I imagine Hedy Lamarr opening the box and wondering who was the mysterious 'G.'" Neither of the two Austrians ever mentioned the box or its message to Fuller until years later, when he was directing his own films at Fox. He ran into Preminger and confessed that he had tampered with his love note. "Otto laughed heartily. He and Lamarr had vowed to never show the faintest distress, thus having the last laugh on the rascal I'd been that day."[17]

Few who met Hedy in her early days in Hollywood saw the moments of humor that Fuller's story suggests she shared with Preminger. Indeed, Fuller's anecdote may not be true. Hedy was single, and Preminger in a marriage that had all but ended, and it is possible the two exiles picked up where Franz Antel suggested they left off in Vienna. On the other hand, many of Hedy's new friends and acquaintances in Hollywood noticed how down-to-earth she could be. Dreamy as she might look on-screen, off the set, she was often dismissive of her burgeoning celebrity and the lifestyle that came with it. In a later interview, Hedy told Gladys Hall, "I am a pest, really, with men. I am difficult. I do not make them feel, as a woman should, they say, big and strong. I have my own mind. If they give me a good reason why they do a thing or think a thing, then I accept it. Otherwise, I argue it out."[18] The new star had an air of determination about her that few could miss. Now all she needed was another hit to seal her success.

7

This Dame Is Exotic

"YOUR NEXT PICTURE AT MGM," Hedy remembers Mayer pronouncing, "must be better than *Algiers*. If it isn't we won't make it. Your next picture must be an artistic triumph, a picture that will make *Algiers* look small. We are now going to give you the biggest stars, the finest writers, and the most talented directors."[1]

In *This Is Orson Welles*, the great raconteur remembers a different version of MGM's response to Hedy's overnight success. "They called an enormous conference," Welles told Peter Bogdanovich. "All the producers, associate producers, casting people, in-laws and relatives, even a few writers—a great council presided over by Louis B. Mayer . . . 'We've got to find another foreign thing,' somebody said, 'This dame is exotic—let's put her in China or someplace like that.'"

And their next big idea was to find an exotic leading man to play opposite her. Welles, then without an agent, seemed like the man. But, after hunting their quarry in a maze of New York fleshpots, they finally asked Welles what he might want. It was not, they were assured, to appear in a movie with Hedy Lamarr.[2]

Mayer ignored the advice he was given and instead focused on a new script that Charles MacArthur had knocked together about a doctor who marries a beautiful European woman with whom he thinks he is in love. She decides she doesn't love him and has to be convinced that she does. With Spencer Tracy on contract, Mayer only needed the right director to ensure Hedy realized her potential as the new Marlene Dietrich. The Austrian Josef von Sternberg agreed to direct what was then called "New York Cinderella." Shooting started in October 1938 and Mayer threw himself into producing the film, probably the only picture he personally produced, even though no producer's name appears on the credits. As Larry Swindell describes it:

He spent his time on the set, taking charge of photography, direction, and anything that concerned Miss Lamarr. On at least two occasions he tried to tell Spencer Tracy how to act a scene. The crew stood and stared in disbelief and so did Tracy. Among themselves they agreed they were probably hatching a monster, and Hedy Lamarr, who was no idiot, was soon feeling uncomfortable.[3]

Germany's invasion of Austria, which occurred just after filming started, preoccupied both Austrians. Von Sternberg's memories of the shoot were characteristically acerbic: "I was asked to act in the supposed capacity of a director on a silly story contrived to glorify Hedy Lamarr. Each detail of this film, on which I worked not more than a week, was predetermined by a dozen others. Other directors were better fitted to participate in this kind of nonsense, though this may well be beyond the ability of anyone."[4]

Hedy was distressed by not receiving her lines until the night before shooting and not being allowed to work with her regular voice coach, Phyllis Laughton, but instead having to make do with Laughton's assistant. By now too, her attention was distracted by the prospect of a new marriage.

On Saturday 4 March 1939, Hedy caused a stir by marrying Gene Markey at the Governor's Palace in Mexico. According to Hedy's account, they had met at a preview of a film, which they both agreed was too dull to watch, and which Markey turned out to have scripted. They dined together that night at Chasen's Restaurant and the next day Markey took Hedy for a drive to Mexico. Swept up in the exoticism of Mexico and sated with sun, a bullfight, dog races, and a jai alai game, Markey came up with an idea:

"Hey Hedy, let's get married and really make it a full day."[5]

In fact, by late January 1939, Markey was reportedly seeing Hedy and in February Hedda Hopper circulated rumors that the two were now a couple. Hedy was also seen around town with the screenwriter Willis Golbeck and with the aspiring English actor Michael Brooke, who was more correctly known as Charles Guy Fulke Greville, the seventh Earl of Warwick. By late February, Hedy had split up with Reginald Gardiner. One legacy of their relationship was an extraordinary painting of Hedy

HEDY LAMARR

in a ruby red, shoulderless dress with a plunging neckline that emphasized her alabaster skin and symmetrical features. Her eyes apparently gazed at a far-off object from beneath her trademark arched eyebrows; her hands, with fingernails lacquered in deep red, were perhaps resting on the arms of her chair, until you realized that one hand was holding a whip, the other a scarlet rose. With her equally dark lips, and her pale face, it is the most gothic of images, forecasting her most gothic roles, in *Experiment Perilous* (1944) and *Strange Woman* (1946).

Gene Markey's career as a Hollywood screenwriter was perhaps what least distinguished him. Not so much good-looking as charming and a committed socialite and playboy, he was a talented sketch artist who authored several novels. He was also deeply fastidious and liked his life to be orderly and ritualized. When he met Hedy, he had already been married to Joan Bennett, with whom he had a daughter, Melinda. That marriage had foundered, possibly because it was destined to, but most assuredly because of Bennett's affair with Walter Wanger, Hedy's director on *Algiers*.

The wedding with Markey was evidently planned in advance and the couple had bought a house on 2727 Benedict Canyon Drive in Beverly Hills in February 1939. An imposing Egyptian-style home on four acres, surrounded by a stone wall, the property was a far cry from Hedy's recent addresses. She in turn rented her old property to Laurence Olivier, who needed his own place while acting in *Rebecca* (1940)—even if her tenant intended to defy David O. Selznick's dictate not to be seen cohabiting with Vivien Leigh, lest it spoil her pristine image in *Gone With the Wind*.

On Friday 3 March 1939, Hedy and Markey traveled to San Diego, where they spent the night, emerging to a barrage of press photographers, who must have been alerted to the impending marriage. Not everyone, however, was in on the plan. Markey dropped a quick, profusely apologetic note to Hedda Hopper, who for once was out of the loop: "We decided late Friday evening that we must get married the next day—or miss our chance. Hedy did not even get a chance to go home to change her clothes."[6]

The ceremony was performed by the Mexican magistrate. The only onlookers were three obligatory witnesses: Gustavo Padres Jr. of the

Mexican Consul, Raul Mateus of the Central Police Department, and Jimmy Alvarez, the manager of a local tavern. "There'll be no honeymoon now; we both have assignments," Markey announced as the newlyweds stepped into a car for the drive back to Hollywood. With his customary dry humor, Markey wired some friends several days later: "WE HAVE BEEN MARRIED NINE DAYS. IMAGINE ANYONE SAYING IT WOULDN'T LAST."[7]

Press releases aside, there may have been a far more compelling reason for Gene Markey and Hedy to rush into marriage, one that only emerged after the actress's death. In 2000, James Loder asserted in court through his solicitor that he was the birth son of his so-called adoptive mother, Hedy Lamarr.

According to Loder's version of events, he discovered his true parentage in 1962 when the U.S. Air Force obtained his birth certificate for him as part of a security clearance procedure. On the certificate, he is clearly designated as James Lamarr Loder, born to Hedy Lamarr Markey and John Loder on 6 March 1939 in the County of Los Angeles; the document was filed on 16 March 1939.[8]

Was Hedy two days away from giving birth to her first child, the son that she later claimed to have adopted, on 4 March 1939? Did Markey believe he was the father? Looking at the press photos taken the day of their wedding, it is hard to reach a firm conclusion. Hedy and her new husband appear seated, so the pictures show her only from midway up her body. Only one photo, taken around the time of the wedding for *Photoplay*, shows her wearing a loose-flowing, ground-length, high-waisted skirt, which could conceal a pregnancy. A picture of her and Gene Markey, said to be the first taken after their marriage, appeared on 10 March in the *Los Angeles Times*. The new bride is shot in profile and is unmistakeably slim.

Even stranger, there is no evidence that Hedy was seeing John Loder at this time. They were not to meet until 1942, and none of the normally eager gossip columnists, who now hotly followed the star's every dinner date, ever intimated the two knew each other before that. John Loder was still working in Britain in 1939; adding to this mystery, the birth certificate lists the parents' address as 919 North Roxbury Drive, the house that Hedy and John Loder purchased seven years later in 1946. Melinda Markey is adamant that her father would not have denied his son his birth identity: "He was a very honorable man, and if he thought for one minute that this boy was his natural child, he certainly would not have denied it at all."[9]

No photographs of either Hedy or Markey with a baby were published around this time; if Hedy did indeed give birth, she must have given the baby up for adoption immediately, as did her prototype Barbara La Marr. She took public possession of the baby in October 1939 but officially adopted him only in 1941. No rumors of her pregnancy seem to have circulated on the set of *New York Cinderella*. Yet, years later, when two journalists contacted the Office of Vital Records in Sacramento, California, they were assured that the certificate was a copy of the 1939 original.[10]

That the birth certificate exists is not in doubt, but its authenticity is questionable. In a March 1940 interview for *Movie Mirror*, Hedy said that her adopted son James was Irish, his father had been killed in an accident before his birth, and his mother died shortly afterward. As of 2010, James Loder has refused to undergo a DNA test and asserts that for him the certificate is sufficient evidence of his legitimacy. The certificate must have been filed after the purchase of 919 North Roxbury Drive in 1946, but by whom and why remains unknown.

One possible explanation is that Markey agreed to marry Hedy so that she might adopt the baby. Realistically, too, there are other candidates who could have parented a baby of Hedy's in these years, if none of them is John Loder. Without a DNA test and with too many key players having taken the secret of James Lamarr Loder's parents to their graves, it seems that this is a story whose full truth will never be established.

Back on the set of *New York Cinderella*, Mayer's project was a growing disaster. After von Sternberg's departure, the mogul viewed all the footage von Sternberg had shot and scrapped everything except a few good shots of Hedy, then hired Frank Borzage. What Borzage didn't realize was that Mayer regarded this as his project and they fought for weeks. Then Spencer Tracy was sent for by 20th Century Fox to work on *Stanley and Livingstone* (Henry King, 1939). Once again production was halted, once again the director left (or was fired, if you believe Mayer's version), and once again, most of the footage was scrapped.[11]

With the shoot in limbo, Hedy was free to act in *Lady of the Tropics*. Ben Hecht, one of the writers at Mayer's "enormous conference," was focusing on writing a role suitable for the exotic dame, while his boss tried his hand at production. Hecht's proposal was to adapt Puccini's opera *Manon Lescaut* to an oriental setting and transform this aristocratic, crystal-white actress into a tropical native. Hedy fully approved of the project and saw in the role of Manon an opportunity to shed any lingering associations between an aristocratic chill and being European: "there was a scene in a clearing after a march through the jungle in which my clothes were pretty sparse; that appealed to me too. I had already been the 'lady' long enough. I wanted some sex appeal."[12] The original story line contains enough echoes of *Ecstasy*—a younger woman becomes the mistress of an older, wealthy man but yearns for her more attractive younger lover—to suggest that Hecht envisaged the film building on Hedy's most notorious production as well as on *Algiers*. The distinction was that now she would be punished for her promiscuity. In the opera, Manon is imprisoned and then dies while escaping across the desert; in *Lady of the Tropics*, Manon shoots one man to save the other and then shoots herself. In a nod to and reversal of the relationships in *Algiers*, Hecht transposed the story line from France to Saigon and reimagined Manon as a mixed-race beauty who dreams of marrying a man who will take her to Paris. Another similarity to Cromwell and Wanger's film is the ending of *Lady of the Tropics*, which is shot in an overheated film noir style and and in which its heroine dies before the ship that would rescue her leaves the port.

The film is imbued with the racial fantasies of the day (particularly around the status of the mixed-race woman), many of them articulated by the priest, Fr. Antoine (Ernest Cossart), whose role it is to explain the "Orient" to the West. "I adore half-castes, they are so vicious and fascinating," murmurs one of the American traveling party, on hearing that the native boy is half French. "No, no, not vicious," the priest responds, "somehow they remind me of, well, flying fish—very harmless. Born to the water, they spend half their lives flying above it, only to fall back into the sea and die there."

Also in the group of Americans is the playboy Bill Carey (Robert Taylor), who is on board the cruise ship arriving in Saigon with his wealthy fiancée, Dolly (Mary Zimbalist). It is Dolly who demands that Fr. Antoine take them to "an aquarium" to see more flying fish and who draws the party's attention to Manon, with a "William, don't look." At that, the soundtrack begins a more exotic beat and the camera cuts to Hedy in medium close-up, costumed in a flowing black gown with an ethereal shawl half covering her dark hair, her face partially concealed by a shadow. Her plunging neckline reveals alabaster skin and, as in *Algiers,* her full, dark lips and perfectly symmetrical eyebrows and hairline are accentuated. Manon pauses, posing at the top of the stairs and with the shadow from the ceiling fan flickering across her face, greets her lover, the local wealthy Frenchman Pierre Delaroch (played by her fellow Viennese actor, Joseph Schildkraut).

Of course William (Bill) does look and falls in love with the exquisite Hedy, one of the film's "flying fish." Little effort was made to disguise the Austrian's whiteness. Her racial mixing is signified by costume; as with so many of Hedy's films, costume supplies the audience with considerable narrative information. Although this is standard filmmaking practice, given Hedy's weak acting skills, it was particularly important that audiences follow her character through what she was wearing. Manon's combination of European clothing and Asian clothing reflects her situation, as does the black (European) gown in the opening sequence, which is dramatically different than the white or pale clothing of the other (purer) women in the room.

Another point of Hedy's costumes was to allow the audience to enjoy some consumerist pleasures. In Dolly's first encounter with Manon, she shows considerable interest in Manon's clothing: "I am dying to go shopping in Saigon. I adore going shopping in strange places. Do you buy your clothes in Saigon, Mademoiselle . . . er?" Soon after, Bill attempts to purchase a hat like Manon's at a native store for Dolly.

Bill easily drops his rich heiress as he falls for Manon and enters a romance complicated by Manon's unhappy dependence on the wealthy and powerful Delaroch, who bathes in her exoticism while reminding her of her position as a "half-caste": "You have the face of the West, but your soul is full of Eastern smoke." Bill, in his American innocence, promises Manon access to that elusive passport to the West, but Delaroch has ensured that she cannot leave the country.

Given Production Code restrictions on interracial marriage, the affair could not be allowed to flourish. To the same end, Schildkraut was made to appear slightly Asian, thus suggesting that he was a more suitable lover for Manon. Submerged in *Lady* is a light critique of racial attitudes in the West. The Harrisons' party is portrayed as both ignorant and consumerist as they interact with the Saigonese. The French colonizers are depicted as little more than sexual opportunists, happy to have affairs with the local women and kiss them good-bye once the babies arrive and their tour of duty is over. The character of Mina (Gloria Franklin), Manon's cousin, embodies this critique; Mina married and had a baby with a Frenchman, who then returned to France, leaving Mina on her own. It is Mina who sings, "Every time you say good-bye, I die a little," in the Saigon nightclub where Manon and Bill meet, foreshadowing the film's finale.[13]

This subtle critique of the careless racism of American tourists and their conflation of purchasing power with entitlement is consistently undermined by the film's intentionally exotic photography, nor are Fr. Antoine's pronouncements on the nature of the "flying fish" and claim that Orientals are "a race as inscrutable and mysterious as its hats and its Gods" ever seriously challenged. Indeed, Mina's inability to say no to her French lovers and a subplot in which Manon leaves Saigon to become one of a wealthy jungle lord's many wives are perhaps truer reflections of Hollywood's racial politics than the script's lip service to liberalism. In another discomforting sequence, Manon greets three local women whose blackened teeth and wrinkled skin portray them as witchlike, causing Bill (and presumably the viewer) to shudder in horror. These women were, she tells him, her schoolmates.

By identifying Hedy/Manon as mixed-race solely through narrative and clothing, rather than skin color, Hedy did not play the kind of over-sexed native she was to portray so outrageously in the later *White Cargo*. Rather, in *Lady* she boasts a European probity and honor that distinguish her from the "true" natives. As the "schoolmates" encounter underlines, her beauty is enhanced by her European qualities. The script also highlights Manon's oriental inscrutability, which might charitably account for the unreadable expression on Hedy's face. However, the reality was that Hedy could produce little else, even under a more committed director. Still, the trade press liked what it saw:

Metro's patience and smartness in grooming her and giving her a vehicle fitted to Miss Lamarr's talents show splendidly in the results, indicating dependability in a wide emotional register and labelling her as a positive money asset. Her performance has honesty, a naturalness most appealing and a distinctive charm which is more than physical allure.[14]

Not all the critics were quite as enthusiastic. *Photoplay* summed up the opinions of other reviewers: "It's still a moot point whether or not it makes any difference that the heady Lamarr can't act worth a tinker's expression of irritation. This follows the only possible formula: lush atmosphere, good acting support, and fine photography, while she looks beautiful."[15]

In June 1939, Hedy wrapped up her role in *Lady of the Tropics*. Looking through a magazine at the pictures from the film, Gene Markey started chuckling. Hedy asked her spouse what he found so funny. "He replied that he was trying to decide which of us, Bob or I, was more beautiful." She also told journalist Bob Edison that she had to teach Robert Taylor how to kiss convincingly.[16] These apparently trivial comments may have been double entendres aimed at an inner circle, many of whom suspected that Robert Taylor was gay (and that his new bride, Barbara Stanwyck, was bisexual).

Remarkably, "New York Cinderella," renamed *I Take This Woman*, was resurrected; though around Hollywood it had acquired the nickname *I Retake This Woman*. The entire original cast, save Spencer Tracy and Hedy, were replaced and director Woody Van Dyke was hired. Known in Hollywood as "One Shot Woody," Van Dyke lived up to his moniker and swiftly pulled the production together and popped it in the can. Hiring Van Dyke was not only expedient but also a reflection of the exotic dame's new standing at MGM. Now that *Lady of the Tropics* was out, no one was certain that Hedy was the new Marlene, least of all Mayer, who finally removed himself, without explanation, from the project.

Although they would act together in three films, Hedy maintained that she and Spencer Tracy never hit it off. He grew irritated when she couldn't understand English and she grew anxious because he slurred his words and she couldn't understand him. When they worked together on *I Take This Woman*, Tracy found a way to pay the new star back for what he saw as her primness:

I thought I'd fix Hedy one day. We had a scene where she had to sit on my lap. The night before we did the scene, I bought a big banana that wasn't ripe yet and was pretty hard. I slipped the banana down the front of my pants, and when Hedy sat down on it, she let out a scream and jumped about ten fuckin' feet in the air.[17]

Tracy's biographer Selden West, however, claims the two stars were "deep in an affair" in early 1938 and that she caused a stir by turning up on the set of *Stanley and Livingstone* in late February 1939; soon after that, apparently, the affair came to an end.[18] If this is true, there is little evidence on-screen. Tracy is dreadfully dull in *I Take This Woman*.

Later that year, Luther Green contacted Hedy to offer her the title role in the stage play *Salome,* which she accepted happily. MGM, however, had other ideas and Hedy was reminded that under the terms of her contract, MGM had exclusive rights to her appearances. Hedy responded by walking off the set of *I Take This Woman,* and once again the production was thrust into limbo. MGM moved swiftly and by mid-November 1939 had acquired a court injunction forbidding her to appear in the play. She returned to work and the picture was started one more time.

In January 1940, *I Take This Woman* was eventually released. Reaction to the film at its Hollywood preview was mixed, which may have been, as the *Motion Picture Daily* reported, "because it was shown on a Friday night in a house mainly patronized by students of U.C.L.A., who are a bit callous to this sort of story and more than a bit demonstrative."[19] The press reviews were equally callous and the film was soundly panned.

Is there anything to be retrieved from *I Take This Woman?* Hedy dismissed it as "nothing more than a soap opera" and, with its play on love versus professionalism and glamour versus working-class values, she was close to the truth.[20] In the final version, Hedy plays Georgi, a Russian who grew up in Paris. As the film starts, Georgi is about to throw herself into the ocean but is saved by a doctor, Karl Decker (Spencer Tracy). Returning to her glamorous life in New York where she models luxury clothing at society events to help attract wealthy buyers for Madame Marcesa's (Verree Teasdale) collection, Georgi feels impelled to visit Dr. Decker. He takes her to his practice in a poor neighborhood, where his colleagues are impressed: "Say, she's not just all looks," Dr. Joe Barnes (Dalies Frantz) comments. "She's like something you'd see in a jeweler's window," Decker responds. "A single flawless gem on a piece of black velvet."

The film simultaneously treats Hedy as an icon—at one point she is shot standing beneath the larger-than-life painting of herself that her former lover Phil Mayberry (Kent Taylor) has on his living room wall—and as a wayward woman who needs the love of a good doctor to save her from herself. If the film's message is ostensibly the valorization of hard work and social commitment, its fascination with Georgi's aristocratic milieu undermines those principles. Everything hangs on Hedy's performance, which is quite unreadable. As a flawless gem, she is unparalleled. Maybe von Sternberg could have molded MacArthur's story into the kind of heightened, unreal melodrama that made his films with Marlene Dietrich so memorable. Maybe too the story's relationship mirrored the Svengali relationship Mayer had hoped for himself and Hedy. In the hands of Woody Van Dyke, however, the film became an average Hollywood production, peopled with actors who turned in routine performances. In her first American-set film, Hedy was so outlandishly different that nothing could anchor her in the story. No wonder it was a critical and commercial disaster.

As war became an ever greater reality, Hedy had to be careful not to appear too foreign, particularly given her native country. Responding to comments on the exotic glamour she imported to Hollywood, Hedy was quick to stress her American qualities. She wore her hair long, she asserted, because of the informality and freedom of her new country, which did away with the necessity of wearing a hat and dressing formally, as she had in Europe. Copying American girls had led her to wear less jewelry, have long telephone conversations, and eat ice cream.[21]

Marriage of convenience or not, Markey and Hedy's relationship was short-lived. Hedy was uncomfortable with her second-wife status, and reminders of Joan Bennett's presence were hard to erase. For instance, Gene Markey's yacht was named *Melinda* after his and Joan's daughter, and when Hedy was on board and dressed for the part of the nautical wife, her sweaters and caps were all labeled *Melinda*. Additionally, Joan Bennett announced that little Melinda Markey most certainly could not see her father in the home of his new wife.

Hedy and Markey did enjoy the social life of Hollywood's royalty, in particular among the émigré set. They were close friends with Myrna

Loy and Arthur Hornblow, whose parties in Hidden Valley attracted the brightest and most glamorous stars. Later, Loy herself married Gene Markey and remembered him as "a brilliant raconteur, a man of unfailing wit and humor, [who] could charm the birds off the trees, although birds were never his particular quarry—women were, the richer and more beautiful the better."[22] Fidelity was not his strongest suit, but neither was it Hedy's. It was only a matter of time before the novelty of their marriage faded.

By July 1940 the couple was separated, and on 4 September, Hedy petitioned for divorce, citing cruelty, which in this case amounted to his being "bored and indifferent" to her. She also alleged that he had spent no more than four evenings at home alone with her.

"When we were first married," Hedy told Superior Court judge William S. Baird, "I used to tell him the little things that happened to me during the day and I thought it was natural for him to do the same, but he never did."

"When I first asked him casually why he never told me about his own experiences, he would say, 'Well I might bore you—besides I forget. I guess I'll write them down next time.'"

Eventually, Hedy told the court, she just gave up asking.

"How many times in the fifteen months you lived with your husband did you two spend the evening at home together?" Hedy's attorney, Lester William Roth, questioned.

"Only about four times," she replied. "He avoided talking to me about private affairs. Therefore, we had people at home or went out to parties and to movies—anything to avoid that. He always invited the guests."

She then went on to explain how Markey used to communicate to her via written messages: "I complained about it. I remember saying to him, 'This is terrible; I'm like a stranger. I have no idea what you are doing— not that it is important. I just like to know about the little things.'"[23]

The end of the marriage came when Markey suggested they play a little game. Surprised by the unusual proposition, Hedy assented. He developed his idea: "Why don't we each take a sheet of paper and write down what is wrong about us. You write down what is wrong about me and vice-versa." Hedy's counter-proposal was that they simply have it out. Words were exchanged and by nightfall, neither doubted that the marriage had been a mistake.[24]

The case was swiftly settled on 27 September since Markey did not contest the charge. The judge advised Hedy that in the future she should spend more than four weeks getting acquainted with a prospective husband, advice that she would forget on more than one occasion. The divorce became final on 3 October and Hedy acquired sole ownership of their home, her own having been sold shortly after their marriage.

At this juncture, Hedy entered into a round of publicity centered on her attempt to prevent her son Jamsie from being returned to the Children's Society, from where allegedly he came. Many fan and other magazines carried the story, always repeating that she was desperate to keep the child and had begged the Society to allow her to hold on to him for another year or until the probation period was over. Even more quaintly, an entire section of *Ecstasy and Me* is devoted to reproducing Louella Parsons's version of the story, first published in *Photoplay* in October 1940, and reprinted verbatim.[25] Apparently, Hedy was successful. Parsons writes, "She called me the day it was all settled: 'I can keep him,' she almost sobbed into the telephone. 'Little Jimmy is all mine . . . I've been appointed legal guardian and later, after the year elapses, the adoption will come up again. But I know in my heart it is all right now. I know it!' "[26] In fact, Hedy spent little time on motherhood, and her understanding of the requirements of parenting would remain poor, and in the case of Little Jimmy, very poor.

Her next film was one of her own favorites, and rightly so. The story for *Boom Town* began with an idea from James Edward Grant and was scripted by Clark Gable's close friend John Lee Mahin. Mahin drew on Gable's early experiences working with his father on an oil-drilling rig in Oklahoma. As Gable later remembered:

> It was a rough business. There were no geologists then. A contractor, like my father, would find a likely place, get someone to finance him and begin drilling a hole. We worked twelve hours on and twelve hours off. There was a sleeping tent and a cook tent and we had two men on each twelve-hour shift. The beds in the sleeping tent never got cold. I'd get up at midnight, and in the freezing cold I'd have to climb a rickety eighty-five-foot wooden tower in the driving wind, to oil the bearings on the rig. There was no light and it was pitch black, and even in World War II I was never so scared.[27]

After the lavish full-color *Gone With the Wind,* Louis B. Mayer was in no rush to spend that kind of money on his latest star vehicle, and *Boom*

Town was shot in black and white. Any social criticism of working conditions in the oil-drilling industry that might have been intended by the scriptwriter vanished as the film became a melodrama of male bonding and rivalry set against a suitably phallic background of gushing oil wells, pumps thrusting into the desert soil, and gleaming oil rigs. Anticipating the themes and style of CBS's *Dallas, Boom Town* had Clark Gable as Big John McMasters and Spencer Tracy as Square John Sand fall in love with the same woman, Elizabeth McMasters, played by Claudette Colbert. Gable gets to marry the girl, but the audience understands that Spencer Tracy might have been the less romantic but certainly more sensible choice. Colbert's Elizabeth is a beautiful, devoted, and much put-upon wife. Repeatedly forced to walk away from luxury as her husband's fortunes wax and wane, and nobly turning a blind eye to his taste for brothel madams, Elizabeth faces the ultimate test of loyalty when Hedy Lamarr's character enters the plot. Dressed in close-fitting dresses and power suits created by her favorite designer and friend, Adrian, Karen Vanmeer (Hedy) is the Mata Hari of the oil business. Her origins are vaguely explained by the entrepreneur Harry Compton (Lionel Atwil) after she has sashayed into his office: "I met her in the Dutch West Indies. She was married to a geologist. She didn't like it there." Hedy played Karen as a smart, assured woman, whose place in the business world is guaranteed as much by her intelligence as by her methods of intelligence gathering. Little doubt is left in the audience's minds as to how Karen pries information out of her contacts; at the same time she is a force to be reckoned with. Her analysis of the information she commands is swift and reliable; enterprises rise and fall on the basis of her insider knowledge. More than that, she evidently enjoys her role, teasing and flirting with Big John in a manner that suggests less coquettishness than confidence in her sexual allure. In comparison, Colbert's stay-at-home wife is vulnerable, both to her husband's whims and to the economic activities of a world in which she plays no part. The moral code of the day dictated that Big John must abandon Karen for Elizabeth, and not before Square John had told the wicked woman what he thought of her. In a scene in Karen's apartment, Square John spells out the nuances: "You know I rang a little buzzer when I came in here but as far as I am concerned, it is an old-fashioned brass bell; and all these lovely flowered curtains around here are red plush for my money." The audience may be reassured by the knowledge that this moral arbiter is, as he says, the kind of guy who knows when a dame needs a wallop to be sure that he's in love with her.

Still, it is hard to argue that Hedy's Karen Vanmeer is anything other than temporarily regretful over losing Big John. Might he creep back to her later when the dust has settled at home? Or will she simply glide on to more powerful men and more influential settings?

Hedy's performance in *Boom Town* anticipates the spider women of the postwar cycle of film noirs—the willful, scheming home wreckers who will do anything to get their hands on money, usually at the cost of any patsies who block their way. Yet, there is a difference. The spider-women are barred from the male world of money-making and can only acquire their fortunes by masquerading as potential wives; Karen Vanmeer moves confidently in that masculine world, and her acceptance of her place in it means that her fall is not nearly as precipitous as that of later femmes fatales who must be punished for defiling the sanctity of the marital citadel. Still with the hint of iciness that marked her earlier performances and overshadowed her transition to Hollywood acting, Hedy was now moving between two performance styles: her favored technique of presenting herself to the camera's voyeuristic gaze, and the new, character-driven Hollywood model. As she teases both the Johns, the viewer knows that she is holding something back from them, retaining her own identity in a manner that Colbert's good wife never can. "Look, you've got to learn to take no for an answer once in a while," John McMasters demands of her. "I wouldn't let *you* give me that answer," Hedy purrs back. It is clear who is in control here.

On the day that Gable was to shoot his love scene with Hedy, a surprise visitor arrived on set. Gable's wife, Carole Lombard, knew her husband's inability to resist any woman he met, and she knew Hedy's reputation from rumors about the content of *Ecstasy*. Claudette Colbert was all right, she was a lesbian, but Carole was going to make sure that Hedy Lamarr didn't get her hands on her costar. Dressed in one of her favorite costumes by Irene, Carole looked in the words of one set worker, "like four million bucks."[28] Nothing apparently passed between the two stars on that occasion, even if rumors that matters were otherwise surrounded their second pairing, on *Comrade X*. Later, Hedy told her friend Arlene Roxbury that Gable had bad breath and false teeth. "He would take his teeth out as a joke, and that turned me off."[29] She also remembered

Boom Town fondly in her memoirs: "I was deadly serious all during the making of it. I needed this one and it had to be good." So it was; and "more important, my acting was praised."[30]

It may have been, but not by any of the more influential critics. Most agreed that the film struggled to find enough plot to keep its star-heavy cast occupied and that Hedy's role was particularly insignificant. Her contribution was dismissed by Bosley Crowther in the *New York Times* as that of a "stunning but routine charmer."[31] *Variety* was no more enthusiastic and *Time*'s review encapsulated many critics' responses: "Like most movies that are built on the theory that four stars are better than one, *Boom Town* is not so much a picture as a series of personal appearances. Stripped to a suit of balbriggan underwear in one scene, Clark Gable reveals a paunch. Fully clothed throughout, Hedy Lamarr still reveals nothing at all."[32]

Ironically, America's increasingly prowar policy offered immigrant actors a new lifeline. Now, suddenly, German actors were needed to populate the new propaganda films with hideous Nazis and treacherous foreigners of all shades. Jewish performers had to reinvent themselves as storm troopers, and Hedy had to reinvent herself as a Russian spy. In *Comrade X,* her first film with King Vidor, she reprized her on-screen relationship and offscreen friendship with Clark Gable.

Comrade X was the first effort of Gottfried Reinhardt, Max Reinhardt's son, as producer. Mayer threw substantial resources at the project; first, he hired Hedy's companion on the *Normandie,* Walter Reisch, who quickly hammered out the story line (which later earned him an Academy Award nomination); then Mayer hired Ben Hecht, Charles Lederer and Herman J. Mankiewicz to write the screenplay. The film was made with more than a passing nod to Ernst Lubitsch's Greta Garbo vehicle, *Ninotchka* (1939), not surprisingly given that Reisch was scriptwriter on *Ninotchka.* However, the two productions have less in common than many commentators have suggested. *Ninotchka* swiftly abandons its digs at Soviet politics ("The last mass trials were a great success. There are going to be fewer but better Russians.") in favor of developing the "opposites attract" love affair between the Russian envoy Ninotchka (Garbo) and Leon (Melvyn Douglas). The film's draw was less its political insights than its promise of Garbo in a comic role.

Hedy, eighteen months old. www
.Hedy-Lamarr.org.

Hedy on a family holiday,
aged circa 16. Courtesy
of the Filmarchiv Aus-
tria, Vienna.

As Eva in *Ecstasy* (1933). Courtesy of the Filmarchiv Austria, Vienna.

New York foyer publicity for *Ecstasy*. Courtesy of the Academy of Motion Picture Arts and Sciences.

A new image in *Die Bühne*. Author's private collection.

On stage as Sissy. Courtesy of the Filmarchiv Austria, Vienna.

On holiday with Trude Kiesler, 1936. Courtesy of the Filmarchiv Austria, Vienna.

With Charles Boyer in *Algiers* (1938). Jerry Ohlinger's Movie Material Store, Inc.

[Left] *Lady of the Tropics* (1939). Author's private collection.

[Below] Advertisement for *Boom Town* (1940). Jerry Ohlinger's Movie Material Store, Inc.

With Spencer Tracy, Claudette Colbert, and Clark Gable in *Boom Town* (1940). Jerry Ohlinger's Movie Material Store, Inc.

In *Comrade X* (1940). Courtesy of the Filmarchiv Austria, Vienna.

With James Stewart in
Come Live with Me (1941).
www.Hedy-Lamarr.org.

In *Ziegfeld Girl* (1941).
Jerry Ohlinger's Movie
Material Store, Inc.

With George Montgomery.
Author's private collection.

Entertaining the troops at the Hollywood Canteen. Courtesy of the Filmarchiv
Austria, Vienna.

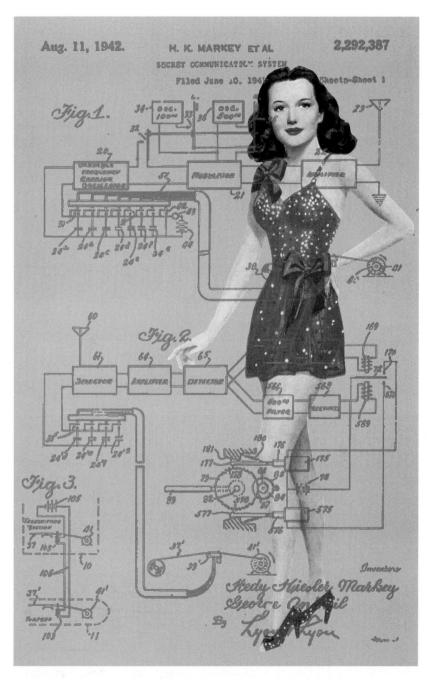

A glamorous patent. Courtesy of the Filmarchiv Austria, Vienna.

[Right] As Tondelayo in *White Cargo* (1942). Courtesy of the Filmarchiv Austria, Vienna.

[Below] With Paul Henreid in *The Conspirators* (1944). Courtesy of the Filmarchiv Austria, Vienna.

In *Her Highness and the Bellboy* (1945) with Robert Walker. www.Hedy-Lamarr.org.

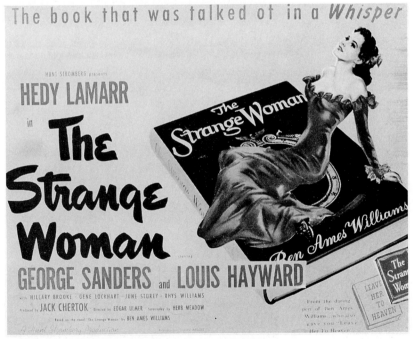

An advertisement for *The Strange Woman* (1946). Jerry Ohlinger's Movie Material Store, Inc.

With John Loder
in *Dishonored Lady*
(1947). www.Hedy
-Lamarr.org.

The star turned
director. Courtesy
of the Filmarchiv
Austria, Vienna.

Jamsie's ninth birthday, with Tony and Denise. Author's private collection.

Let your own _TASTE_ and _THROAT_ be the judge!

There's never a rough puff in a Lucky

Because Lucky Strike Means Fine Tobacco!

LUCKY STRIKE

[Right] Advertising Lucky Strike (1949). Author's private collection.

[Below] Painting on holiday in Southampton (1950). Author's private collection.

Quick sketch (1950). Author's
private collection.

The mystery of the missing jewels (1955). The actress
told reporters that the missing jewelry was worth about
$250,000. Courtesy of the Filmarchiv Austria, Vienna.

[Above] Holding a press conference following the shoplifting charge (1966). Author's private collection.

[Right] Hedy in her old age. Courtesy of the Filmarchiv Austria, Vienna.

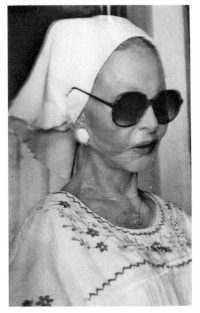

Comrade X, on the other hand, is set almost entirely in the Soviet Union. Its cast was its main attraction, but they carried an unexpected seriousness that disturbs the light tone of what was intended as a routine screwball comedy. Another talented immigrant and former Max Reinhardt protégé, the Viennese Oscar Homolka, played Commissar Vasiliev as a Stalin look-alike, while the German émigré, Sig Ruman, appeared as Von Hofer, a humorless, monocled Prussian. The local Russians are charming, double-crossing scoundrels. Gable plays McKinley B. Thompson, an easygoing journalist by day and Western spy (Comrade X) by night. Hedy makes her entrance as Golubka, the cable-car driver, as did Garbo, in drab, communist clothing. She is known, she explains, as Theodore since the workers' council only lets men drive cars. This plot device allowed Adrian to dress the star in startlingly androgynous clothing. Her father, played by Felix Bressart, knows that the wind of orthodox thought is turning against his daughter and blackmails Thompson to sneak her out of Russia to convert her to good, democratic, American values. To secure her exit visa, Comrade X has to marry her. Of course, he falls in love with the Russian, their romance signaled by a series of slapstick sequences that suggested Hedy's talent for comedy, hinted at in her Weimar films, might transfer to Hollywood. In a bizarre plot twist, the two are thrown in a Soviet jail, where they witness innocent men and women being led by the guards to their deaths. This is a truly chilling sequence, quite at odds with its preceding light-hearted comedy.

For all its slapstick, *Comrade X* is a much darker film than *Ninotchka,* if less conventionally constructed, even to the point of incoherence (notably the tank chase at the end). It is as if, for once, the émigré mind-set could not quite render world affairs as a light-hearted joke played out by foreigners with funny accents and bad dress sense. Nevertheless, in the end, Theodore is fully integrated in American society, her transition sealed by her enjoyment of the Brooklyn Dodgers.

On set, Hedy and Clark Gable enjoyed each other's practical jokes— once Gable led his costar to a door and holding his finger over his mouth, opened it. "Inside, to my consternation," Hedy said, "stood Felix Bressart, the actor who played my father in the film. Only he wasn't exactly standing. He was bent over, as a nurse administered a hypodermic needle. Felix suddenly looked up, his dignity intact, but I fled with embarrassment as Clark's gutsy laughter followed me." Although rumors continued to intimate an offscreen relationship, Hedy maintained that she never quite understood Gable's sex appeal: "I thought he was one of the nicest people I'd met, and a great practical joker."[33]

The film "kept us all, Clark Gable, Felix Bressart, and the rest of the cast in laughter most of the time," Hedy recalled shortly after its completion. "I love to laugh. I hope I will be often given comedy roles."[34] She was right, comedy suited her best, but that was not why she had been contracted by Mayer.

The critics saw in her performance the fulfilment of a promise that had been all but buried by Hollywood: "What she does in *Comrade X* is to suggest for the first time (since *Ecstasy*) that she is an actress as well as a museum piece."[35] *Variety* agreed: "Miss Lamarr is handed the strongest role of past pictures on her home lot, and demonstrates she can be more than decorative by a good display of both deadpan comedy and romantic antics."[36]

One of the film's more unexpected admirers was the photographer Joseph Cornell. A cineast and creator of experimental films, Cornell liked to fashion exhibitions around lesser-known talents or forgotten historical figures. Developing a technique that later became associated with "found art," Cornell would search through archives and newspaper cuttings, gathering an inventory of secondary materials—clippings, other written materials, press photos—that he would then place in files, or boxes, or drawers and put on display, taking the observer on a journey through his subject's life. In this way, the viewer is both voyeur and biographer as they reconstruct a person's identity from still images. In 1941–1942, Cornell invited readers of the surrealist journal *View* to follow him on a journey around the "Enchanted Wanderer," as he termed Hedy Lamarr. The one-page advertisement urged readers to remember the beauty of silent cinema. "And so," Cornell continued:

> we are grateful to Hedy Lamarr, the enchanted wanderer, who again speaks the poetic and evocative language of the silent film, if only in whispers at times, beside the empty roar of a sound track. Amongst screw-ball comedy and the most superficial brand of clap-trap drama she yet manages to retain a depth and dignity that enables her to enter this world of expressive silence.
>
> Who has not observed in her magnified visage qualities of a gracious humility and spirituality that with circumstance of costume, scene, or plot conspire to identify her with realms of wonder, more

absorbing than the artificial ones, and where we have already been invited by the gaze that she knew as a child.

Her least successful roles will reveal something unique and intriguing—a disarming candor, a naivete, an innocence, a desire to please, touching in its sincerity. In implicit trust she would follow in whatsoever direction the least humble of her audience would desire.[37]

In the final sequence of her next film, *Come Live with Me*, Cornell saw in the contrast between the pallor of Hedy's skin, her rich, dark hair, and her glowing eyes, echoes of Snow White in her crypt, and an effect of chiaroscuro worthy of the disciples of Caravaggio and Georges de la Tour. Her androgynous costume in *Comrade X* reminded him of paintings of Renaissance youths; while a scene where her face lights up in the prison cell was for him a moment of pure artistic creation.

If Cornell was happiest worshipping Hedy from afar, he also wrote letters to her, which she answered. It seems, however, they never met. In any case, it was her image that captured him; and as that image grew in importance it increasingly threatened to usurp the reality of Hedy's daily life. Her beauty alone did not define how she was viewed; others detected more complex undercurrents in her look. In the first issue of *Batman* (Spring 1940), Bob Kane introduced the world to a new superhero; also in this issue, "Cat," who later became Catwoman, appeared alongside Batman. Her real name was Selina Kyle and her nocturnal activities were inspired by her boredom with the privileged social life to which she had been born. Kane had long admired Hedy's "feline beauty" and the figure of Cat/Catwoman was largely inspired by her and by Jean Harlow. As the series developed, Catwoman's relationship with Batman was marked more and more by undertones of sadomasochistic sexual gameplay and by her suggestive costumes.

Hedy next worked with director Clarence Brown and a rising star named James Stewart. *Come Live with Me* (1941) has survived as little more than a footnote in the illustrious careers of its director and young male lead and is most interesting for our purposes for its biographical turn. In the film, Hedy plays Viennese-born Miss Johnny Jones, now exiled in America since her father was "liquidated" for standing up for what he believed in (the film's only reference to the political events coursing around it). Her lover Barton (Bart) Kendrick (Ian Hunter) has an "open marriage," which, in a risqué challenge to the Production Code, permits him to live with his wife, Diana (Verree Teasdale), and enjoy the pleasures of a mistress. Hedy's character is carefully crafted as a woman of honor, refusing to marry Bart lest his wife be hurt; she is also once more represented as a precious object, here via a dancing ballerina figurine that Bart winds up and sets in motion. Once again, too, she has a male name, Johnny, though her costumes (by Adrian) spell out her sophisticated, feminine elegance.

The happy state of affairs between Johnny and Bart comes under threat when an officer from the Department of Immigration comes to the apartment with a warrant for Miss Jones's deportation. "I guess you like it here, don't you?" he inquires. "You don't ask somebody in heaven if they like the place," she responds. To stay, she needs to marry and on the double. While Bart is considering this, she falls in with a penniless writer Bill Smith (Stewart) and, for a small consideration, he agrees to marry her. By fortunate coincidence, his book is taken up by Bart and his wife's publishing company and Diana ensures its success, thereby furnishing him with the wherewithal to marry Miss Jones and allowing her husband to return to the marital bed. This auspicious premise turns into a predictable comedy, its frisson residing in its references to Hedy's own life story. "Unless I can get an American husband right away, I'll get sent back to . . . to what used to be Austria," she explains to Bill. The second half, in particular, is intensely mawkish; Bill brings Johnny on a visit to his grandma (the screen debut of Clarence Brown's elderly discovery, Adeline de Walt Reynolds), who lives in a quaint homestead decorated by samplers offering homespun truths such as "What Fools These Mortals Be" and "Time Heals All Wounds." In this all-American environment, Johnny realizes that she is indeed in love with good ol' Bill and they duly pair up, this time for real.

No doubt her foreignness, combined with her apparent wealth, were an adequate diversionary tactic from the film's plot, in which Hedy played, as in *Boom Town,* a woman with a moral code at odds with America's idealization of female propriety. That she, a foreigner, could effectively buy James Stewart for $17.80 per week was also a narrative flashpoint that the film had to negotiate with care. The final result so strenuously papered over the moral cracks in the story it all but fell apart in the effort. Not surprisingly, the trade papers were unimpressed by what they saw: "It is a silly piece," *Variety* wrote, "never believable for a moment, and its romantic and humorous shortcomings are the more conspicuous because of the apparent earnest effort to give the production good settings, fine technical trimmings and polish."[38]

Hedy, too, was to embrace the principle of marrying Americans, though she reserved them for later in life. For now, though, she was occupied with career considerations.

8

The Siren of the Picture Show

BETWEEN SEPTEMBER 1940 and January 1941, Hedy was busy shooting *Ziegfeld Girl*. She had pressed Mayer for a part in the film: "Mr. Mayer, I've done several dramatic roles. Now I'd like to do something Viennese style, a light, airy musical," she recalled telling him.[1] Mayer had assembled a team of writers to work on the script and was not amused when its producer, Pandro S. Berman, suggested that the Lamarr story line was dull and should be dropped. If Hedy was hot at the box office, she would stay in the picture; not only that, a rewrite would cost thousands. The mogul was proved correct in his prediction. *Ziegfeld Girl*, made at a cost of $1,468,000, was a hit, grossing $3,901,000 on its initial release. Berman's opinion was unchanged: "Hedy has no talent and is not an important person in any way. Film acting has more to do than looking icy beautiful."[2]

Hedy had not been first choice for the role of Sandra, nor were Judy Garland and Lana Turner the first choice for the parts of Sheila, Susan Gallagher, the daughter of a struggling vaudeville artist, and the Irish girl from Brooklyn, respectively. Initially the leads were to be Joan Crawford, Margaret Sullivan, Eleanor Powell, and Virginia Bruce, but by the time the production was ready to film, MGM had a new generation of stars they wanted to cast in the parts. Similarly the original lineup of male stars, Walter Pidgeon, George Murphy, and Frank Morgan, was replaced by James Stewart, Tony Martin, and Charles Winninger.

Ziegfeld Girl is a showcase film; directed by Robert Z. Leonard and choreographed by Busby Berkeley, it was a "backstage musical," whose main focus was on what it took to create a musical, highlighting the emotional melodrama of success and failure. From the start, the film spotlights the process of becoming a Ziegfeld Girl. "Take off your hat and smile winningly," all prospective dancers are instructed as they line up to audition. A running stream of banter allows the girls to hint at just what being a Ziegfeld Girl entails, information that the film's prospective audience would have recognized, given the real-life Mr. Z's well-known penchant for indulging in affairs with his pick of the troupe. The Ziegfeld tradition had already been the subject of the enormously successful *The Great Ziegfeld*, also directed by Leonard, in 1936. The new film clarifies its relationship with its predecessor by incorporating scenes from the former, notably the giant wedding-cake finale, this time with Judy Garland singing from atop the cake. More than that, each of the three central female characters was cast in a role that drew closely from her real-life persona. They were each also easily recognizable as bearing the traits of their real-life Ziegfeld counterparts. Lana Turner was the Irish "Red," who is spotted working in an elevator, and removed from her working-class home, finds herself unable to cope with the attentions of wealthy male suitors and the temptations of drink. Eventually she collapses in an alcoholic daze onstage. As audiences would have known, the actual Ziegfeld Girl, Lillian Lorraine, destroyed her career with public drunkenness and disorderly behavior and, as Sheila does, would show up for years afterward haunting the corridors of the Follies. So strong were the resonances between Lana Turner's offstage affairs and her onscreen character, that her role was expanded as the film was made.[3] Judy Garland's struggles with stardom were already becoming public, and Hedy's foreignness and standoffishness were now considered her defining traits.

Lest the audience fail to make the connection between Hedy and her character Sandra, Sandra is distinguished from the other performers by her accent, elegant clothing, aristocratic bearing, and Germanic fiancé, Franz (Philip Dorn). True to the profile of the new immigrant, Franz is a talented jazz guitarist, and Sandra is discovered when she accompanies him to an audition. "Kookatacha, look at that one! She looks better all wrapped up than the rest of them do unwrapped!" Jerry Regan (Jackie Cooper) gasps, drawing the attention of the other performers and the audience to Hedy on her belated entry into the story. Franz is rejected but Sandra is instantly swept backstage and signed up. Now she will earn enough money to buy back his classic violin from the pawnbroker, and her success, accompanied by her flirtation with the lead tenor, Frank Merton (Tony Martin), will threaten their relationship. In words that echoed Hedy's dismissive attitude toward her profession, Sandra explains her new job to Franz: "It's a little silly, you put on some beads or something, and walk up and down like this [placing a book on her head], that's all, and people pay money to look at you."

Berman may have been dismissive of Hedy's iciness, but here it defines her, and reminds the film's audience of her other roles. But in this film her character gives up her liaison with Frank and returns to Franz; in fact, she even gives up her career to follow his. For any filmgoers who have still failed to link the fictional Sandra with the real Hedy and invoke her colorful past, one of the film's numbers, composed by Roger Edens and sung by Judy Garland, runs like this:

> They call her Minnie from Trinidad
> She wasn't good but she wasn't bad.
> Calypso Joe was so very sad
> When one day Minnie upped and left Trinidad.
> In Hollywood Minnie traveled far
> They changed her name to Minnie Lamarr
> And pretty soon she became a star
> The siren of the picture show.

In this number, Garland presents a kitschy exoticism emphasized by noticeably fake palm trees and a real white donkey, which she caresses as she sings. Garland, made up with a touch of blackface, would later become a much discussed gay icon,[4] but the song, as its lyrics make clear, had two functions. It not only commented on Judy Garland as a performer but also on Hedy Lamarr's double makeover: first as a Hollywood immigrant performer and second as an exotic icon.

Hedy's main function in *Ziegfeld Girl* is as a mannequin, just as the real-life Dolores of the *Follies* was. Again Adrian clothed Hedy, this time in costumes that were at once high camp and excessively glamorous. If her narrative contribution was minimal (much less than that of either Judy Garland or Lana Turner), Hedy's visual display was magnificent. With her showstopping headgear suggestive of a peacock's feathers, Hedy was presented as a chillingly beautiful natural creation, refashioned by artifice. Never could she be mistaken for an American, and throughout the film, she remains isolated from the main drama by her foreignness. The image of Hedy gilded in the peacock/jeweled headdress became her trademark. Endlessly reproduced, it catches the roots of her camp legacy, which would become a considerable part of her later life.

Hedy, however, remembered the shoot mostly for its uncomfortable costumes: "The director, Robert Z. Leonard, had instructed me to walk down them [the steps] regally, with Lana on one side and my dear friend Judy on the other. I was to float with my head erect, arms disdainfully away from my body in the accepted Ziegfeld manner, and never, but never, look down to see where I was going. The fact that I couldn't see in the blinding light, even straight ahead, was small consolation." The only way to keep her headdress from falling off as she descended the steps was to fasten it to a board that was strapped to Hedy's back. "My bosom was taped from behind and I felt a little like some religious penitent in the 10th century walking in a torture procession."[5]

She took a break after the filming of *Ziegfeld Girl* and flew to the Riviera, where she said she met Anthony Eden, then British Foreign Secretary, who asked her opinion on European attitudes. According to Eden's biographer, Richard Thorpe, this may well be true. "He always liked getting opinions from all kinds of people he met. He also had a liking for stage and cinema (he was later President of the Royal Shakespeare Company) and would certainly be interested in meeting stars."[6]

In 1942 Warner Bros. was casting their forthcoming war propaganda picture, then titled "Everybody Comes to Rick's." Jerry Wald, one of their senior producers, noted that "This story should make a good vehicle for either [George] Raft or [Humphrey] Bogart. I feel it can be easily tailored into a piece along the lines of ALGIERS, with plenty of excitement and suspense in it."[7] With Bogart on board and the name changed to *Casablanca*, Warner turned to finding a suitable female lead. "Try to get a foreign girl for the part," advised the Epstein twins (Warner's cynical resident scriptwriting duo), who were working on the screenplay in Washington. "An American girl with big tits will do."[8] Warner's first choice of a foreign girl was Hedy. Louis B. Mayer refused to loan her out and informed Warner that he would not loan her to anyone. While this might seem like outrageous paternalism, one ought to remember that *Casablanca* was only considered a minor production, with no one anticipating the extraordinary cult status it would later attain. It's unlikely that anyone realized this was Hedy's greatest missed opportunity.

• • •

In her next film, and one of her best, *H.M. Pulham, Esq.,* Hedy played a role that portrayed the pleasures and dilemmas of being a modern American girl. She played it with a gentle irony that reflected the intentions of the novel it was based on. King Vidor, Hedy remembered, pushed her to take the part, pressing her over dinner at Romanoff's to take the role because it involved being a little less formidable than she was offscreen. Realizing that this was indeed a hot property, she agreed.[9] Her casting as Marvin Miles, the ambitious but charming advertising agency copywriter, was not, however, welcomed by all concerned. In 1940, John P. Marquand, author of the novel *H.M. Pulham, Esq.,* was startled to hear the Viennese actress had been cast as the female lead in Vidor's screen adaptation. He dashed off a quick letter to the director, "I am . . . wondering, although I knew you were leaning that way, whether you are seriously going to have Hedy LaMarr play Marvin Miles or whether this is merely an artistic impulse which you are reconsidering."[10]

Dismissing Marquand's reservations, King Vidor managed to take a swift dig at the author in defending his choice, and the skills of Marquand's wife, Elizabeth Hill, who had written the script. *Pulham* had been a best-selling novel, abridged for *Reader's Digest,* and appeared serially in *McCall's Magazine* in September 1940 under the title "Gone Tomorrow"; overall, Marquand's characters were prosaic, Vidor declared, and Hedy would add much-needed color to the tale. "It's an interesting idea," Marquand muttered, "and not bad, if you can make Miss Lamarr into a young American businesswoman. She is certainly the sort of person a man might remember for twenty years."[11]

Next, Louella Parsons entered the fray. Her column reeks of the casual xenophobia of the day, a reminder to Hedy that she need not consider herself accepted by American society, even if this was, of necessity, her new home. Hedy was not an American girl, Parsons insisted, and Marvin typified the "100 per cent American girl." She should not have the role.[12]

Marquand's Marvin Myles was a very particular kind of American girl. In the novel, as in the film, the narrative is told from the perspective of Harry Pulham. A modest Bostonian, endowed with an increasingly old-fashioned integrity, he realizes that he is part of the "lost generation" and "the life we had learned to live was gone."[13] This is the life of privilege that barely survived the First World War and was falling asunder by the end of the Second. In the interval between wars, Pulham defies his family's expectations and moves to New York, where he obtains a job in an advertising agency. There he meets Marvin Myles. If her name is, characteristically for Marquand, androgynous, her demeanor is not. Harry falls in love with Marvin, who, to his astonishment, reciprocates. She is in every sense the modern woman, ambitious, smartly dressed, and with a taste for highballs and New York glamour. Everything about her is at odds with Harry's background and this in the end drives them apart. He wants her to live in Brookline with his family and she knows she can never leave New York or her career. Eventually, Harry returns to Boston and marries his childhood friend, Kay. What only he knows is that he is still in love with the girl in New York. One doesn't discuss these things:

> I was taught that telling was one of the things a gentleman did not do, and I still agree. I was also brought up in the intolerant school that has a contempt for cry-babies. This sort of training could lead to only two results: You either got used to taking what was coming to you in a conventional way which troubled nobody like a gentle-man . . . or else you revolted from it entirely and became what we used to call, among other things, a "mess." You became a Socialist for instance.[14]

Pulham was fashioned from Marquand's own background as were many of the characters in the novel. Its author attended Harvard and later worked with the J. Walter Thompson agency in New York. Unlike his central character, Marquand harbored strong reservations about his social circle, particularly the old Harvard brigade with their inability to move past their college days.

Vidor and Elizabeth Hill remained faithful to the spirit of the novel, but omitted one complication. In the original, Harry is unaware that his wife too hankers after an old flame, a man he regards as a friend, and with whom she eventually has a short-lived affair. This particular twist resulted in the Catholic cardinal of Boston, William O'Connell, denouncing the book, which was almost banned in Marquand's hometown.[15]

Aside from a crisp, ironic writing style, Marquand's virtue is his refusal to judge his characters, either his slightly dim hero or Kay; nor is Marvin Myles vilified for her modern-American-girl aspirations. In the film, Robert Young played Harry Pulham with a kind of sleepy good nature that is taken directly from the original. Marvin Myles now becomes an immigrants' daughter rather than the small-town American girl who makes good in the city. Vidor told Hedy afterward that this was the best film she had ever done and he may have been right. This was in no small part due to his own careful handling of the star. For once, Hedy plays her part with animation; she makes eye contact with the other actors and under Vidor's direction, she adopted some wholly American tics, such as winking cheerfully at her friends when out for a night at the agency. With her hair in a bob, and, to Pulham's surprise, given to adjusting her make-up in public, this was a role that for once allowed Hedy to play the smart professional that she was. Her discomfort in the woolly winter garb she is forced to wear when the Bostonians go tobogganing is tangible, as is her pleasure in her work. The film, as the novel, is entirely in sympathy with its career girl's ambitions: to become a partner in the agency and have a car waiting on her, to mix with artists and writers, to have a butler and a yacht. "I know that if I didn't feel independent," Marvin Myles says, "I'd feel unhappy." All of this made her, as Jeanine Basinger said, "a truly subversive heroine."[16]

Here was a role for Hedy in which her identity was not defined by her beauty, but by her ambition and intelligence. This transforms her performance in Vidor's film. She is no longer simply presenting herself to the camera, to be admired as an objet d'art, but instead actively engages the film's narrative. It was, also, a moment in American film history that would soon pass. After the war, Hedy, along with so many women on-screen and in real life, would be forced to once again acquiesce to an image that demonized ambition and lauded domestic responsibilities.

Of all her directors, Vidor seems to have best understood Hedy. Writing about his experience working with her, he compared her with Jennifer Jones. Both, he said, were beautiful but had little acting ability; a director had to use patience to coax a performance out of either. It was Hedy's note of uncertainty in her acting that most struck Vidor and that he played on when directing her. Most perceptively, he noted: "Her inter-est seemed to be divided between the part she was playing and another career as an inventor or discoverer of some fascinating new soft drink or useful invention. Although Hedy was a tremendous sex symbol to mil-lions of movie-goers, she presented quite a different image to those work-ing with her on the set."[17]

Just how different Hedy was offscreen from on, Vidor illustrated by relating an incident that occurred after the wrap party for *H.M. Pulham,*

Esq.: "When I arrived home about two hours late for dinner, my wife was in a forgiving mood but she couldn't help calling attention to some lip rouge on my shirt collar. My defensive reply which came forth quite spontaneously was, "Don't worry, it was only Hedy."[18]

Was *H.M. Pulham, Esq.*—perhaps Vidor's comment on his increasing sense of anonymity at MGM—a reluctant insistence on the virtues of hard work and steadfastness? "Maybe I'm dead and I don't know it," Pulham sighs as he returns home one evening. It was rumored, too, that Mayer wanted Vidor to direct one big failure to cut him down to size. In the end, this wasn't it.

Despite Louella Parsons's views, the trade press were nothing short of positive in their reviews of the film and Hedy's part in it:

> The manner in which Miss Lamarr comes through puts to a glorious end all the controversy, leaving her critics with a lot of words to eat. She does Marvin Myles, the girl Pulham might have married, so that it is impossible to imagine another actress in the part—that's how excellent she is. Hedy Lamarr's beauty has never been questioned, only her acting ability. Her advancement in this appearance advances her screen career a good three years.[19]

Marquand, too, was bowled over by Hedy and, according to his biographer, "he told her gallantly that she seemed exactly right."[20]

Hedy was now becoming a regular on radio; just after the release of *H.M. Pulham, Esq.*, she appeared on the Edgar Bergen/Charlie McCarthy show, with the ventriloquist Bergen playing the stern father figure to his dummy, the errant Charlie McCarthy. In the episode with Hedy, she has fallen in love with Charlie, "Hollywood's Casanova," and is pressing marriage; he is terrified of the idea and runs away from her. The slot was a success and Hedy was back on the show in February 1942, this time so dedicated to her Red Cross training that all she wants to do is practice on Charlie and the show's new dummy, the dopey Mortimer Snerd. By September 1943, she was holed up on a desert island with Charlie McCarthy and the show's regular guest Don Ameche. The banter was permeated with racist asides—in one exchange, Charlie asks Dale Evans (Lucille Wood Smith) if she is a full-blooded princess. "No," comes the reply, "me half caste." "Well," Charlie counters, "come back when you're finished." Hedy here has little to add to the content other than being a foil for the men's gags. Still her persona worked well and she returned several more times to the show.

In February 1941, Hedy legally changed her name from Hedwig Kiesler to Hedy Lamarr. In November, she officially adopted James Lamarr Markey. She had met his mother in a hospital, she now said, and after the woman had died, she took the boy to her home.[21] No one questioned her story, though it sounds, in hindsight, more like the plot of a minor woman's picture. If it seemed an odd decision for a newly arrived starlet with no guaranteed future and an erratic love life to adopt a baby, no comments to that effect were made by any of Hollywood's main players. Her mother later told Gladys Hall that Hedy had always liked dolls and treated them as if they were alive, which she apparently believed supplied explanation enough for Hedy's adoption of a small baby. That this baby was not only sweet but also "unbelievably clever" confirmed the wisdom of that decision.[22]

The family was complete when, in early February 1942, Hedy's mother arrived in Los Angeles. She had been living in London with relatives for several years, and since 1938, Hedy had been expecting her to join her in California. She moved in with Hedy but soon afterward moved out to live nearby. Despite warm words for the press, the two kept in touch but were never close.

By late 1941, Hedy was already giving interviews in which she tended to discuss herself in the third person, an affectation that also marked *Ecstasy and Me,* which suggests that the book's voice was, at least to some extent, hers. She was also encouraging her fans to make the connection between her incarceration at the hands of Fritz Mandl and the wider loss of civil rights in Europe under fascism: "Hedy is no longer a little girl living in a land of rigorous discipline and hidebound restrictions," she said of herself in one such article. "She is now a woman living in a democracy instead of under despotic conditions which made her a woman watched and guarded and without really anything of her very own."[23] Hedy's statement suggests that coming to America enabled her to mature and become a woman, while living with little freedom in prewar Europe she was forced to remain a child.

On 24 March 1942, Hedy and George Montgomery announced their engagement. They met at a friend's tennis party and had known each other for three months. The blond-haired, blue eyed Montgomery, the son of Ukrainian émigrés, stood six feet two inches tall and had a frame to match. An outstanding high school athlete, particularly skilled in baseball, football, and boxing, he had been raised on the family ranch in Montana, the youngest of fifteen children. Hollywood knew him as a former cowpoke, but there was certainly more to Montgomery than this. "I wanted to become a boxer and study under Jim Jeffries," he told a reporter:

> But the fight promoters stalled me with promises. So I tended bar for a while at the Club Troika and worked as a carpenter and painter when the Bublichki night club was being remodeled. I thought a zombie was a dead man walking, but I needed that job as a bartender badly and I bought a book and memorized recipes. Either my memory or the recipes failed me. I was fired. Meanwhile, I'd gotten another idea from the girls who patronized the Club Troika. "Say, Gable, shoot us another martini!" they'd say. That was when I started touring the studio offices looking for a job.[24]

Hired as a horse rider and then a stunt man, Montgomery soon moved through the ranks of "B" movies to stardom. He was also a fine craftsman, and in later life made a good living as a cabinetmaker and sculptor.

Their engagement was short-lived and by the end of May, Hedy returned Montgomery's ring. She next met the French actor and professional charmer Jean-Pierre Aumont. Aumont, who was Jewish, had been forced to flee France after the Nazi invasion. He found America in general, and Hollywood in particular, to hold fairly prudish ideas regarding the proper conduct of relationships. It was left to Charles Boyer to take the new arrival aside at a Hollywood party where Aumont was enjoying flirting with Gene Tierney. "Watch your step," Boyer warned him, "she's a married woman. It simply isn't done here."

"What a strange country!" Aumont mused.[25]

He was more at home with Hedy, with whom he now shared an MGM contract.

During dinner at Hedy's home in Beverly Hills, according to Aumont's memoirs, which are almost as racy and probably as unreliable as Hedy's, she brushed her knee against his. The following week, they were engaged. Aumont gave her a diamond ring and they planned an early July wedding.

"But, beautiful as she was, the moodiness of the Austrian star began to worry me," Aumont wrote. "One evening, when we were driving back from a concert, I braked too quickly. Hedy became hysterical, claiming that I had purposely tried to throw her against the windshield because I was jealous of her beauty."[26]

Aumont had summoned his father, also newly arrived from France, to meet his future bride. Heading to the airport to pick up his father, Aumont suddenly realized that the meeting between Hedy and his father would make the whole event somehow official. " 'You take care of her,' I said with cowardice unbefitting a gentleman, 'I've had enough.' I jumped on the first plane for San Francisco, leaving the poor man standing there with his mouth open." Aumont spent the weekend reconsidering a future with a "Tyrolian temptress already three times divorced and nursing in her personality all the complexes and insecurities of our old Europe."[27] He returned to Hollywood; Hedy threw the ring in his face, then picked it up and walked out.

Aumont's tally of Hedy's marriages suggests their encounter took place in the late 1950s, as she also remembered it,[28] though newspaper reports place them together in 1942, when Aumont first arrived in Hollywood. Aumont married Maria Montez in 1943, and they remained married until the latter's tragic death in 1951. Aumont remarried in 1956, so it seems unlikely that he became engaged to Hedy in the late 1950s; she was herself experiencing a succession of chaotic marriages in the early 1950s. Aumont would have certainly met Hedy working at the Hollywood Canteen (see next chapter) and it seems more likely that this engagement, if it ever happened, occurred during wartime.

Aumont's description of Hedy's personality generally agrees with that of others. There is her grasp of the monetary value of her beauty,

HEDY LAMARR

allied to a deep insecurity about future income as expressed by an unappealing pursuit of material goods: she grabbed back the ring. And there is her moodiness, explained in part, by the largely unacknowledged circumstances of her background as a European Jew. Even among her fellow exiles, Hedy could expect little understanding of how tough she needed to be to survive.

Still, the now-famous star seemed most comfortable in the company of fellow exiles and old lovers. On 6 August 1942 she attended the opening of *Tales of Manhattan* at Grauman's Chinese Theatre on Sam Spiegel's arm. She kept up with Erich Maria Remarque, who was now living in Hollywood and part of the film colony; he went to see her films and they met at social events.

Like so many of her peers, Hedy had to threaten her employers with lawsuits to ensure that she was paid according to her contractual agreement. In September 1942, she walked out on MGM, demanding that her pay raise be honored. Promised $2,000 per week, the studio was holding her salary at $1,500. MGM claimed it was unable to pay her more because of President Roosevelt's wartime executive order limiting all salaries to $25,000 a year. Hedy's challenge to MGM was viewed in some quarters as evidence of un-American tendencies:

> The Hedy Lamarr thing is entirely out of line, as is Miss Lamarr with the filing of such action. It would seem to us that such a test case, if there is necessity for such action at this time, might far better be filed by one of our own people and not by a foreigner, nor even by a foreign-born American citizen. Miss Lamarr, with her action, tells the world she does not like our laws, that she resents the President or anyone else meddling with her $2,000-a-week salary, and wishes the court to straighten out the President, the Salary Stabilization Board, the Treasury, the Government and MGM. Each of these might well say, "Look who's talking," and suggest that if she does not like our way of doing things, she go back to her native country, try her talents on that government and question its rights, rather than offer criticism of this land in its war effort.[29]

Only in May 1943 did the suit close and then because Congress lifted the limit and MGM could no longer claim they were legally constrained from giving Hedy her raise. In hindsight, it is remarkable that Hedy could have been accused of being disloyal to her adoptive country. Her full-hearted immersion in wartime activities, detailed in the next chapter, would years later win her recognition at home and abroad. Yet, for the American public, she would always remain a foreigner, too different and too difficult to be anything else.

9

The Rather Unfeminine Occupation of Inventor

HEDY WAS CONDEMNED to watch the battle in Europe from the distance of America. Like so many other émigrés, she threw herself into the war effort; in her case, serving in the Hollywood Canteen and selling war bonds. It also meant using the intellectual property she had taken with her from Mandl's castle, but we'll return to that.

The Hollywood Canteen was set up in autumn of 1942 on Cahuenga Boulevard, just off Sunset, by Bette Davis and John Garfield, after the latter had been turned down for war service. Inspired by New York's Stage Door canteen, it was decorated in the style of a New England barn, and entertained upwards of three thousand soldiers every night. Some hitched in from camps fifty miles away, some were heading to the war, others returning. Their hosts, be it Bing Crosby, Basil Rathbone, Eddie Cantor, or Fred MacMurray, kept the show rolling: "Fellows, we hate to do this, but a thousand of your buddies are outside, waiting to see the show. We're going to ask all of you who have been here an hour or so to leave now, so they can come in."

Once indoors, an array of celebrities, from Abbot and Costello to Rita Hayworth and Joan Crawford, dished out food, danced with the troops, and scrubbed the floors. A passing soldier could ask Betty Grable to dance, while her husband, Harry James, played in the orchestra. Newsreel footage shows a smiling Hedy signing autographs and giving a shy young soldier a kiss. Indeed for her and other high-profile Germans and Austrians, notably Marlene Dietrich, this was a chance to remind their hosts where their allegiances lay. "I constantly worked at the Canteen and I worked hard," Hedy remembered. "Some nights I signed so many autographs I thought my arm would drop off, but I couldn't resist those boys, and, in the end, I was able to dance with pleasure."[1]

Hedy also actively participated in the national war bonds drive. Along with her old friend Greer Garson and others such as Irene Dunne and Ronald Colman, she was one of the headliners in the Stars over America tour. Hedy visited sixteen cities in ten days and is credited with selling $25 million in bonds. In one day alone, according to most accounts, she sold $7 million worth of bonds. Titus Haffa, a Chicago businessman, made the headlines by suggesting that he would buy a $25,000 war bond if Hedy kissed him; later he reneged, saying that he would kiss her if she bought a bond to that tune.[2] Hedy was welcomed to New York's City Hall by Mayor Fiorello La Guardia and feted up and down the country. Next she headed a drive to persuade everyone at MGM to write friends in the service. The press reported that 2,144 letters had been mailed since she started her campaign.

Hedy also unintentionally lent her name to a gadget designed to create confusion in public spaces and thus facilitate the escape of a spy. The "Hedy" was a firecracker, which, when lit, made the sound of a falling bomb and sent crowds running for cover. Its inventor so named it because he said Hedy Lamarr triggered panic among men wherever she went.[3]

In an equally bizarre use of her name, Hedy became the subject of a short story in which she and a G.I. capture Adolf Hitler. Penned by Ben Hecht for *Collier's* magazine and published in 1943, "The Doughboy's Dream" was later distributed as a pamphlet for the American troops. Hecht was unhappy with the end result, which he rightly considered to be poorly written; what is of greater interest now is less its hackneyed dream narrative than what it reveals about Hedy's position as a wartime icon. The story is composed as if it were a script for the stage or screen and is set in a regimental camp. One of the privates, Cookie Johnson, has fallen into an exhausted sleep from which he is woken by his sergeant, who sends him to a meeting with Franklin Roosevelt. The president entrusts him with a mission to fly that night to Germany and bring back Adolf Hitler; traveling with him as his companion will be Hedy Lamarr.

On the airplane, the beautiful Hedy confides to Cookie that she has loved him since the second reel of *Tortilla Flat*, when, looking out of her cabin window, she saw him sitting on the fourth row end seat chewing on peanut brittle. Kissing Spencer Tracy was, after that, just business, it was him she loved.

The twosome are captured, and after getting some mileage out of the Germans' funny English accents, Cookie squares up against Hitler in the boxing ring; Hitler is wearing swastika-embroidered underwear. Cookie knocks out the fuehrer and the two rush Hitler onto the plane. Once on board, Cookie flies the plane, leaving Hedy sitting beside the captive. As soon as he regains consciousness, Hitler starts sweet-talking Hedy, impulsively seizing her hand and covering it with kisses. For a moment, Hedy seems to fall for him, stroking his cheek affectionately. Cookie is horrified: "If I'd took Lana Turner along she would have remained true blue. Or Betty Grable or anybody."[4] It transpires that Hitler has hypnotized Hedy by playing "The Blue Danube" and once the tune reverts to "I'm a Yankee Doodle Dandy," she comes to and resumes her patriotic duties. They return home to great fanfare, which switches to a camp bugle as Cookie awakes from his dream.

As much as the piece recognizes Hedy as *the* wartime fantasy figure for the troops, it also touches on a subliminal concern that neither she nor the other émigrés could shake—where did their allegiances lie? If they spoke German, could they be lulled into sympathizing with the enemy? Here, Hedy is redeemed by a double whammy of Americana, the love (for which she must plead) of an honest G.I. and a dose of patriotic music. Try as she might, the role of exotic or threatening outsider, depending on time and circumstance, was always shadowing her.

In a more considered move, Hedy became a member of the Los Angeles Austrian group, whose members were proposing that she and Franz Werfel appear together in a short German-language film to promote the cause of recent Austrian immigrants in America. But it was when Hedy applied one of her less-vaunted talents to aiding the American war effort that the actress created a legacy that has come to define her quite differently.

During the war Hedy persuaded the composer and concert pianist George Antheil to work with her on the invention of a radio-controlled torpedo-guidance system, commonly referred to as the "Secret Communication System." This startling fact has only become widely known in recent years; at the time it was reported in the news as a lesser item of interest.

Frequency-hopping, the system which has become associated with the actress and the composer, is a fairly straightforward process, although, in the years preceding and during World War II, its finer points eluded the scientists of the day. The procedure involves sending a series of signals from a transmitter to a receiver in a manner that cannot be intercepted, thus allowing for a torpedo (for instance) to be dropped remotely. Not only is it essential that the information pass from transmitter to receiver, it is also crucial that the message cannot be jammed by a third party.

From the mid-1930s, the German navy had been working on a device that would allow them to launch missiles at sea. The most obvious idea—tying a rope or wire to the device—was impractical. The rope or wire could be cut or become entangled in intervening objects. Radio control offered another solution, and German engineers had developed a three-hundred-foot-long antenna that would attach to the torpedo. The next challenge was to control this.

According to Professor Hans-Joachim Braun, a substantial contract was awarded to the German firm Siemens and Halske to develop missile-guidance technology. It was just as war was about to break out that the idea of frequency-hopping was broached:

it was definitely discussed at a meeting in July 1939, and it seems likely that the notion had already come up in Fritz Mandl's conversations a few years earlier. Siemens and Halske was supposed to have a radio-control system ready by the end of 1939, but the outbreak of war redirected military R&D priorities, and the project went by the wayside amid continuing uncertainties about jamming, cumbersome transmitters, and underwater penetration.[5]

If the German military technicians had given up on the idea, Hedy saw an opportunity to demonstrate, once and for all, her loyalty to her new country while also satisfying her own intellectual curiosity and restlessness. She may well have also sought this opportunity for personal financial gain, which indeed, half a decade later, came to fruition. In the early years of the war, however, she was having difficulty refining the details of frequency hopping. She needed the help of George Antheil.

Today, George Antheil is best known for his composition of *Ballet Mécanique*, but in the years before World War II, Antheil, who was born in 1900 in Trenton, New Jersey, performed as a concert pianist across Europe. During the 1920s, this pint-sized prodigy with his blonde hair and childlike blue eyes acquired a reputation as not only the most unorthodox but also the most talented American composer of his time. Nothing about his music conformed to the expectations of the classical audience, least of all his use of the piano as a percussion instrument. Riots among the surrealist crowd regularly accompanied a night out at an Antheil concert, and his group of friends included Gertrude Stein, Ernest Hemingway, James Joyce, Ford Madox Ford, Ezra Pound, F. Scott Fitzgerald, and Sylvia Beach. Living in an apartment above Sylvia Beach's bookshop, "Shakespeare and Company," Antheil was particularly close to Ezra Pound, who wrote several treatises placing Antheil's work at the center of modernist musical composition. Antheil also composed for Joyce and W. B. Yeats. Antheil's Paris debut was in the famed Champs Elysées Theatre, where he played three of his sonatas. The event was filmed for and included in the surrealist movie *L'Inhumaine* (Marcel L'Herbier, 1924). Drawn by the suggestion that the concert would be included in a film, the bourgeois élite of Paris arrived and found themselves rubbing shoulders with surrealists and Dadaists. Others attended because they had heard of the notorious American composer, who attracted riots wherever he played. Ezra Pound was there, as were the surrealist Ferdinand Leger, the composers Erik Satie and Darius Milhaud, and James Joyce. So great was the hullabaloo that from the end of the opening sonata's first movement, no one present could hear the music. As some audience members shouted, whistled, and yelled in indignation, Antheil's defenders roared back. Delighted with the effect, Marcel L'Herbier requested that they repeat their performance for the film; they obliged, with the effect now immortalized, even if only for lovers of French surrealist cinema. Always one to capitalize on notoriety, Antheil would lock all the concert hall doors before he performed and place a revolver on the piano as he readied to play. It was in Paris that he composed the first version of *Ballet Mécanique* as a soundtrack to the surrealist film of the same name. The piece required one player piano, two pianos, three xylophones, electric bells, a small wood propeller, a large wood propeller, a metal propeller, a tam-tam, four brass drums, and a siren.[6]

Antheil's reputation did not last much longer than his early performances (with their inevitable riots) of the *Ballet Mécanique*. He returned to America penniless. In 1934, Antheil tried his hand at composing film scores, starting with the music for two films by Ben Hecht and Charles MacArthur, *Once in a Blue Moon* (1935) and *The Scoundrel* (1935). He even began cowriting the advice column "Boy Advises Girl" for the *Chicago Sun* syndicate. His wife, Böski, niece of Arthur Schnitzler, also cowrote the column. It was Böski, Ben Hecht remembered, who took care of Antheil: "She was shapely, cultured, elegant and able to double as cook and char woman without dropping a smile. Böski cooked and cooked, produced and nurtured a son; worshipped, coddled, applauded, and forgave her Georgie through thirty-five years of living, much of which was like going over Niagara Falls in a barrel for two."[7] After a visiting endocrinologist left a stack of books in his house, Antheil began familiarizing himself with the then-popular discipline of endocrinology, focusing especially on its criminal aspect. A good portion of Antheil's future income came from articles he wrote on the topic for *Esquire*. In the articles, he restricted his knowledge to advice on how to use an understanding of hormones to pick up women. In 1939, however, he published *Every Man His Own Detective: A Study of Glandular Criminology*. Its premise was that a glandular criminologist could solve crimes by analyzing forensic evidence to determine what hormonal type had committed the deed. In 1940 he followed his first book with *The Shape of War to Come*, on international strategy.

It was through his work on endocrinology that he met Hedy. According to his aptly named, if unreliable, memoir, *Bad Boy of Music*, Antheil's friends Adrian, the dress designer, and his wife, Janet Gaynor, approached him in the summer of 1940 with a request from Hedy Lamarr to talk to him about her glands. A dinner meeting was arranged:

> I sat down and turned my eyes upon Hedy Lamarr. My eyeballs sizzled, but I could not take them away. Here undoubtedly was the most beautiful woman on earth. Most movie queens don't look so good when you see them in the flesh, but this one looked infinitely better than on the screen. Her breasts were fine, too, real postpituitary.[8]

"Postpituitary" in Antheil's analysis of hormonal types equated to being excessively sexually available with a tendency to nymphomania. Hedy was apparently impressed; she also may have believed him when he assured her that he could recommend a cream that would increase her bust size. Scrawling her phone number in lipstick on his car, Antheil tells us, she demanded that the composer call her. He did and the next evening found himself dining with the star at her Benedict Canyon home. Nervously, he advised her on some activating substances that would do the trick.

Whether or not there is any truth to this version of how they met, it makes for a good yarn; elsewhere Antheil wrote that "it seems that Hedy had discovered that somewhere along the line of my perhaps not too nefarious but certainly varied past I have at one time been a government inspector of U.S. Munitions. Albeit . . . my knowledge of the same was at this particular moment . . . a bit dusty, nevertheless I was undoubtedly the only 'munitions brains' available at the time, and Hedy had decided that I would have to do." In this version, it seems that Hedy invited Antheil to visit. To his surprise, he found her drawing room filled both with unreadable books and very usable drawing boards that looked as if they were in constant use. Hedy, he discovered, was not going out nights; she was sitting at home working on her inventions.[9]

If Antheil was a disappointment when it came to breast enhancement, he was infinitely more useful when it came to developing frequency-hopping technology. Hedy explained to him that she felt uncomfortable sitting in Hollywood when Europe was in such need. She knew, she said, a great deal about munitions and secret weapons and was considering quitting MGM and heading to Washington, D.C., to offer her services to the newly established Inventors Council. Antheil suggested she could do more for the war effort by staying in Hollywood. Hedy disagreed; though in the end, she insisted that Antheil be responsible for contact with Washington.

Although most accounts ascribe Hedy's motivation for inventing the "Secret Communication System" to a general desire to avenge herself on the Nazis, and particularly on her ex-husband, Fritz Mandl, Antheil believed there was another reason behind her efforts: "Hedy, for all her sweetness, does not forget that the Germans free hired, misrepresented, and tricked her into appearing most vastly to her early disadvantage in a film called Ecstasy!"[10] The Hedy that decided the Germans must be bombed because of *Ecstasy* is perhaps more fantastical than true.

Whatever the motivation, Antheil was struck with Hedy's ideas. The two had much in common, a love of music and of Europe, and a slightly different perspective on the world. Both, too, liked the idea of exploiting their talents for money. Antheil appreciated Hedy's intelligence and his correspondence is peppered with warm mentions of her personality, even if they occasionally had a falling out. Unusually, there was never any suggestion that the two had an affair. Still, this new friendship was hard on Antheil's wife. As he recollects in his memoir, Böski would come home in the evening only to be told her husband couldn't dine with her; he was expected at Hedy Lamarr's, and she was not invited. They were too busy working on something.

"Oh, so you're going to be busy!" Böski exclaimed. "What doing, dare I ask?" She was a trifle sarcastic.

"We are inventing a radio-directed torpedo," I said.

"Indeed," said Böski frigidly.

"Yes," said I. (Anybody who knows me will tell you that I would not tell a lie to Böski.)[11]

As it turned out, Antheil was telling only the truth. What he contributed to the invention of frequency-hopping was the notion that swift changes in radio frequencies could be coordinated just as he had coordinated pianos and other instruments for Ballet Mécanique. A rapidly changing frequency, they both agreed, could not be jammed. The two spent many hours in Hedy's villa with used matches and a silver matchbox laid out on her carpet, considering how to develop her initial concept. Antheil's proposal was to place a paper roll in the transmitter and another in the receiver. Each roll would be perforated with a pattern that appeared random. The transmission would switch from channel to channel in a secret sequence that was too complex to be intercepted. Clearly, the transmitter and receiver had to be perfectly synchronized using a precise mechanism that remembered the sequence of channels. If the two rolls were started at the same time, one staying at the launch point and the other being launched with the torpedo, they would remain in synch, just as the player piano rolls did in Ballet Mécanique. The system used eighty-eight frequencies, the number of keys on a piano.

Encouraged by the much-vaunted launch of the National Inventors Council earlier that year, the twosome sent a description of their ideas to Washington in December 1940. The chairman of the council was Charles F. Kettering, research director of General Motors. Kettering was initially enthusiastic, encouraging Hedy and Antheil to work toward a patent. While most of the initial proposal was patentable, one or two of its clauses were too similar to other patented ideas and had to be altered. They worked together throughout 1941, with Hedy dropping by Antheil's latest home (he enjoyed changing addresses) to refine their design. By June, Hedy urged Antheil to head to Washington to lobby for their patent, but Antheil preferred to rely on William C. Bullitt, special assistant to the secretary of the navy, to exert his influence. Bullitt was an old friend from Antheil's Paris days and had served as U.S. ambassador there; Antheil flooded him with correspondence about the invention.

Surprisingly, Colonel Lent of the National Inventors Council leaked the story of the invention to the press in October 1941, before it had been completed. The idea was taken up with enthusiasm, mostly because of Hedy's name: "so vital is her discovery to national defense that government officials will not allow publication of its details," advised the *New York Times*.[12] "Her invention, held secret by the government, is considered of great potential in the national defense program," the *Los Angeles Times* agreed.[13] Under normal circumstances, the Patent Office would issue a secrecy order. One might speculate that the Inventors Council leaked the information, not because they planned to use the invention, but for public relations purposes. How bizarre and exciting to have Hedy Lamarr devising a wartime invention!

Dr. MacKeown, a professor of electrical engineering at the California Institute of Technology, helped them iron out the bugs and the patent (no. 2,292,387) was granted on 11 August 1942. The names listed on the document, titled "Secret Communication System," are Hedwig Kiesler Markey and George Antheil. It specifies that a high-altitude observation plane could steer the torpedo from above.

Anxious that measures be taken to develop their invention, Antheil lobbied for funds for further research from, among others, his friend Bullitt. In a series of strongly reasoned letters, Antheil contended that America needed to redress Germany's superior naval technology. But the war effort was not yet to benefit from Hedy and George Antheil's ideas and the twosome found themselves being stonewalled by higher-ups.

No doubt, the National Inventors Council in Washington could not fathom that a proposal by an Austrian film star and a down-at-heel pianist could have merit. Antheil tried in vain to argue their case: "Likewise, a curiosity of this idea is that its co-inventor is Miss Hedy Lamarr, the motion picture actress (who is a good friend of mine), who, curiously enough, has had considerable experience of a second-hand nature concerning this subject. Her first husband, Fritz Mendel [sic], was once one of the largest munition [sic] manufacturers in Austria, besides which Miss Lamarr has a natural aptitude for the rather unfeminine occupation of inventor."[14]

The navy replied that the proposal was unworkable and was too bulky to be used inside the average torpedo. Antheil was enraged by their folly:

> Now if there's one single criticism that they could not, nor should not have made, it was THAT one.
>
> Our fundamental two mechanisms—both being completely, or semi-electrical—can be made so small THAT THEY CAN BE FITTED INSIDE OF DOLLAR WATCHES!
>
> I know (or I think I know) why they said that. In our patent, Hedy and I attempted to better elucidate our mechanism by explaining that a certain part of it worked not unlike the fundamental mechanism of a player piano. Here, undoubtedly we made our mistake. The reverended [sic] and brass-hatted gentleman in Washington who examined our invention read no further than the words "player piano."
>
> "My God!" I can see him saying, "we can't put a player piano into a torpedo!"[15]

The Secret Communication System was not the only invention Hedy and George Antheil worked on during the early 1940s. Another project was an antiaircraft shell that would explode automatically not just when it hit the plane (they regularly missed), but when it came near the plane. A magnetic device attached to the missile would cause it to explode when it achieved the same altitude as the enemy aircraft; should this device not be triggered, the missile would self-destruct so as not to fall to the ground and destroy friendly targets. A timing device would ensure the missile remained inactive before it was fired.

Hedy and Antheil were excited about their proposal and after Antheil submitted it, Hedy pestered him nightly by phone to ask whether he had heard back from the Inventors Council. They agreed to divide any monetary benefit they might accrue fifty-fifty. The council, however, showed less interest in the antiaircraft shell than in the Secret Communication System, and Hedy began to suspect her friend George of secretly taking the entire credit for the invention. In January 1941, at a dinner in his house, the dispute came to a head. Antheil made accusations that he soon regretted and the friendship briefly cooled.

Although Hedy remained a difficult invention partner, the Antheils and the Loders continued to spend time together. They regularly met for dinner and Hedy took a close interest in Antheil's compositions. On occasion, they were joined by the flamboyant conductor Leopold Stokowski, who would later conduct the premiere of Antheil's Fourth Symphony. Hedy was bursting with suggestions for the composition, so much so that Antheil announced that he would dedicate his nearly completed Fifth Symphony to her. In fact, he may have intended to dedicate "Heroes of Today" (1945) to Hedy for her commitment to patenting the antijamming device, which made her a war hero in his eyes. That overture became the first movement of the Sixth Symphony; hence, in the end, she received no dedication.[16] By now Antheil had fallen out of love with musical Dadaism and embraced a more populist and accessible style, a change of heart that corresponded to the political moment but might equally have been inspired by his friendship with Stokowski.[17]

Antheil introduced Hedy to his circle; among his friends were Ethyl and Saul Chaplin. When they visited the Chaplins' bohemian residence for the first time, Hedy hung back shyly, as she often did. Saul had been tinkling on the piano; Ethyl took her place at the second piano and the couple launched into a duet from Kurt Weill's *Threepenny Opera*. One of the other guests, Farley Granger, was amazed to observe the Austrian's transformation: "She joined in with complete animated abandon. If only she had been able to bring some of that joy to her screen roles, there would have been no stopping her."[18]

After the publication of Antheil's memoir in November 1945, there was a brief renewal of interest in their work together and Hedy phoned Böski to investigate. Again, Hedy suspected Antheil might be secretly profiting financially from their invention. He quickly wrote to her to explain that this was far from the case.[19] In fact, the memoir recollects Hedy with great sympathy:

The Hedy whom we know is not the Hedy you know. You know something which the MGM publicity department has, in all its cunning, dreamed up. There is no such Hedy. They have long ago decided that, in order to give her sufficient sex appeal, they will make her just faintly stupid. But Hedy is very, very bright. Compared with most Hollywood actresses we know, Hedy is an intellectual giant.[20]

Antheil also agreed with an opinion shared by many others and often expressed by the star herself, that Hedy was not hugely interested in acting.

It seemed that the Secret Communication system proposal had died. But in the 1950s, before the patent expired, it was used, without the inventors' names, on equipment designed to communicate between aircraft and sonobuoys—cylindrical devices dropped from planes into the ocean to search for enemy submarines. The engineers at the Hoffman Radio Corporation, who won the contract to manufacture the devices, were unaware who had invented the communication system.[21] In 1957 the concept was again adopted by engineers at the Sylvania Electronic Systems Division in Buffalo, New York. By now the first computer chips were in use and the invention, using electronics rather than player piano, ultimately became a basic tool used for secure military communications. Although the system was commonly called frequency-hopping, its official name was CDMA (Code Division Multiple Access). It was installed on ships sent to blockade Cuba in 1962, about three years after the Lamarr-Antheil patent had expired.

Subsequent patents in frequency-changing, generally unrelated to torpedo control, refer to the Lamarr-Antheil patent as the foundation for the field. In 1985, the system was declassified for military use, just as the emerging mobile telephone industry was warring over which system to employ. After a lengthy process, CDMA was adopted as the standard and Hedy Lamarr and George Antheil's invention became the base of all modern telephone technology (or spread-spectrum technology). Frequency-hopping technology is crucial to Global System for Mobile (GSM) telephones because it allows privacy for callers. Their concept is also the basis of the main jamming device used today, for example, in the Milstar defense communications satellite system used by the United States.

Scientists disagree on the impact of the Lamarr-Antheil invention on later technologies, including today's mobile telephone technology. Certainly, the actress and the composer were only two of many who helped develop frequency-hopping during the war and interwar years. Certainly too, Hedy Lamarr was the most glamorous name associated with this work, and her legacy is contained in the very concrete evidence of patent number 2,292,387.

It was most likely Hedy's glamour that dispatched competitors for the legacy; neither the field of amateur invention nor the technology industry have been much associated with Hollywood pizzazz, most particularly feminine beauty and stardom. It has well suited these industries to elevate Hedy Lamarr (with suitable accompaniment from George Antheil) to the position of emblematic figure. As the final chapter details, Hedy insisted that they pay to do so. Curiously, Hedy does not mention her work with Antheil in her autobiography and for many years she never publicly referred to the Secret Communication System.

10

Enter: Loder

HEDY WAS BECOMING as well known for the roles she did not play as for those she did. If her most famous missed opportunity was the role of Ilsa in *Casablanca*, other films she reputedly rejected included *Gaslight* (1944) (ironically, she starred in *Experiment Perilous*, a film often compared to *Gaslight*) and *Saratoga Trunk* (1945). She apparently turned down *Laura* when Preminger sent her the script: "I think it was a lousy script, and still do. If only he had sent me the music!"[1] How much leeway Hedy had over such decisions is debatable. Claiming to have turned down a role was part of the stardom package, actually doing so was less commonplace and such decisions were usually made by studio heads. George Cukor, for instance, said that when he came to *Gaslight*, Hedy was not mentioned as a casting possibility.[2] However, it is fair to assume that Hedy, who was clearly regarded as troublesome by most who worked with her, made her preferences clear.

Other circumstances also intervened in casting decisions during these years. When Niven Busch pitched his story *Duel in the Sun* (1946) to RKO, he aimed to provide an opportunity for his wife, Teresa Wright, to break from her "good girl" roles. RKO was instantly interested in the project but wanted Hedy and John Wayne in the leads. Hedy too was keen but became pregnant and had to withdraw; then Teresa found she was pregnant. In this instance, the role was memorably filled by Jennifer Jones, in a career-altering performance.

On Christmas Day 1942, Hedy met John Loder at the Hollywood Canteen. Loder was an easygoing Englishman from an impeccable military background, who inherited his dark good looks from his Sicilian grandfather. Educated at Eton, he received his military training at Sandhurst and served with distinction in World War I. In April 1916 he joined his father, who was in command of the British troops in Dublin, in time to witness the Easter Uprising and stood by his side as the Irish revolutionary leader, Padraic Pearse, surrendered to him. As his father's aide-decamp, he took Pearse to Kilmainham Gaol to execute him. When they reached the gates, the rebel leader had not finished writing his last message to his family, so Loder (still known by his real name, John Lowe), instructed the driver to keep driving. When Pearse had finished, he turned to Loder and said, "That indeed was kind of you. I would like to give you a small token of my gratitude." He then took off his Australian-style hat, removed the Sinn Fein badge, and handed it to the young officer.[3]

After the war, Loder resigned his commission and left the army; it had been, after all, the war to end all wars, and he saw little future in military service. Instead, he entered the pickle business with a German friend. For a short period, they made a fortune bottling and settling "Harris & Williams Pickles," but the devaluation of the German mark forced them to liquidate and Loder turned to another minor interest, acting. A happy encounter with the flamboyant Hungarian producer Alexander Korda put him on the road to a life of modest fame, largely gained from playing romantic British leads. Loder's looks fitted the debonair image of the day and he was cast in a succession of films, including Hitchcock's *Sabotage* (1936) and John Ford's *How Green Was My Valley* (1941).

Loder was inevitably drawn to Hollywood, where he easily fit in with the set of expatriates known as the English Colony. But his circle of friends stretched beyond his fellow countrymen; on arriving in Los Angeles, he began an affair with Marion Davies, which he claimed took place under the nose of William Randolph Hearst at San Simeon, the millionaire publisher's baroque mansion.

Loder's friend, director John Farrow, warned him off this activity, reminding the young Englishman of the fate of one of Davies's other lovers, the celebrated silent-film director Thomas Ince. Ince disappeared overboard while on the Hearst yacht and was never seen again. Loder simply relocated his assignations with Marion, or so he claimed, to her sister's house. By 1941, he had been joined by his wife, the French actress Micheline Cheirel, and their daughter, Danielle.

In 1942, Loder made his mark on Hollywood in the role of Elliott Livingstone opposite Bette Davis in *Now, Voyager*, playing, as he so often did, the jilted lover. Soon after returning to America from shooting *Passage to Marseilles* (1944) in England, he was introduced to Hedy. Meeting the Austrian film star was, "as the French so aptly put it, *un coup de foudre* [bolt of thunder]."[4]

Compared to the macho charms of George Montgomery, Loder was cut from an altogether different cloth. It was his Englishness that Hedy found so attractive, with its intimation of discretion, a quality that Hollywood clearly lacked (she also credited him with having a knighthood, which he did not). At the same time, Loder was no puritan: When Hedy and Loder met, he was recently divorced from Micheline Cheirel. He also had a son from an earlier marriage to Sophie Kabel. Hedy remembered Loder as being something of an intellectual, though there is little to suggest that he was. In fact, Loder resembled Hedy's other flame Reginald Gardiner, another urbane Englishman with a useful line in handsome, one-dimensional romantic male leads. What distinguished Loder from the run-of-the-mill Hollywood crowd was his refusal to take either his or his future wife's world seriously. This was not a problem when it came to Hedy's next film, *Crossroads* (1942), in which she starred opposite William Powell.

Crossroads stemmed from an original script by Hedy's fellow Viennese émigré Hans Kafka. The tale had already seen the light of day as *Carrefour* (1938) in France and *Dead Man's Shoes* (1939) in England. Unusually for a film with Hedy as the female lead, in *Crossroads,* William Powell's character, David Talbot, supplied the narrative's enigmatic center. Powell, already well-known for his "Thin Man" roles, starred as a French diplomat who suffers from memory loss and is blackmailed by a couple claiming he killed a man. Hedy is his new wife, Lucienne, who slowly comes to suspect her husband. The other two key roles were played by Basil Rathbone and Claire Trevor, although it was rumored that MGM had offered Trevor's part to Marlene Dietrich, who sharply refused to play second fiddle to Hedy. Despite an intricate plot, *Crossroads* is a light thriller in which Hedy only shines in the early sequences where she jokes with Powell by pretending she doesn't know him. After that she is almost entirely sidelined by a plot that focuses on the interplay between the two debonairs, Rathbone and Powell.

Mayer's prevarications over the direction of Hedy's career had resulted in throwaway roles such as Lucienne Talbot in *Crossroads.* But her role in

Tortilla Flat (1942) suggested that varying her "exotic dame" persona was a stronger commercial decision. In undistinguished peasant garb and coated in makeup, Mayer's aristocratic, Jewish-Austrian star once more made a memorable young native woman. MGM initially planned to borrow Rita Hayworth for what was, in the original story, the minor character part of Sweets Ramirez. The focus of Steinbeck's novella is the transformation of its central character, Pilon, from a venal manipulator of his peers in the *paisano* community of mixed-race Mexican Americans to a man touched by God and content with what life has given him. Steinbeck scholars have since widely critiqued it for its sentimentality, but during the war it would become one of many such escapist films that MGM, in particular, felt would take viewers' minds off their troubles.

Steinbeck had been surprised by the warm critical response from the press to his latest publication: "Curious that this second-rate book, written for relaxation, should cause this fuss," he wrote to his literary agent, Elizabeth Otis.[5] Like many writers, he was happy to disparage popular cinema and even happier, when the opportunity arose, to accept its checks: "You ask me why I don't take Hollywood's filthy money," he wrote to his friend and fellow author Louis Paul. "I like to think I wouldn't take it but I probably would. I've been around there quite a bit and I dislike it so much that I wouldn't want to. On the other hand, we've been so filthy broke for so long that I would probably go nuts if anyone waved a ten dollar bill."[6] Mayer did better than that, he waved $4,000 before Steinbeck for *Tortilla Flat*. Its author didn't hesitate to sign the contract. "I am not proud of this sale of *Tortilla* to pictures," was his response, "but we'll slap it into government bonds which are cashable and forget about it."[7]

MGM's adaptation was even more sentimental than Steinbeck's original. Pilon, under Victor Fleming's direction, was played by Spencer Tracy, and his nemesis, the young and innocent Danny, was played by John Garfield. The film focused on Pilon's resistance to change and his manipulation of Danny after the latter learns that he has inherited two houses. Only when Pilon tries to scam the holy fool Pirate (Frank Morgan) does he regret his ways and accept the need to make an honest living. Sweets Ramirez was a secondary character in the original plot; little in Steinbeck's prose suggested that this would be a suitable role for Mayer's star:

She was not pretty, this lean-faced paisana, but there was in her figure a certain voluptuousness of movement; there was in her voice a
throatiness some men found indicative. Her eyes could burn behind
a mist with a sleepy passion which those men to whom the flesh is
important found attractive and downright inviting.[8]

In other ways, Hedy was cast to form, as the strong woman who is
determined to marry well and has little time for Danny's layabout friends,
especially Pilon. Once again, her "foreignness" is contrasted with Spencer
Tracy's workingman image, although this time it is his character that
must adapt to the new ways she represents.

The script developed the character of Sweets Ramirez in a manner
quite at odds with the original; in the screen version she has a job in a
tuna factory and convinces the men of the value of paid employment
over casual swindling. This plot maneuver offers a nod to the wartime
imperative of having women work outside the home.

Hedy welcomed her peasant role as an opportunity to break from her
glamour girl image. This she did with vigor, her hair tied back in pigtails
and her lavish gowns traded for more earthy clothing. As she so often
would be, she was most convincing when stamping her feet and scolding
Pilon and his circle of feckless comrades, and least persuasive when she
crumbles as Danny is threatened with death. In another familiar pattern,
Hedy was required to provide little more than a disruptive female presence in a narrative that largely focused on power relationships between
the men. On set, she was increasingly upset by the news from the war,
breaking down in tears on several occasions as the situation grew worse.

In a review of this "good-natured and engaging minor novel by
Steinbeck, turned into a good-natured and engaging (though corny and
quaint and picturesque) film," Pauline Kael rated Hedy's performance as
"unusually animated."[9] Other critics agreed:

> Hedy Lamarr's stature as an actress increases with her portrayal of
> the fiery Portuguese girl loved by Danny and disapproved of by Pilon
> because she works in a canning factory—or merely because she
> works (period). It is surprising how far Miss Lamarr has advanced in
> her last few pictures. She is now more than simply a beautiful girl.[10]

It was her next movie that would cement Hedy's reputation as an
erotic fantasy in the minds of filmgoers. Perhaps Loder was right to

urge Hedy to reject the role of Tondelayo in *White Cargo*, but Hedy claimed she saw it as a way to finally silence those whispers that she was made of marble. No doubt, Mayer did. The film bore the tagline, "It wasn't the heat that drove Ashley crazy. It was Tondelayo!" Of course, Hedy was the exotic native woman, Tondelayo, who drove white men crazy. "I thought with some interesting makeup, a sarong and some hip-swinging I would make a memorable nymphomaniac," she said later.[11] She was right.

Tondelayo marked a new stage in Mayer's construction of Hedy's exotic-dame persona. Gone were the aristocratic demeanor of her European identity and the sensual contrasts between the very whiteness of her skin and her dark gleaming hair and full lips. Even in *Lady of the Tropics*, discussed in Chapter 7, she retained many of her European traits; and as Sweets Ramirez she still looked white. Her Tondelayo, on the other hand, was simply defined by desire. Once in "blackface," Hedy was reduced to America's most unreconstructed image of the sexual female— the native woman. Although some audiences complained her makeup was too dark, others saw the role as the true unmasking of her foreignness. Once again, as one reviewer noted, she:

> portrays the seductive siren which has long been the popular picture of her personality. The role doesn't call for words; it doesn't call for acting ability. Tondelayo is simply a half-caste native girl whose indolent, erotic nature causes men to throw away pride and ambition for her love.[12]

The film was a remake of an earlier British production of the same name, which had been distributed independently in the United States in 1930. Many American states had banned it, while in others it was severely censored. The genesis for the story was a novel by Ida Vera Simonton called *Hell's Playground*, which had been transformed into a successful stage play in the early 1920s. Not simply exploiting the white world's fantasies of the oversexed native woman, *Hell's* also reflected the colonial world's ambivalence about what happened to the white man when he spent too long in the tropics, particularly if he "went native."

In July 1940, the stage version enjoyed a run at the Beaux Arts Theatre in Los Angeles. Theatergoers were deemed sufficiently educated and respectable to resist being led astray by the loose morals of the play they were consuming. Filmgoers, by virtue of their lower social status, needed to be protected from the influence of the same sinful entertainment. As Joseph Breen sourly commented during the theater run of *White Cargo*, if a motion picture were accompanied by such publicity (an image of Tondelayo with breasts exposed), "this office would be swamped with protests from all over the world."[13] Production on the film commenced on 18 May and continued until early July 1942.

One of the many problems associated with the original version was that Tondelayo was, in the language of the day, a Negress. To have a white man willingly enter into a sexual relationship with a woman of color was completely unthinkable under the restrictions of the Production Code, which specifically banned miscegenation. Louis B. Mayer was adamant from the beginning of the production that the part should be played by Hedy. If this was because Mayer hoped to divest his star of her icy aura, it also toned down the film's queasy racial politics. Would anyone in the audience seriously mistake Tondelayo for African when she was played by one of Hollywood's whitest actresses?

Once Mayer accepted the project, he chose Victor Saville, one of Hedy's companions on the *Normandie,* to produce it. One of the first changes the scriptwriters were told to make was to devise a plot twist whereby Tondelayo turns out to be white after all. In fact, they fudged the film's revelation, introducing a narrative twist that revealed Tondelayo to be half-Egyptian. When Saville asked the director, Richard Thorpe, to test Hedy's new look, they discovered that under the studio lights she looked "like Hedy Lamarr in dirty makeup." The solution was to shoot her only in night scenes. They then saturated her in oil and shone a light on her to simulate moonlight, creating the effect now familiar to audiences of her gleaming, shadowed body.[14]

White Cargo takes place in 1910 on a West African rubber plantation, where a group of hard-bitten expatriates sits drinking whiskey and awaiting the arrival of Langford (Richard Carlson), a replacement for the washed-up Wilbur Ashley (Bramwell Fletcher), whose tour of duty is over. Witzel (Walter Pidgeon), the plantation manager, is unhappy about the prospect of a new arrival, who will bring with him, he predicts, all the idealism of a new arrival to Africa. Witzel's foreboding turns out to be well-placed as Langford pays no heed to his warnings of the "damp rot" that destroys white men's souls. As the men gather the night before Ashley's departure, their evening is disturbed by the arrival of the local native seductress, Tondelayo. Hedy's first appearance is signaled well in advance as the old hands warn the newcomer about Africa's darkest danger, the woman whom Ashley describes as a "chocolate Cleopatra." She has, the padre (Henry O'Neill) warns Langford, "the undeveloped mind of a child made dangerously vain by the attentions of white men." Our first glimpse of this chocolate Cleopatra begins with a movement behind the mosquito netting over the cabin. The camera swiftly moves into a close-up of her face, her features darkened and almost unrecognizable, shadows falling across her oiled skin. She takes one look at Langford and announces herself with the film's famed line: "I am Tondelayo!" Her hair is now lightly waved and all that is left of Hedy's whiteness are the whites of her eyes and her gleaming teeth. Her clothing, as befitted her calling, was minimal, and she moved with the lissomeness of a dancer, all the time jangling her many bangles and necklaces.

In case the audience had failed to pick up the clues, soon it is obvious that it is she who will cause the rot in Langford's soul as he becomes enchanted by the sinuous native woman. "She knows how to purr her way into your mind and scratch her way out," the doctor (Walter Pigeon) warns him. To spite Witzel, Langford announces that he will marry Tondelayo. If at first this torments the other white men (for whom sex with natives comes without the commitment of marriage), Langford's bride soon torments him as she begins to complain that he is not giving her enough bangles and gifts. Throughout this scene, which has Hedy sitting on the floor pouting and running her fingers through a pile of jewelry, there is the unspoken suggestion that Langford is also not providing her with enough sex. Maybe Witzel was a more fulfilling lover; in any case, she tries to allay her boredom by approaching him. He rebuffs her and her only recourse is to poison Langford. Witzel recognizes her methods and makes her swallow her own "berry fruit" poison. Performing one last agonizing dance, Tondelayo falls to the jungle floor and dies.

Hedy's sensual dances provide the focal point of the film's entertainment; her choreographers were two fellow exiles and Max Reinhardt alumnae, Maria and Ernst Matray. Both sensed the star's discomfort with her role: "She would have preferred Viennese waltzes," Maria commented.[15] Indeed, despite her best efforts, and those of the makeup department, Hedy is a ludicrous Tondelayo. With her expressive range restricted to some eye flashing, pouting, and hip wiggling, recycled in each appearance, she never remotely conjures the Arabian Nights allure that was evidently intended. At a preview in Westwood, the audience responded by laughing uproariously in all the wrong places; Hedy's appearances gave particular rise to mirth.

The only sequence that lends an edge to her performance is one that introduces a theme, the pleasures of a good beating, that would weave throughout Hedy's on- and offscreen persona. Trying to reignite her husband's passion, Tondelayo falls to her knees and begs him, "please beat me, then maybe you feel much better." They have been married five months, she further reminds him, and he still hasn't beaten her. Witzel on the other hand had offered her those pleasures in abundance.

Unsurprisingly, the film held little appeal for up-market critics. The *New Yorker*'s review was typical:

> White Cargo, which has been on both the stage and the screen before, is suffering, in its latest film version, from the same complaint as ever. There's still the native girl, Tondelayo. This time Hedy Lamarr has the part and is just as unable to keep from sounding foolish as her forerunners were.[16]

How far Hedy had traveled from her days in the Theater in der Josefstadt! How could she have imagined as she took the stage to perform before cultured, appreciative theatergoers in Vienna that, within a few short years, she would be appearing on the world's screens, barely dressed, covered in oil and makeup, playing a character named Tondelayo. One has to imagine her day: listening to the latest news from the war as she rose from bed; being chauffeured to MGM, her thoughts preoccupied with her fallen country and not yet fully aware of the fate of her childhood Jewish friends and neighbors; being greeted as Miss Lamarr (no longer Hedy Kiesler); and setting to work as the makeup artists and costumers removed the last markers of her old, white Jewish identity.

Increasingly, it seemed the only roles considered suitable for Hedy were those of the prostitute, the exotic dame, or the aristocratic foreigner— and ideally some combination of these. What MGM chose to overlook, over and again, was that comedy was her forte. Glamorous beauties were no more allowed to be smart than they were funny. Carole Lombard and Barbara Stanwyck were funny; Katharine Hepburn could play Cary Grant off against a leopard in *Bringing Up Baby* (1938); a younger generation had been brought up with a wise-cracking Mae West; and Lucille Ball was to make a career as a comedienne that would transfer effortlessly to television and make her a millionaire. Hedy's comic roles were her least significant, sandwiched between her exotic dame parts. Her potential as a comedienne was lost on all but the most sympathetic writers such as Walter Reisch and a few of the more discerning of the film critics.

"Rumor has it that Hedy Lamarr will marry John Loder," Hedda Hopper wrote. "Personally I doubt it. There's no gold in them thar hills!"[17] Although relying on Hedda Hopper's judgment of Hedy's character would be foolish, John Loder recalls that on the day before they were married, Hedy sent him a bill for $350 to cover the cost of his nightly dinners at her home: "She said it was exactly half the price of the food and wine we had consumed together, and explained that she had also divided her cook's wages in half for the month I had been dining at her house." Somewhat taken aback, Loder wrote the check; then his phone rang. It was Marion Davies. "John, is it true you're marrying Hedy Lamarr tomorrow?" she asked. On hearing that it was, she hung up, just leaving time to add, "You old bastard, I hoped you were going to marry me, but good luck."[18] Like most of the Hollywood tales Loder recounts in his cheerful *Hollywood Hussar,* one may take this anecdote with a pinch of salt. But if the detail was probably short on accuracy, there is a grain of truth to Loder's account of his early days with Hedy. She was determinedly materialistic, a trait that most commentators found unseemly. At this point, however, she was the greater earner of the two.

In her turn, Hedy remembers them debating whether a happy marriage was fueled by sex, a conversation inspired by a man they had met at a party who claimed the secret of his marital success was making love to his wife every night, except for when she was "incapacitated," and nineteen times on a two-day weekend during their honeymoon.[19]

It was John Loder's good friend Errol Flynn who predicted most accurately the consequences of marrying Hedy; enjoying a last drink together in the Polo Bar of the Beverly Hills Hotel, Flynn wished his buddy good luck and, with a wide grin, added, "I suppose you realize, old boy, from tomorrow on you'll be known as Mr. Lamarr."[20] Years later, Princess Margaret confessed to John Loder that every time she and her sister Elizabeth, the soon to be Queen of England, saw his son Robin Loder on duty outside Windsor Castle, they would tease him and ask, "How does it feel to be Hedy Lamarr's step-son?"[21]

Around this time, Hedy became friendly with actress Ann Sheridan. Hedy called her friend "Pluto" because of her sad eyes while Ann responded by naming Hedy "Double Ugly." Ann would stop by and watch Jamsie and the two women went on double dates, Ann with Hedy's next-door neighbor, actor Robert Sterling, Hedy with Loder. Both also met up in the Hollywood Canteen.[22]

Undaunted, apparently, by the Englishman's low-key career, Hedy married John Loder in May 1942, according to him, and on May 27, 1943, in her account. On this occasion, Hedy's memory was faultless; this was also the day Loder's divorce from Micheline Cheirel was finalized in Chihuahua, Mexico. The couple had a quiet civil wedding on May 27 at the home of Lily Veidt (whose husband, Conrad, had recently died). There were only five witnesses: the famed interior decorator Elsie de Wolfe, otherwise known as Lady Mendl, and her husband, Sir Charles Mendl, who was best man; Hedy's mother; and Loder's friend, the actor Sam Pierce. Hedy wore a simple black velvet suit with a plain white silk blouse. They did not immediately honeymoon as Hedy was in the middle of filming *The Heavenly Body* and just took the day off for her wedding.

The Heavenly Body reunited her with William Powell and was best remembered afterward for Edith Head's designs and appropriately frugal use of cloth, given the prevailing wartime conditions. In fact, the film gave Hedy another opportunity to show off her skill at light comedy, again as penned by Walter Reisch (coscriptwriter). The plot was a marital farce that revolved around Vicky Whitley's astronomer husband William's (Powell) fury when she turns to an astrologer for life guidance. At the heart of her discontent, as in so many of her films, was the suggestion that Whitley was not providing her with sexual satisfaction. He, in turn, is apparently more than content to peer at his wife from the safety of his observatory through a powerful telescope. Enter a handsome stranger, Lloyd Hunter (James Craig), in the temporary guise of an air-raid warden and Vicky's longing appears to be on the verge of satisfaction. Needless to say, Hollywood morality dictated that matters should remain otherwise but not before some appropriately screwball chaos had shaken the certainty of the otherwise complacent Whitley.

Hedy and John Loder's marriage began ideally. After filming wrapped, the couple honeymooned in a log cabin at Big Bear where Hedy surprised Loder with her ability to cook. Her gift to him was a golden key to the door of her house and once they had settled into the Benedict Canyon home, they adopted a lifestyle far removed from the Hollywood glamour from which they had both so recently emerged. Their ranch house at 2707 Benedict Canyon Road in Beverly Hills was named "Hedgerow Farm." Visitors traveled up a long drive to reach the hideaway, which was unseen by most passers-by. Those who made the trip found an L-shaped single-story building with shuttered windows surrounded by six and a half acres of land. The grounds included a wide front lawn with a swimming pool and tennis court. If this was standard fare for a Hollywood star, the accompanying chicken and duck coops were a little less predictable. This was a home, comfortable but not luxurious, with a walnut-paneled living room and a fireplace framed by a carved English mantelpiece. The walls in most rooms were white, as was the furniture, though it was enlivened by stenciled sprays of flowers. The bedroom was as close a re-creation as Hedy could manage of her bedroom in Vienna, with rag rugs on the floor, hanging bookshelves, and a desk where she managed the household bills.

Hedy and John Loder had three servants, one who had been with Jean Harlow until her death in 1937, and the couple kept a Great Dane. They also had a ready-made family with little Jamsie at its heart. John Loder adopted him, and the child now became James Lamarr Markey Loder. Jamsie attended Black-Foxe Military Institute on Wilcox Avenue, a popular school (now closed) for movie industry kids.

Their lifestyle was widely described as resonant with domestic bliss. Hedy preferred to stay home in the evenings, reported numerous lifestyle articles, and on the cook's day off, she enjoyed cooking dinner for herself and her new husband. Around the house, she wore slacks, sweaters, and flat-heeled shoes; most of all, she liked to spend hours on the telephone, and on days when she was not filming, she occupied herself with extended early morning calls. In the afternoons, she listened to the radio, always tuning in, if she could, to Orson Welles's broadcasts. Loder, in turn, was comfortable with his habitual pipe and circle of friends from England and elsewhere. Both loved music and books.

If the release of these kinds of details was sanctioned (and often created) by the MGM publicity machine, they may not be entirely untrue. Still, Hedy was seldom contented for any great period of time and, as will be detailed, she soon tired of Loder's "slippers in front of the hearth" presence. Meanwhile, she had the freedom to explore her many creative pursuits, from designing jewelry to mixing her own perfumes and writing poetry, habits she maintained, along with lengthy telephone calls, on and off throughout her life.

In company, she was happiest discussing politics or just about any other topic and, as Loder acknowledged, she was never ostentatious or out to catch the limelight for herself. Like so many of the people who knew her well, Loder was adamant on another point: "Hedy's best quality was that she was completely unimpressed by her own outstanding beauty. Indeed she seemed oblivious to it." He also adds that, "she never flirted with other men, but then I think she was much more interested in success as a movie star than the opposite sex."[23] Was that true? During this time period it seems to be, as Hedy truly believed that she could make something of herself in the American star system. For now too, rumors of her profligate sexuality were hushed.

The couple kept up with old friends. Erich Maria Remarque notes in his diaries that he met with the twosome in New York in October 1943 and spent the evening chatting.[24] Another regular was Bette Davis, whom Hedy admired for being the "one actress who has lived up to her expectations, both on and off the screen."[25]

Money remained an issue between John Loder and his wife. According to him, on their first Christmas together, he bought her a diamond ring and she promised him a Cadillac. On Christmas Day, he handed her the box with the ring and she, in turn, handed him a small box. He opened it to find a little toy car.

Both agree that Hedy persuaded Loder to leave Warner Bros. Where they disagree is on the consequences of that decision. He blamed it for his slide down the B list, even if it temporarily led him to more lucrative work in radio. She wrote that "Even after we were divorced, he said it was the smartest career move he had ever made."[26] Hedy was still appearing regularly on radio, both in dramas and on comedy slots.

In October 1943, while she was shooting *The Heavenly Body*, Hedy appeared on the Burns and Allen show, sponsored by Swan Soap. Newly revamped as a soap opera revolving around the scatterbrained Gracie Allen and her foil, her on- and off-the-air husband George Burns, their show enjoyed top ratings on CBS. Guests played themselves, coping as best they could with the mayhem generated by Burns and Allen. In Hedy's episode, Gracie's friend, Tootsie Sagwell, is running as "Queen of the Fleet." The only other contender is Hedy Lamarr, and Tootsie has declared that she isn't afraid of her, even if all the other contenders dropped out once they heard who they were up against. Gracie visits Hedy to ask her to withdraw and is instantly caught up in paroxysms of admiration for her clothing. When she eventually remembers why she is visiting, she invites Hedy to her house. Misunderstanding follows misunderstanding with the full value of Hedy's complexion used for Swan Soap product placements. Throughout, all Hedy is expected to do is play up to her beautiful-but-foreign persona, allowing for multiple cultural and situational misunderstandings.

In a short while, it seemed that Hedy had found both happiness and celebrity. She was making good money (considerably more than her husband), and offers of work were flying in the door, along with her considerable fan mail. She had a home in an environment that was as close to the Vienna Woods as she could re-create, a charming child, and, nearby, her mother. Even as the war in Europe destroyed everything she remembered from her childhood, she was, for now, secure in Hollywood.

11

Exit: Loder

IN 1944, Hedy compensated for her missed opportunity to act in *Casablanca*. In January, she, Alan Ladd, and John Loder reprised the lead roles in the Lux Radio Theater adaptation of the film, produced by Cecil B. DeMille. Soon after, filming started on *The Conspirators*.

Suddenly aware of the value of the small film they had virtually thrown away, Warner Bros. proceeded to capitalize on the need for wartime propaganda by reassembling much of the cast for what they advertised as a *Casablanca* reunion. Originally, Warner Bros. planned to feature Humphrey Bogart, Helmut Dantine, and Ann Sheridan in their adaptation of a recently published novel, *The Conspirators*. Frederic Prokosch, its author, was known as a brilliant writer and poet; his Austrian father was a respected academic who had suffered from anti-German prejudice in his early career; his mother, a well-known pianist. Prokosch held a doctorate from Yale and might have followed his father into academia had he not found early success with his poetry. A poorly timed trip to Europe as war loomed saw him flee from border to border, eventually settling in Estoril, a small town just outside Lisbon in Portugal, best known for its ritzy casino. Estoril is the setting for *The Conspirators,* and the novel and film adaptation draw closely from the rich cast of characters Prokosch observed around him:

> The Palacio was filled not only with the wealthy refugees but with certain more ambiguous and slippery personalities. There was the sinuous Mrs. Grigoresco from Bucharest with her pearls, and the swarthy Mrs. Suleiman from Ankara with her parasol. There was the one-eyed Signor Katz from Trieste with his Utrillos, and there was the tweedy Mr. Abercrombie from Edinburgh with his golf

clubs. And who was that willowy Danish girl with the Pomeranian, and who was that rat-faced Fräulein Torok with the sunglasses?[1]

Prokosch's environment was translated into a swiftly written anti-Nazi novel, peopled by Prussian officers with cruel scars, duplicitous foreigners, and secret documents relayed by shadowy couriers; the book was duly banned by a number of unsympathetic governments. Ripe material indeed for Hollywood, as Warner Bros. realized.

When Hedy's friend Ann Sheridan was ruled out for the female lead, Joan Fontaine was approached next. Eventually, Jack Warner settled for Hedy (swapping her for John Garfield, who had to make two pictures for her one), with Ida Lupino as a reserve if MGM were not amenable. Paul Henreid starred as Vincent Van Der Lyn, aka the Flying Dutchman, a Dutch schoolteacher on the run from the Nazis. Sydney Greenstreet played the head of the Portuguese Resistance, Ricardo Quintanilla. Peter Lorre was his simpering henchman Jan Bernazsky. Hedy took center stage as the mysterious Irene von Mohr, who is married to a double agent within German High Command. She, of course, falls for Van Der Lyn, and the film's narrative struggles thereafter to integrate the spy story with the romance. If the casting was meant to invoke *Casablanca*, it also strongly echoed *The Maltese Falcon* (1941), boasting many of that film's twists and turns, as well as its film noir look. With Hedy, Henreid, Lorre, and Berlin-born editor Rudi Fehr all involved, the set was also referred to as "Reunion in Vienna."

From the beginning of the project, the film was dogged by difficulty. According to director Jean Negulesco, Hal Wallis had been its initial producer. That year Wallis had collected Academy Awards for two earlier productions, *Casablanca* and *Dark Victory*, awards that his boss, Jack Warner, had himself anticipated he would receive. "During the festivities of Oscar night, the repeated calling of the name of Hal Wallis aroused long applause and laughter. This was regarded as a covert slap at Jack Warner. Warner was humiliated and Wallis was fired the next day."[2] In fact, Wallis's acrimonious departure from Warner Bros. played out more slowly than Negulesco remembers. The upshot for *The Conpirators* was the same, however. Jack Chertok was then appointed producer; any footage that had been shot under Wallis was discarded; and the pace of the story was changed: "My job as a young director became a nightmare. Secretly the film became known as *The Constipators*, with 'Headache Lamarr' and 'Paul Haemorrhoid.'"[3]

The film was shot between March and June 1944, using stock footage in lieu of overseas locations. The finished result looked like the thrown-together, studio-shot spy story that it was. But its climax, at the casino in Estoril, in which the double agent has five minutes to pass a secret message to the Nazis before the eyes of both sides of the ideological divide, is genuinely thrilling. In this sequence, as Hedy noted, one can see *The Conspirators* as an early precursor of the Bond films.[4]

Hedy's character was presented as a potential traitor until the film's ending, which gave narrative weight to her inexpressive features. She is a more active participant in *The Conspirators* than was Ingrid Bergman's Ilsa in *Casablanca* and a more sophisticated figure, with her clothing (by Leah Rhodes) once again doing much to explain her character. In one sequence she is dressed all in flowing blacks, her hair covered by a sequined mantilla; in another she wears equally striking whites, offset by chains of large pearls. Her Irene is as beautiful and elegant in this film as was her Gaby in *Algiers*, though her presence is often little more than a distraction from what is essentially a boy's story of secret messages, hidden signs, and derring-do. Negulesco (who had briefly worked on *The Maltese Falcon* before he was replaced by John Huston) relied on lighting to pick up the whiteness of Hedy's face amid the dark, shadowy settings. Unlike Huston, however, Negulesco found it challenging to combine artistry with conventional storytelling, and under his direction the actors did little more than retread other, similar parts.

Paul Henreid later blamed the director for the finished product: "his accent was atrocious and his command of English even worse."[5] Hedy remembered the film for her first inklings of morning sickness.[6] Despairing of coaxing any kind of facial expression from his leading lady, Negulesco apparently turned to the more experienced Henreid for help. In one sequence, Hedy was to wear a flimsy white negligee and look flustered and embarrassed as she saw Henreid. Take after take produced no alteration in her demeanor until Henreid leaned over and whispered something in her ear. Hedy reacted at once and the camera captured a perfect show of flustered embarrassment. "Negulesco was enraptured. 'Pauli . . . ,' he pulled me to one side. 'What did you whisper to her? What magic word made her act?'

"I grinned and said, 'I told her that with the lights behind her I could see right through her negligee, as if she were naked.'"[7]

Continuing his reminiscences, Henreid comes to the hardly surprising conclusion that Hedy was quite unsure of herself and needed help with her acting technique. With discreet coaching, all went well until Hedy realized Negulesco and Henreid were discussing her behind her back. At that point she threw a fit of rage and was only eventually calmed down by apologies from all concerned. Henreid's account is less than reliable in some of its details (there is no sequence in the finished version with Hedy wearing a negligee), but it is partially confirmed by the production schedule reports, which note that from her first day on the set, Hedy slowed the shoot as she required considerable rehearsing and tired quickly. Tensions also mounted on set and one evening, after the day's work was over, Paul Henreid got into an argument and hit another actor, Otto Reichow, who had to be taken to the hospital to have his chin stitched. Meanwhile, according to the *Press Book*, Hedy learned that her previous stand-in, Lisa Isl Steffi, was reportedly executed by the Nazis. She had been known as Steffi Golz.[8]

What can life have been like for this group of émigrés working together on *The Conspirators* set? Each one was in exile; each one must have feared for their friends, family, and neighbors left behind in Europe. Did they share reminiscences of their days in Vienna and Berlin, or news gleaned from home? How did they react when hearing of the deaths of loved ones—silently, communally? Did they realize then that few if any of them would ever return home, if home was still their city of birth?

"Emigration in itself, whatever the reason, inevitably disturbs the equilibrium. On alien soil one's self-respect tends to diminish, likewise self-assurance and self-confidence," Stefan Zweig, the exiled Austrian author, wrote in his recollections of these traumatic years. "Losing one's native land implies more than parting with a circumscribed area of soil."[9] No wonder the set was fraught with tension, though those involved may have consoled themselves that they were working on anti-Nazi propaganda.

On its release, however, *The Conspirators* was greeted with little warmth from the press, which was now tiring of war stories:

Despite its topflight cast and a generally good production quality, "The Conspirators" does not come off. It is in fact, rather a boring and annoying affair. This unhappy condition is due largely to a very tired, dated story, weakly scripted, and even more dated, inept direction which tries desperately to be arty and succeeds only in being irritating.[10]

Prokosch was equally dismissive, writing to the *New Republic* that, having just seen his film after a year and a half of traveling:

All I felt when I rose to go was weariness, intense boredom and certain amazement. Weariness and boredom, after the preposterous rubbish I had been observing; amazement at the mentality which can concoct such nonsense with a straight face; amazement also at the mentality which is willing to pay to see such tedious stuff.[11]

Hedy remained on friendly terms with Henreid and his wife, Lisl. One afternoon, the actor recalled, she appeared at their house with a bagful of her laundry. "'Your girl does such a beautiful job of ironing,' she told Lisl. 'Let's you and me chat over some coffee while she does these things.'"

Lisl was too stunned to protest, but the second time Hedy tried it, Lisl told her, "'no, once and for all!' Hedy shrugged it off and still remained friendly."[12]

Alongside her service in the Hollywood Canteen and her work with George Antheil, Hedy became increasingly involved with aiding artists who had remained in Austria and were endangered by fascism. In October 1945, she was one of a group of people who gathered at the left-leaning Actors' Laboratory in Los Angeles to create an organization that would, as Hans Kafka noted, "assist in the development of a democratic, cultural, internationally-minded Austrian theatre; and it should also send relief to needy persons who are creatively connected with the Salzburg and Viennese theatre and who have an unblemished record."[13] The chair was Paul Henreid; vice-chairs were Fritz Kortner, Peter Lorre, and Hedy; and the secretary was Leo Reuss (known in Hollywood as Lionel Royce).

MGM lent Hedy out once again, this time to RKO for *Experiment Perilous,* which was filmed between July and October 1944. This was, Hedy said, the picture she liked herself best in. It was also the first time she had worked at RKO where "everyone treated me like a queen. Never did a movie go so smoothly."[14] Based on the best-selling novel by Margaret Carpenter, the film's director was Jacques Tourneur, now celebrated for his B-movie film noirs and horrors. Hedy played the mysterious heroine Allida Bederaux, with George Brent in the male lead as the psychoanalyst who investigates the mystery of a gothic heroine. *Experiment Perilous* was a classic women's film of the 1940s. Its cinematic predecessors are *Rebecca, Suspicion* (1941), and *Laura* (1944) and it has most often been compared with *Gaslight*. Like these films, in *Experiment Perilous* the woman is the mystery around which the male protagonists revolve. Brent was Warner Bros.' dependable good guy and had memorably played the solid doctor to his then-lover Bette Davis in *Dark Victory* (1939). Like Hedy, he was regularly critiqued for his wooden acting, though often it was this solidity that defined his characters. In any case, he was a favorite with female filmgoers in the 1940s and a familiar face in women's pictures.

One of the disorienting aspects of *Experiment Perilous* is its sense of period; there is something a little off in its historical detail, as if it were taking place simultaneously in the 1940s and at the turn of the century. A pedestrian explanation for this is that Warren Duff shifted the setting from the 1940s to 1903. It was also rumored that Hedy felt she would photograph better in period costumes. But the decision to shift the story's location in time may have been due to the slightly dated feel of the original story. As the executive producer, Robert Fellows, explained: "It was felt that the slightly archaic quality of the heroine, who appears in the book as a cloistered and frustrated orchid, would lend itself to a clearer expression on the screen if presented against a less realistic background."[15]

But the feeling of disorientation that the film creates was caused by more than just set design (for which the film received an Academy Award nomination). Jacques Tourneur's reputation now rests principally on three films: the elegant horror films made with producer Val Lewton at RKO, *Cat People* (1942) and *I Walked with a Zombie* (1943), and his film noir masterpiece, *Out of the Past* (1947). There is a convincing case to be made for the inclusion of *Experiment Perilous* in the canon. The film bears all the hallmarks of Tourneur and RKO's emphasis on visual storytelling. Like the better known of the Tourneur–Lewton collaborations and *Out of the Past, Experiment Perilous* relies more on what is suggested than what is seen; even the film's obvious gothic qualities are not as exaggerated as they are in other films of that genre.

Experiment Perilous revolves around an enigmatic heroine, Allida Bederaux (Hedy), who is married to a wealthy but slightly sinister older man, Nicholas Bederaux (Paul Lukas). One or the other must be insane and the reliable psychiatrist, Dr. Huntington Bailey (Brent) is sent to investigate, after his chance encounter on a train with Cissie Bederaux (Olive Blakeney), the sister of Nicholas. Cissie's unexpected death then sparks a series of events that creates a traumatic link between the past and the present.

Curiously, in this film, Hedy was cast as an American, whose trip to Paris as a newlywed is the reason for the murders that follow (Nicholas Bederaux is, however, Viennese). This casting decision adds to the film's overall disorientation, as does Tourneur's play on her marmoreal beauty. Allida (Hedy) is, the sculptor Clag (Albert Dekker) says, a "work of art"; Cissie refers to her as a "jewel" that Bederaux is determined to polish. Bederaux has also hung a portrait of Allida in the gallery that Bailey studies, in a sequence that anticipates Hitchcock's *Vertigo* (1958) and Tourneur's own *Out of the Past*. "It has a disturbing beauty," Bailey muses. Later, the solid Bailey bursts into an unexpected lyricism as he declares aloud that he would have painted her in a field of daisies; and the film's ending suggests that he and she will at last find happiness in the American pastoral setting of his new practice. Yet the viewer must question this optimism.

To intensify the mystery around Allida, Tourneur makes the most of his star's inability or refusal to express anything beyond the most limited emotional range. She is a beautiful object that men want to own, whether through making her the subject of their poetry (as does her unfortunate Parisian admirer Alec Gregory [George N. Neise]) or of their painting or through marriage. The whiteness of her skin contrasts with the over-furnished Bederaux mansion, with its heavy drapes, book-lined walls, and deep shadows; and her pallor finds its echo in the snow falling ceaselessly on the streets outside. Most of those who meet her will die during the course of the film, yet their deaths are not directly caused by her. This intense link between beauty and death would be reprised in *Strange Woman* (1946), another gothic romance, in which Hedy played a more active, if less innocent part.

Hedy's next film, on the other hand, offered slender pickings. Produced by the Hungarian Joe Pasternak and directed by Richard Thorpe, *Her*

Highness and the Bellboy (1945) is a tale about a "lovely, lovely princess," who, in the opening sequence is seen looking longingly from the balcony of her castle. Interpreting this sequence as a subtle allusion to Hedy's much-publicized relationship with Mandl probably ascribes too much intelligence to an excruciatingly corny narrative. The Princess Veronica (Hedy Lamarr) comes to America on a state visit and falls in love with the hotel's bellhop, Jimmy Dobson (Robert Walker), with whom she enjoys some plebeian fun slumming around New York. But she is only putting off the day she must face her royal duty and marry the dull suitor considered appropriate by her entourage. The bellhop, in turn, falls disastrously for the princess, causing him to abandon his girl (June Allyson), a dancer who is suffering from a psychosomatic disorder that has left her disabled, and which is diagnosed by the doctor as being caused by a deficit of love. She is the darling of their tenement neighborhood, whose members gather around her bedside to hear the bellhop tell her fairy stories. When Jimmy falls for the Princess, he abandons his sweetheart, bringing on the opprobrium of their close-knit circle. Designed as escapist entertainment for wartime audiences, the film played to poor reviews and poorer box office takings.

In *Ecstasy and Me,* Hedy rued her casting: "Though I had star billing, the June Allyson role was really better." [16] She was wrong; June Allyson as Leslie barely kept her clichéd part on the right side of gratingly lachrymose. Allyson in turn simply remembered her terror at the idea of appearing alongside the more-established star:

> In 1945, *Her Highness and the Bellboy* thrust me up against the greatest competition of that era, Hedy Lamarr, said to be the most beautiful woman in the world. I would just stare entranced at her profile. No doubt about it, she was stunning and she knew how to look at a man with an intimate little smile that turned him on.
>
> Every time I tried to copy that kind of look, it was viewed as comedy—Junie, the clown. Junie trying to look cute. I resigned myself—it would never be June the sexpot. [17]

Caught between the sexpot and the sweet American girl was the character of the bellhop, played by the then extremely troubled star Robert Walker. David O. Selznick had long staked out Walker's wife, Jennifer Jones, and would later marry her. Walker, always insecure and prone to self-doubt, responded by annihilating himself with alcohol. During the making of Pasternak's film, he was in the habit of disappearing from the set for extended periods. On one occasion, the cast and crew found him sitting on the roof just surveying the world; on another, they located him in a little café around the corner from the MGM lot. He had smashed his hand through a mirror and required numerous stitches. Later Walker was to die tragically after an emergency injection of sedatives.

Still, Walker largely carried the film, though its real strength was Pasternak's decision to center Hedy's performance around her talent for light comedy. Here was a chance to have some fun, and Hedy took it. Her execution of a thigh-slapping song-and-dance routine and the twinkle in her eye as she delivers her lines is so far removed from her ice-queen performances as to startle. "Hedy Lamarr," noted the *Hollywood Reporter*, "comes out a real winner. Now why didn't anyone ever think of having her play gentle comedy before?"[18] Why not, indeed? Hedy had already delighted audiences in her slapstick routines with Clark Gable in *Comrade X*. But Hedy had been hired to look beautiful; beautiful women, as she discovered when she invented a device that could have revolutionized the American military, couldn't also be clever. Nor could they be funny. MGM firmly ignored their star's sense of humor, particularly when it undermined their carefully constructed image of classic beauty in which they had so strenuously invested.

For a short while, Hedy and John Loder's career differences were pushed aside by the joy of having a daughter, Denise, who was born on 29 May 1945. Bette Davis was asked to be godmother and a photograph taken of the 9 April christening shows the star holding the howling baby at arm's length, while the new parents look on cheerfully.

Hedy was to suggest later that she suffered from postnatal depression; emotionally fragile as she would become, this may well have been true.[19] It's hard to gauge Hedy's response to motherhood. She definitely wanted children, yet, like so many of her generation, she seems to have expected them to reflect well on her, to be her satellites. Otherwise, they were to be seen and not heard. Jamsie, for instance, was reported in several press interviews to have been raised with a taste for classical music, as Hedy had been. The children later remembered her returning from

HEDY LAMARR

the studio in the evening and singing them Viennese lullabies to put them to sleep.[20] Yet, like Trude Kiesler, Hedy could also be cold and demanding, her love was always conditional, her career her priority. In this, she was only outdone by John Loder, whose attention to parental detail seems to have approached nonexistent.

The immediate effect of having children was that Hedy adopted a new perspective on life. Bolstered by one of her many consultations with a psychiatrist, she determined to make some changes. First of all, came the contract with MGM. Squaring up against Louis B. Mayer in 1947, she demanded to be released from her contract so that she could freelance. Referring to herself in the third person, as she often did, Hedy recalled the occasion: " 'Hedy Lamarr,' I said under perfect control, 'is grateful for everything Mr. Mayer has done. But she feels both the studio and she have prospered with their contract and now it's time to move out.' "[21]

Mayer agreed on the condition that Hedy would make three pictures for him over the next five years as an independent producer. This type of arrangement was becoming more common in Hollywood as the formal structure of the studio system crumbled. Producer Hall Wallis had enjoyed such an arrangement, for instance, since 1944, as had director, screenwriter, and producer Leo McCarey. It was more unusual for actors to make this kind of deal, particularly for female stars of Hedy's status. The only other comparable star was Bette Davis, for whom in June 1943, Warner Bros. established B. D. Inc. It would fund thirty-five pictures in return for 65 percent of the net profits. In the end, Davis made only one (*A Stolen Life,* directed by Curtis Bernhardt in 1946), and there is some doubt as to whether she had any production involvement. As the next chapter details, Hedy's deal was less generous but more fruitful.

The second victim of Hedy's clear-out was John Loder. According to her autobiography, Hedy determined to have a second child and then to divorce her husband. Once she knew she was pregnant, she rounded on the unsuspecting Loder who was reading a book and puffing on his pipe. "I am pregnant," Hedy announced, "and I want a divorce."[22] Removing his pipe long enough to tell her that she was a cold bitch, Loder returned to his book. The matter was, apparently, decided. Loder, however, remembered the sequence of events somewhat differently. According to his account, he was performing in a play in Montreal when Ronald Button, Hedy's lawyer, called him: "Hello John, this is Ronnie speaking—your wife wants to divorce you." Why, Loder wanted to know, did she want a divorce? "I really don't know, John," was the response. "All she said was that you were a mediocre actor and a crashing bore in private life. She also mentioned that you always fall asleep in an armchair after dinner."[23]

As early as January 1946, Hedy confirmed rumors that she and Loder had been estranged for two weeks, following a dispute. The catalyst for the partial separation was a car accident involving their adopted son, James. James, now six years old, was briefly hospitalized after he and his nurse were involved in an accident in Beverly Hills, and Hedy claimed that her anxiety following this incident sparked a row with Loder. Soon after, Jamsie had an accident while bicycling and Hedy once again made a great deal out of the event, proclaiming her upset while suing the driver of the car who had allegedly knocked her child off his bicycle. This too, apparently, came between her and John Loder.

By March, the papers were reporting their reconciliation; it was to be another eighteen months before the couple divorced. Hedy was not pregnant with her second child when her marital difficulties were first reported.

In August 1946, Hedy and Loder sold their property in Benedict Canyon Road to Humphrey Bogart. Ever aware of the value of money, Hedy attempted to pull a fast one on the estate agents by pretending to withdraw from the deal and then selling privately to Bogart, thus avoiding the 5 percent commission owed to the agency. Loder and Hedy then moved to 919 North Roxbury Drive in Beverly Hills. There, on 1 March 1947, their son Tony was born.

In the spring of 1947, Loder toured with the stage production of *Laura*. On 17 April, he was in Hartford, Connecticut, where he sent a letter to Hedda Hopper, informing her of the success of *Laura* and his eagerness to rejoin his "blushing bride" in New York City, when the production opened there. "I miss her like hell," he wrote, adding, "hope we don't immediately launch another offspring!"[24]

According to Hopper, in May Loder returned home unexpectedly from New York only to face Hedy and her lawyer, Ronald Button, who were in cahoots about a prospective divorce and settlement. Loder moved out and stayed at his friend Arnold Phillips's house, and on this occasion, the couple were not reconciled.[25]

Hedy filed for divorce, citing "great and grievous mental suffering," on 3 July 1947. At the court hearing, she testified that Loder was indifferent toward her and the children.

"Was he in the habit of falling asleep about 9 o'clock in the evening while conversing with you when both of you sat in the living room?" Button asked her.

"Yes, except that he was usually lying down," the star replied. "He would fall asleep even in picture shows."

The divorce was finalized on July 17. Hedy gained custody of the children and Loder was ordered to pay $300 per month for their support. Hedy acquired sole title to their home, two cars, business properties, and four insurance policies valued at $30,000 each.[26]

12

Independence

While the rifts in Loder and Hedy's marriage were becoming public, Hedy was busy developing her own production company, Mars Productions Inc. Her partners in the venture were Hunt Stromberg and Jack Chertok. Stromberg was one of Hollywood's most successful producers and had recently split with MGM after a dispute with Louis B. Mayer. According to some sources, Mayer may not have been sorry to see his once-gifted producer leave, as Stromberg had taken to dosing himself with morphine to treat a slipped disc and was hallucinating at meetings.[1] Chertok too had come from MGM, where he had produced, among other films, *The Conspirators*. The company arranged for their films to be distributed by United Artists.

The move to production was perhaps a clear one for Hedy but, as the example of Bette Davis was to prove, a challenge that few women in Hollywood, with its overwhelmingly male management structure, would have considered in the 1940s. Hedy was now confidently rejecting acting roles: In March 1945, Paul Kohner sent her the play *Great Love* by Ferenc Molnar, which her agent, George A. Lovett, declined on her behalf. Earlier she had said no to another Kohner property, "Madame Bovary of Greenwood Manor." In September 1945, she turned down two more scripts, "Ave Maria" and "Elisabeth von Osterreich." She was determined to produce her own films.

In *Ecstasy and Me*, Hedy writes, "when I first came to this country, I acted because I needed a job and afterward I had to support my children. It was usually a chore otherwise. I feel like a puppet, to be moved around as a director says. I much prefer to be on the outside of it all, the creative part, as you put it."[2] There was always a chance that, behind the camera, she might find the satisfaction that acting so evidently did not offer her. Interestingly, on the films that she produced and starred in, she tended to be written out of the picture. By the time *The Loves of Three Queens/ Femmina* (1954) was being filmed, it is probably true that she engineered her own downfall. Though, as will be detailed, by then her psychological state was too frail to withstand the demands of filmmaking. In the mid-1940s, however, Hedy was still able to focus on the work at hand. Unfortunately, she was also capable of stirring enmity, not least by having affairs with her directors and leading men.

Her first film with Stromberg and Chertok was *The Strange Woman*, to be directed by her compatriot and fellow refugee, Edgar G. Ulmer. Hunt Stromberg had purchased the rights to Ben Ames Williams's novel of the same title, following the recent success of the author's *Leave Her to Heaven*,³ which was an overheated melodrama about a daughter's fixation on her father. Williams took his title for *The Strange Woman* from Proverbs 5:3–5: "For the lips of a strange woman drop as an honeycomb, and her mouth is smoother than oil: But her end is bitter as wormwood, sharp as a two-edged sword. Her feet go down to death; her steps take hold on hell." The informed reader, therefore, knew what to expect; they were not disappointed.

The Strange Woman is set in Bangor, Maine, and opens in 1824 with young Jenny Hager playing with her childhood friend Efraim Poster. She is the daughter of the town drunk; he, the son of a respectable shopkeeper. She taunts Efraim for being a coward and pushes him off the bridge; when he surfaces, she pushes him under again. Only when the Judge (Alan Napier) happens by, does she hurriedly rescue Efraim and take the credit for saving his life. Meg Saladine, the Judge's daughter, invites Jenny to attend boarding school with her but the Judge amends the offer to a job in the kitchen, which Jenny refuses. Her father overhears this conversation and, as Jenny assures her father that she will do well in later life, she preens herself and admires her reflection in the water. Ripples break up the image and a dissolve brings viewers to the present, with Jenny's assertion of the value of her beauty accompanying the time lapse. "Men like me," she tells Tim Hager (Dennis Hoey), "and it's the men who have the money in this world."

Jenny is now clearly marked as a loose woman, as a scene where she flirts with sailors at the docks further emphasizes. Efraim's father, Isaiah (Gene Lockhart), relates what he saw on the docks to Jenny's father, who beats her; directly afterward he dies. At the decision of the town elders, Isaiah marries Jenny, who appears to acquiesce to the arrangement. However, she has other plans and dispatches a letter to Efraim (Louis Hayward) begging him to return from England, where he has been at college. Meanwhile, she takes etiquette lessons from her neighbor, Meg Saladine (Hillary Brooke). When the townsfolk gather in church, the minister, Reverend Thatcher (Moroni Olson), asks his congregation for money to fund church repairs. As the rest remain silent, Jenny stands up and pledges Isaiah's money; the other parishioners are shamed into contributing too.

When Efraim returns home, Jenny begins seducing him, planning that her husband will die and they will live off his money. When Isaiah's health turns out to be robust, she persuades Efraim to drown him on a canoe trip, despite Efraim's already-established fear of water. Meanwhile, Jenny whiles away her time seducing Meg Saladine's fiancé, John Evered (George Sanders). When Efraim apparently accidentally drowns his father, Jenny throws him out of the house and he turns to drink, eventually committing suicide. This frees Jenny to marry John; however, while their marriage is happy, she is unable to conceive. Told by a traveling preacher that an evil woman cannot bear children, she is driven crazy and confesses her deeds to John; he briefly returns to Meg and, when she finds out, Jenny attempts to run over the two of them; instead, she herself is driven over the cliff and dies.

With a script as powerful as this, Mars needed an experienced director. The choice of Edgar Ulmer to direct was Hedy's. Shirley Castle has said that Ulmer and Hedy knew each other from "way back, when they were kids," though Ulmer was ten years Hedy's senior.[4] It is possible they met in Berlin, though Ulmer was in America while Hedy was working in Germany. Later Hedy would claim she had discovered the director, though it is more accurate to say that she offered him an opportunity to move from Poverty Row B movies to the A list. Hedy insisted Ulmer direct her in *Strange* after watching him work with Loder on *Bluebeard* (1944). Between those films, Ulmer made what was to become his most celebrated picture, *Detour* (1945).

When Hedy hired Ulmer through Mars Productions in autumn of 1945, he was years away from becoming the darling of the indie set. In

1933, he had notoriously incurred the wrath of Carl Laemmle, president of Universal, by running off with Shirley Castle, the wife of Laemmle's nephew Max Alexander. Laemmle ensured that Ulmer and Castle were blacklisted by all the major studios and the pair wound up on Poverty Row making B movies for Leon Fromkess's Producers Releasing Corporation (PRC). As Ulmer told Peter Bogdanovich, Fromkess loaned him to Lamarr and her coproducers for $1,500 per week while paying him just $250 per week: "I made more money for PRC on *The Strange Woman* than they had paid me the whole time I worked there."[5] Furious, Ulmer left PRC.

Filming commenced in early December 1945 and ran through the winter of 1945–1946, with a break during Christmas when Hedy contracted the flu. Ulmer's sets tended to be family affairs. Shirley was always at his side and worked as his script supervisor; his daughter, Arianné, frequently joined them. According to Stefan Grissemann, the eight-year-old Arianné was fascinated by Hedy's beauty and the pair enjoyed long walks with the dog. On these outings, they found they had an issue with freckles in common. Hedy later gave the girl a black-and-white cat, which was named Monte Cristo.[6] More damagingly for the "family" set, Hedy was rumored to be having a relationship with Ulmer. Later, Shirley Castle conceded that this could have been true, but that the relationship was short-lived and her husband never much liked Hedy.[7]

Hedy may have been having an affair with Ulmer but she was also rumored to be enjoying a brief fling with George Sanders, no departure from form for either of them. Apparently, a number of their friends knew of the affair, including Zsa Zsa Gabor, who would marry Sanders in 1949.[8] By this stage, Sanders was battling a drug problem and Castle remembered him being a "very cranky, difficult guy."[9] He was badly miscast and appears awkward and unkempt as John Evered. Only Louis Hayward seems to have been able to deflect the tensions of this stormy group, whose members each operated strictly to their own agenda.

Further problems arose around the casting of Arianné in the part of young Jenny. After the opening scenes were shot, either Hedy or Hunt Stromberg, depending on sources, objected to Arianné's playing of the child and demanded that a professional child actor be cast in the part. The scenes were then reshot, this time with Jo Ann Marlow in the role and Douglas Sirk behind the camera. Whether Sirk filmed this sequence because Ulmer refused or because Ulmer had completed his contract and moved on to his next project is unclear.[10]

If all of this led to tensions on the set, there were light moments too, as the following poem reflects:

Poem:
Supervised by Hedy Lamarr
Instigated by Blanche Smith
Written by Johannes [John] Loder

I'M QUITE SURE THAT ALL MY LIFE
I'LL ENVY EDGAR ULMERS [sic] WIFE
HER HUSBAND'S ALWAYS ON THE GO
WORKING HARD AND EARNING DOUGH
HE'S NOT TOO BUSY THOUGH TO THINK
MY SHIRLEY SWEET WOULD LOVE A MINK[11]

For Hedy, the challenge of working independently, without the safety net of studio backing, meant a change in production practices: "I was in business for myself now and had to hold down the pampering. When my mother called collect from the East Coast, I told her to drop some coins in the slots instead and I'd give the money back to her." She also recalled the difficulties she had with her part, abandoning her persona for that of Jenny Hager; Ulmer advised her to be a tigress: "We did the bedroom scene over and over so often I could do it now, twenty years later, in one 'take.' Anyway, it didn't work. I just wasn't a tigress. All the talent at my disposal couldn't make me one."[12]

She remembered, too, rewriting the part of Jenny when she felt it wasn't working. Stromberg, Chertok, and Ulmer had all already edited the script, most notably downplaying the incest theme. Hedy's alterations were to clarify that Jenny Hagar was infertile, thus making her more sympathetic. She also had a scene in which she hit a neighbor's child removed. Ulmer's original ending had Jenny die, swearing her love to John and begging him not to let her be buried alongside Isaiah and Efraim. Apparently, this was too grim for the French distributors of the film, who insisted on ending on a note of redemption, with a funeral sequence where the townsfolk declare how good and charitable she had been.[13]

•   •   •

Being frugal, being in control, being the star—Hedy had at last found herself at home in Hollywood. For a brief moment, she was able to exercise her unmistakable abilities and, under Ulmer's direction, she even gave a competent performance (even though a more gifted actor might have guaranteed *The Strange Woman* the classic status it deserves). As for her predilection for having affairs, this could be dismissed as meddlesome gossip, though it may well be true. There's no denying Hedy was promiscuous; had she been a man, it would have hardly been worth a mention.

The film improves on the book insofar as it grants Jenny greater agency. For instance, in the novel, Jenny inherits her wealth; in the film, she is a successful businesswoman. More than the narrative, the visuals and acting endow the final result with a dark, gothic atmosphere that swirls around the protagonist. However much the sadomasochism in the novel was tempered in the transition to Hollywood, the sequence in which Hedy's father beats her is transparently provocative. "There's a devil in you, Jenny Hager," Tim Hager tells her, grabbing hold of her arm, "and I'm going to whip him out of you." As he pulls her to him, she turns and squares up to Hager, her face lighting up. "You're going to beat me?" she taunts suggestively. "This is one beating I'll not like," he responds, overturning the table. At first, as he whips her, Hedy's face registers what seems like pleasure, then turns to pain and a mixture of fear and invitation, as he continues his assault. Eventually she frees herself by biting his wrist and as she runs from the balcony, the film's score reaches its melodramatic climax and Hager falls dead.

Jenny runs to Isaiah Poster, displaying her bruises ostensibly to his housekeeper but most directly to him. He too seems hypnotized by her damaged flesh. Further, Jenny's letter to Efraim outlines their new relationship (of stepmother and son) in the terms of domination and submission that she clearly relishes. It is this intense engagement with pain and fear that marks the film and renews the terms on which the characters desire each other. When Jenny eventually kisses Efraim, his father sees them and collapses against the gatepost; and as Efraim urges her to call the doctor, the camera closes in on her look of thinly concealed triumph.

The town is the locus in equal measures of puritanism and temptation, the latter imported with sailors and lumberjacks who wash in and out of the taverns. Riots break out as the men become crazed with alcohol, evoking a spectacle that brings Jenny close to swooning in apparent pleasure before she steps in to rescue Lena (June Storey), the brothel madam.

What is enacted outdoors and inside saloons transfers to the shuttered, gloomy interiors of the allegedly respectable citizenry. From outside, the Posters' house is a pretty, solid brick building, surrounded by a veranda, suggesting a settled permanence; indoors, it is cluttered with gothic furnishings and a claustrophobic jumble of possessions from past generations. The moment she lays her eyes on Meg's fiancé, we see Jenny's desiring gaze fasten on him. Soon after, as she watches Efraim pack, she glides down the stairs to the living room, snuffing out candles as she goes and moving from mirror to mirror, only pausing to preen herself. Now is the moment for her to plant an idea in Efraim's mind as he complains about his father: "How long must he live?"

Looking—at herself and at others—further awakens Jenny's desire. "Don't look," John tells her on seeing Efraim's dead body, but again a sensation of rapture crosses her face. As John goes outdoors a bolt of lightning sets a tree ablaze and they embrace in the storm. "Your beauty has made you evil," the fundamentalist preacher thunders—for which, in true gothic fashion, Jenny must ultimately be punished.

The volatile mix of desire and loathing that infiltrates *The Strange Woman* was replicated on set. Not only was infidelity the order of the day, Ulmer had a trick up his sleeve when it came to directing Hedy. With more money at his disposal than he normally enjoyed, he was determined that this film would return him to favor with the Hollywood majors; still his swift shooting style needed actors who were in tune with what he was doing. To an extent, he could compensate for poor performances through the use of montage, different camera angles, and suspense. Inevitably, however, he complained that Hedy was wooden; his solution was in tune with the film's atmosphere. No coaching here, instead he timed her delivery with a baton and rapped her on the knuckles or around the ankles if she didn't seem to be taking her acting seriously. One can only imagine how this went down with his star and occasional lover.

Although Ulmer's admirers do not rate *The Strange Woman* as highly as his other films, this rich melodrama abounds and delights in the kind of moral ambiguity that was his trademark, in this case, creating an Old Testament world of good and evil with an absent but punishing God. For Hedy, this was the first time she was required to carry a film, rather than simply appear as a plot device and aesthetic object. Ulmer clearly borrowed from the gothic look of *Experiment Perilous,* but unlike Tourneur, he attempted to make Hedy a participant in the drama rather than one of its furnishings. In doing this, he exposed her limitations as a performer, but his ability to manipulate camera angles and keep the plot whipping along effectively kept his star from slowing the story line.

The critics, already familiar with the novel, found Hedy adequate to the task: "As the grasping, wily wanton, Hedy Lamarr is beautiful, even in peplum and bustle. She is a desirable, sagaciously vicious and passionate woman, who very conceivably might captivate men easily," even if they remained unsure about the overall achievement of Ulmer's film. "Like Mr. Williams' prose, 'The Strange Woman' is expertly handled, but somehow the excitements of her life are rarely projected from the screen."[14] Some were more enthusiastic about the lead performance: "Hedy Lamarr scores as the scheming Hager. Two-sided character obtains plenty of realism in her hands. Her capacity of appearing as a tender, ministering angel and of mirroring sadistic satisfaction in the midst of violence bespeaks wide talent range."[15] Others were less convinced: "While the plot of The Strange Woman goes busily along assuming that the heroine is outrageously clever, Miss Lamarr's beautiful face never manages to express anything at all except its own uncommon beauty."[16] The film ran over budget by $1 million, which significantly diminished its $2,800,000 box office take.[17]

What was running through Hedy's mind during this period? According to John Loder, who spoke to a journalist about the reasons for their marital breakdown, his estranged wife was becoming increasingly reliant on therapy. More than this, he said, she appeared to be having dreams in which her father beat her. That she was experiencing these recurring dreams while she was working on *The Strange Woman* may be coincidence. But her psychiatrist's theory that the dream signaled her fear of her husband could not have helped. Loder's opinion was that their marriage was in trouble from the moment Hedy began psychoanalysis.

In Loder's version of the break-up, Hedy told him that she had become afraid of him after the children were born. He argued with her, he said, reminding her that she had always said her father had been wonderful to her and that it was her mother who had been cruel. Hedy responded that she had come to realize that it was not her mother but her father who was cruel, and that she now understood that her husband was assuming the personality of her father in her eyes.

The second reason Loder gave for the end of their marriage was economic. As the relationship faltered, he felt increasing stress over his lower income. In the first three and a half years of their marriage, Loder contributed $45,000 to the upkeep of their home. After his break with Warner Bros., Loder's salary dipped and he found himself increasingly out of work. Performing in *Laura* was a last-ditch effort to rescue his finances and remind Hollywood of his talent. However, he quit the show when he heard Hedy was planning to divorce him.

While they lived in the little house in Benedict Canyon, Loder added, he could keep the place going. Their household costs were about $800 per month. But the big new house in Beverly Hills was well beyond his means. The monthly upkeep there ran to about $2,000, and he didn't make that kind of money. To appease his wife, however, Loder said he had signed a promissory note to pay the $20,000 he was in arrears. Then, he added, Hedy demanded he pay his room and board when he wasn't working, even if he couldn't handle the upkeep. He agreed to this, too. She had become obsessed with money, Loder said, yet she was now a successful producer.

Hedy, for her part, said that she had tried to find something for her idle spouse to occupy himself with around the house. She asked him to hang curtains, "the simplest thing in the world, and he couldn't do it."[18]

The visits to the psychiatrist had been precipitated, according to *Ecstasy and Me,* by the pain of giving birth to Denise; though it seems likely that Hedy was suffering from more than postnatal depression. Around this time, she started seeing the Beverly Hills psychiatrist Dr. Philip Solomon, who treated her for many years.[19] Only Solomon knows what passed between the two, but he must have recognized how Hedy's émigrée status affected her moods and behavior. Her financial anxiety is hardly surprising given the sudden and almost unbearable loss of status she experienced in interwar Vienna. Not only had Hedy seen her gilded childhood vanish before her eyes, she learned that nothing was permanent; anything could be taken away from you. By now, she must have known of the deaths of friends and neighbors in the concentration camps, of the treatment of the Viennese Jewish community under Hitler. Yet, she could not allow herself to be traumatized; she had to move on; she had to keep working.

With *The Strange Woman* a moderate success, Hedy moved forward with her production plans. Her next film, *Dishonored Lady*, was rooted in what was allegedly a real-life murder case. It was also based on the successful Broadway play of the same name, written by Margaret Ayer Barnes and Edward Sheldon, and played to enormous acclaim by Katharine Cornell (often considered to be America's greatest stage actress of the twentieth century) in 1930. In the original, the heroine poisons an Argentinean cabaret dancer with whom she is having an affair to free herself to marry an English lord. She stands trial for the crime and is acquitted after several close friends perjure themselves on her behalf. After the trial, however, these same friends despise and shun her.

The original murder case was also the unacknowledged source for MGM's Joan Crawford vehicle *Letty Lynton* (1932, directed by Clarence Brown), which Hunt Stromberg produced. Stromberg had long planned a remake and from 1942 was feeding news of his forthcoming production to the press. Bette Davis and Greta Garbo were rumored to be interested in the lead role, and at one point it seemed that the Hungarian refugee Andre de Toth would direct. Hedy too had sensed that this was a chunky role for a woman and purchased the story *Madeleine*, based on the same case, from the exiled German-Jewish writer Paul Schiller in 1944.

Letty Lynton had fallen foul of the Hays Office and also become tangled in a legal dispute over its source material. Stromberg knew he was in danger of having the same fate befall his version of the story. He hired Sophie Treadwell to write a script but she too was unable to satisfy Joseph Breen, who objected to the story line on all fronts: "The basic story . . . is thoroughly and completely unacceptable under the provisions of the Code, because it is a story of gross illicit sex, with insufficient compensating moral values. In addition it is the story of an unpunished murderer."[20] Stromberg hired Ben Hecht, who made amendments, including altering the story so that Madeleine is punished. Breen was unmoved and scented a happy ending for the irredeemable lead female:

As we read it, this is the story of a young girl who is suggestive of a kind of nymphomaniac, and who, when she falls in love with a fine, decent fellow and wants to completely sever her relations with her former lover, attempts to kill the former lover, fails and becomes involved in a court trial which eventually establishes the fact that she is not the murderer, and is permitted to go off scot free, with the suggestion that she will finally get together with the decent man. This basic story, of course, could not be approved.[21]

Breen was further incensed that the script refused to condemn its heroine for her "lewd" activities, which included multiple love affairs in New York and Mexico City.[22] Hecht reworked the script while retaining its overheated, exotic tone, in particular Madeleine's "night of passion" with the Mexican dancer Moreno, whom she shoots and believes she has killed. This was still unacceptable to Breen, who refused to sanction the depiction of Madeleine's profligate sexuality and unsavory family background. The final script entirely removed the scenes in Mexico City, the character of Moreno, and the night of sordid passion. A disgusted Ben Hecht asked that his name be deleted from the credits (David Lean's 1950 *Madeleine* is closer to the original); the end result is credited to Edmund North.

Hedy hoped that Ulmer would direct her in this film too, but he was involved in another project. Instead, she hired the British expatriate Robert Stevenson. She chose Elois Jenssen to design her costumes and, in a startling act of provocation, chose her former husband John Loder to play the part of Felix Courtland, a substitute for the original character of Moreno.

A dispute with Stromberg shortly before shooting was scheduled to begin threatened to derail the production. But Stromberg and Hedy resolved their differences and filming commenced. *Dishonored Lady* was shot between May and July 1946 at California Studios and was released on 16 May 1947.

Hedy told the press the new production was an opportunity for her to play a role closer to her true identity:

I have never been so excited over any picture, because, you see, I have a chance to do something other than merely be a clothes horse or look pretty. I have always wanted to do character parts, and this gives me the chance I have been waiting for for so long.

At least, Jack Chertok thinks I have some intelligence, and it is up to me now to prove it to him.[23]

Writing later in *Ecstasy and Me*, however, Hedy credited her desire to play Madeleine Damien to a need to demonstrate that she could be sexy, rather than aristocratic and cold on screen.[24]

Given the distance *Dishonored Lady* traveled from conception to execution, it is not surprising the finished result was a disappointment. Oddly, the film's story line reflects that of the failed *I Take This Woman*, in which Hedy played a would-be suicide whom the doctor saves and who then must choose between a life of honest endeavor or society's pleasures. The biggest change to the original story and Hedy's role in it was its theme that sophistication and sexuality, when combined in one woman, are a curse and not a pleasure. From the moment the viewer encounters Madeleine Damien, she is under investigation; in this instance, by two traffic cops, who are curious why this beautiful woman is sitting immobile in her car. The viewers' perspective of her is therefore theirs, looking down at her framed through the driver's-side window, as she will later be framed for Courtland's death. In a sudden movement, Madeleine puts the car in gear and attempts to commit suicide. Her rescuer conveniently turns out to be a psychiatrist and he will pop up at key moments in the narrative to explain the characters to themselves. First it is Madeleine's turn and Dr. Caleb (Morris Carnovsky) is swift to diagnose her discontent as "a disease of the times." "Many women," he pronounces knowingly, "haven't the courage to face themselves, so they look for excitement in one excitement after the other."

The specific source of Madeleine's unhappiness is revealed shortly after as viewers learn that she is the art editor of a city magazine. This setting allows Hedy to reprise the dynamism of her strong female characters, notably in *Boom Town* and *H.M. Pulham, Esq.*, and to model a series of elegant outfits that express a modern and exciting urban cosmopolitanism. Madeleine is surrounded by a constellation of men, all of whom are in love with her in one way or another. The most unpleasant of these is the jewel baron Felix Courtland, whose reasons for seducing her seem motivated by little else than a desire to control. This was the role given to John Loder, who acquitted himself decently, even if the part was just another variation on his usual theme of tarnished debonair. There is, in the masochistic interplay between the now estranged husband and wife, a frisson of power-playing that no doubt reflected their offscreen relationship. The sequences between these two have a charge quite lacking in the rest of the drama, which is often emotionally inert.

The actors were hamstrung by a wordy script that relied on a three-act structure (as one reviewer noted, the three acts were almost like three separate stories).[25] All the action was compressed into the final thirty minutes. The message of *Dishonored Lady* was clear: Hedy's Madeleine Damien was a woman in a man's world and it would take a decent sort of guy to put her right and return her to some down-home values. Cue Dennis O'Keefe as the wholesome David Cousins, a small-town doctor, temporarily working in the city on a research project, who falls in love with Madeleine. She by now has given up her glamorous profession to develop her talent as a painter, a skill she inherited from her Hungarian father, who, she tells the psychiatrist, committed suicide. Madeleine had given up painting so that she would not become like him.

With her new occupation comes a new name, Madeleine Dixon, and a refreshed outlook on life. Now she can contentedly play second fiddle to the brilliant and dedicated doctor (she casually mentions in one scene that she has sold a painting, but the film focuses on Cousins's success).

A brief obstacle to the consummation of this relationship occurs when Courtland is murdered and the blame falls on Madeleine. Cousins abandons her as the trial approaches and is reminded by the psychiatrist that Madeleine is sitting trial not for her alleged crime but for the life she has led. The responsibility now falls on the good doctor to "forgive" his fiancée by reconnecting with his emotions and solving the murder, which was actually committed by Jack Garet, one of her coworkers.

All is happily resolved, and viewers may assume that Madeleine will devote the rest of her life to her painting and her husband's career, leaving behind the demands of the city job that had so damaged her psyche.

Dishonored Lady is notable for its reflection of an increasingly conservative trend in mainstream cinema. In a comment dripping with irony, given the reasons for Loder and Hedy's marital problems, one of Madeleine's many suitors complains to her as they dance: "It's awfully hard making love to a woman who is making more money than you." She has, Courtland remarks dismissively, a man's mind. Her response is that she does a man's work. The film could have hardly made its point more succinctly: a woman's place is in the home. Compare this with *Boom Town*, made just seven years earlier, and one can see how far society's attitudes toward women had shifted. Hedy played a much more subversive character in *Boom Town* who escaped relatively unscathed. In *Dishonored Lady*, the message was that with the war over and the men home from the front, it was time for women to get back to the kitchen and leave their jobs to the boys. What's more, it is the city, with its bright lights and all-night allure that blinds ordinary Americans to the values on which their country is built. Any woman who participates in these corrupt pleasures is likely to lose sight of these values. The change from her roles in *Boom Town* and *H.M. Pulham, Esq.* could hardly have been more marked.

Trade reviews for *Dishonored Lady* were upbeat. *Variety* predicted it would play well with female filmgoers and lauded its lush production values, Elois Jenssen's gowns, and Hedy and John Loder's performances, the latter approvingly described as Mephistophelian.[26] The *Hollywood Reporter* predicted an Academy Award nomination for the film.[27]

Mainstream critics, by contrast, saw little merit in the film: "She moves to a Greenwich Village garret, becomes involved in a murder, is proved innocent, and winds up refreshed and bubbling with euphoria. I doubt that you'll be in the same condition if you sit through this one."[28]

Stromberg earned some of the blame for the failure of *Dishonored Lady*—it had run $1.2 million over budget.[29] Unlike *The Strange Woman*, it performed poorly at the box office, and United Artists refused to deal with the former darling of MGM and his copartners any further. Without a distribution deal, Mars Productions was on a much less secure footing.

Even on radio, Hedy's persona was growing more domesticated. In a 1946 appearance on the Edgar Bergen/Charlie McCarthy Show, she marries Charlie. The show is interesting for its play with domesticity and its consequences. The new Hedy is motivated not by sexual attraction (much hinted at in the earlier shows) but by the promise of "an ultramodern, postwar home" as the script has her declaim.[30] The show plays off her supposedly natural female desire to live in such a commodity, with

Charlie quipping, "Yes, I hear the modern house comes equipped with self-winding stair cases and even plastic termites." But she pushes on, and they marry and move in, followed by a line of salespeople determined that the couple buy a pool for the garden. Now even Hedy is dubious about this excess consumerism, while Charlie is increasingly threatened by his feminine environment, even more so when Hedy's Aunt Minerva moves in.

If women, the scenario suggests, were to become the vanguard of consumerism and domesticity, the home must be ceded to them, while men should stick to what they knew best—making money and staying out of the kitchen.

Hedy next purchased the story, film, and stage rights to Don Tracey's novel *Last Year's Snow,* entering into a complex contract with Douglas Sirk and his producer, Arnold Pressburger, to make the film, in which she would star. Hedy's connection with Pressburger dated back to her Vienna days when he was a producer at Sascha Film Studio. Now, however, she was pregnant again and needed to take a break. Sirk and Pressburger refused to release her from the contract and only after a court case were both sides able to reach a compromise. The film was never made.

Hedy approached Paul Kohner to see what he might have on offer. He reminded her of her longtime interest in *Hedda Gabler,* to which he could now purchase the world rights for $35,000.[31] Nothing came of this, nor of Kohner's hopes that she and Ulmer would work together again on "The Last Empress of China." It too was not made.

Still, Hedy was doing well enough to join several Hollywood stars in investing in a new restaurant. The funds would allow restaurateur George Tchitchinadze, better known as Gogi, to begin a new venture, buying the celebrity hot spot The Larue on New York's Park Avenue. Hedy was also seen around town with Billy Wilder, which gave the press free rein to speculate on another marriage. She had a brief affair with actor Mark Stevens, to whom she was introduced by Hungarian director Michael Curtiz on the set of *Passage to Marseilles* (1944). Stevens was a few years her junior and just beginning his short-lived Hollywood career, primarily in film noir. Given that he was married to actress

Annelle Hayes and the couple had a young baby, it was just as well the relationship did not last. Stevens returned to his wife and Hedy embarked on an equally brief affair with businessman Howard Klotz.

With her hopes of a career in production fading, Hedy was forced to appear in other people's productions. When the actor Robert Cummings set up a company, United California Productions, with Eugene Frenke (an émigré producer, who was married to the Russian actress Anna Sten), they asked Hedy to take the lead role in *Let's Live a Little*, released by United Artists in 1948. Frenke also ensured a small role for his wife, whose Hollywood career had never taken off.

In another nod to her Viennese heritage, Hedy played a psychiatrist, Dr. Loring, who is the author of the book *Let's Live a Little*, an early version of a self-help manual. The part gave Hedy the opportunity to perform in the more comfortable role of a professional woman, if only one whose profession was not taken seriously. Cummings played the hapless Duke Crawford, who is romantically tied to his advertising agency's model Michele Bennett (Anna Sten). Crawford is breaking under the dual pressure of a personal and a professional relationship and winds up being treated by Dr. Loring. Needless to say, they fall in love.

With his talent for light comedy, Cummings made the most of his role and Hedy was a good foil for his "little boy lost" charm. But difficulties with the script (scriptwriter Edmund Hartmann blamed Cummings's interference) helped neither actor—a shame since the role-reversal premise and a cheerful desire to poke fun at Freudian cinema (notably Hitchcock's *Spellbound* in 1945) was rich territory for the mining. "The not too discriminating filmgoer," the *Hollywood Reporter* commented, "might reasonably find it much to his liking."[32]

Before *Let's Live a Little* was released, another event occurred that would cause Hedy anger and hurt in equal measures. *Look* magazine published an article entitled "Broken Faces, Broken Futures" suggesting that she had had her nose altered with plastic surgery. In April 1948, Hedy hired celebrity lawyer Jerry Geisler to sue *Look*. The public, she contended, knew her as a natural beauty and her reputation as well as that of her three children was in danger of being undermined by such a claim. The case would rumble on throughout the summer, offering the press, who scented a juicy news story their readers would appreciate, the opportunity to fill empty summer columns with cruel speculation about Hedy's disintegrating career and declining beauty. More than ever before, she needed a major role, one that would restore her reputation and her position on the Hollywood A list.

13

No Man Leaves Delilah!

C<small>ECIL</small> B. D<small>EMILLE</small> had been contemplating another lavish biblical epic for a number of years. His reputation for large-scale biblical films had been cemented in the prewar era with the release of *The Ten Commandments* (1923), *The King of Kings* (1926), and *The Sign of the Cross* (1932). The story of Samson and Delilah eluded him in 1932 and only in 1947 did he manage to persuade Paramount to finance it. They were tempted by a text that had been shorn of any complexities and amounted to little more than a narrative of marital revenge, set against an extravagant Technicolor background.

"The moment I heard it would be in Technicolor, I wanted to do it," Hedy said in *Ecstasy and Me*.[1] She didn't just want to, she needed to make *Samson and Delilah*. With the promise of major production values and a director whose name conjured the great days of Hollywood, here was a chance to put her career back on track.

DeMille's longtime actor Henry Wilcoxon vividly described De-Mille's painstaking casting process. For this cherished project, numerous stars were considered and then rejected. "He didn't like Marta Toren's teeth. He viewed Viveca Lindfors's first test and said she was a fine actress but that it would be a year before she would be ready for an American audience. Later he didn't find Lindfors sexy enough."[2] Lana Turner, Rita Hayworth, and (more surprisingly) Nancy Olson were all in the running, but each became unavailable or were rejected. Other names included Susan Hayward, Ava Gardner, Jane Greer, Greer Garson, and Maureen O'Hara.[3]

From May 1948, DeMille was in negotiations with Hedy's agent, Joe Schoenfeld, at the William Morris Agency. Schoenfeld sent him photographs from *Let's Live a Little*, which hadn't yet been released. But the stills that he really urged DeMille to consider were those from *The Strange Woman*. As Wilcoxon remembered: "It was a disheartened De-Mille who walked across the lot that day to a screening of *The Strange Woman*. They were either too young, too nice, or not sexy enough. Where was his Delilah? *The Strange Woman* starred Ian Keith (whom Cecil B. De-Mille was considering for the Saran) and Hedy Lamarr. When the lights came up after the screening, DeMille said but one word: 'Delilah.' Hedy was in discussing the part with him the very next day."[4]

Nor was her eventual costar, Victor Mature, DeMille's first choice; DeMille's eye had been caught by the young bodybuilder, Steve Reeves, but after two auditions, he realized he needed to look elsewhere. Doug-las Fairbanks Jr. and even Cary Grant were mentioned for the part, but in the end Mature was cast, primarily on the strength of his *Kiss of Death* (1947). His refusal to wrestle a lion left DeMille out of sorts with his lead-ing man.

In June 1948, Hedy was contracted for the role for a sum of $100,000 for ten weeks.[5] In July, Hedy vanished. Reports reached DeMille that she was in hospital and he was much relieved to receive a cable from her from Paris, where she was staying at the luxury Hotel George V and, she said, having the time of her life. In August, she took another three-week holiday, this time in Lake Tahoe, missing her early wardrobe fittings.

Shooting started on 4 October 1948 and, contrary to Wilcoxon's and Lasky's accounts, Hedy recalled that she and her director were on a colli-sion course. Costume became the battleground, with Hedy complaining that her gown was too drab and claiming victory when DeMille gave way and ordered Edith Head to alter it.[6] The designer was further en-raged when Hedy insisted that she take on Elois Jenssen, who had worked on *Let's Live a Little* and *Dishonored Lady,* and responded by refusing to let Jenssen touch anything. Nevertheless, Jenssen shared the Academy Award for Best Costume Design in a Color Film with Head, and the two later became friends.

Although Head's work was honored with an Academy Award, she remembered the shoot with little warmth, referring to her director as "a freak trying to play God."[7] She was particularly bothered by the famed peacock gown (created with feathers from DeMille's ranch), which did not fit with her understanding of dress in the historical era.

What she produced turned out to be the epitome of camp chic, set against a noticeably creaky, overdesigned set, and peopled with

DeMille's inevitable cast of thousands. Censorship restrictions prevented Head from baring Hedy's navel and she negotiated this by encircling the offending area with a selection of deliriously suggestive narrow jewel belts.

Nor was working with the Austrian ever easy: "Hedy spent a good part of each fitting on the horizontal. Under my spotlights in a slinky gold-beaded gown, she'd look like the all-time femme fatale. Then, suddenly, she'd turn those great translucent eyes on me and say, 'Edith, I must rest. When you have had children, you have backaches.'" Even though they might only be half-finished, down she would lie. And, if she was unhappy with her costume, she would lie for longer. And she would eat: "A Hedy Lamarr fitting meant food shuttled in every hour or so, Viennese pastries, pot-roast sandwiches, anything to eat; and while she rested, the sultry, exotic temptress munched and talked of her three children."[8]

When Head sketched costumes that incorporated a voluptuous bust line, Hedy intervened again: "I'm not a big bosomy woman, if you pad me I'll look ridiculous. I won't be able to act. I'll feel as if I am carting balloons."[9] Head redesigned her costume so that it fell in a way that suggested the kind of Rubenesque effect DeMille sought.

If Hedy remembered the shoot as fiery, others felt that her casting was a success. Wilcoxon wrote about Hedy warmly later and Jesse L. Lasky Jr., the film's scriptwriter, had equally fond memories of her participation: "De Mille was not sure how good an actress she was, but that was never his first consideration. She filled the eye of the beholder with such breathless beauty that her acting hardly mattered." Nor did she seem wooden to him: "The spectacular face and figure were enhanced by a miraculous grace. She could fall into a pose as naturally and easily as though she had been rehearsing it for weeks. She seldom needed correction. De Mille said she was like a gazelle—incapable of a clumsy or wrong move."[10] Telegrams between the director and his leading lady suggest that Hedy responded flirtatiously to the sixty-seven year old, referring to herself in correspondence as Delilah to his Samson.

Once again, she was costarring with her old lover George Sanders. If this was a prospect they both found agreeable, Sanders's then-fiancée Zsa Zsa

Gabor was less enthusiastic. Deciding a visit to the set might be opportune, Gabor soon bumped into DeMille's Delilah:

> "Who is this beautiful blond bitch?" Hedy demanded to know. "Get her off the set."
> George said, "This is the woman I am going to marry, Mrs. Conrad Hilton."
> Hedy looked momentarily taken aback, then rallied, shook hands with me, and said, "Can I meet Mr. Conrad Hilton?"[11]

A few years later, when Zsa Zsa Gabor and George Sanders were married, Hedy called on them. Their daughter Francesca, who was three, was on her way to bed. Hedy volunteered to say good-night to her, since it was the nanny's night off. Then as an afterthought, she asked, "Does Francesca know the facts of life yet?" Perturbed, Gabor shook her head. "The next morning Francesca came downstairs with a balloon stuck inside the front of her dress and informed me that she was now pregnant. Hedy Lamarr had told my three-year-old daughter the facts of life. I was livid."[12]

Victor Mature remembered that Hedy had appeared unwell on the set of *Samson and Delilah*, "Nothing chronic, she was just somehow out of sorts. Let me put it another way: she was not exactly a ball of fire—she just seemed to be loping along."[13] Maybe as a result, or maybe by design, she became a languorous Delilah, whose contribution to the story was to drape herself casually in a series of poses that allowed her to appear more as a tableau than a flesh-and-blood biblical character. Still, Hedy was right about Technicolor; the whiteness of her skin set off Head's vivid costumes, and her jeweled headpiece reminded audiences of her prewar seductresses and guided their eyes to her gleaming black hair. Her look, in particular her harem tops, drew strongly on the orientalism of her best-known performances, now with the added glamour of vivid color. Similarly, the peacock-feather gown recalled her equally camp headgear in *Ziegfeld Girl*. Given the popular and commercial (if not critical) success of *Samson and Delilah* and the vivifying effect it had on her career, it is tempting now to see this role as the summation of all her parts to date. Nor would it be surpassed by anything that followed. "That year of *Samson and Delilah*," Jesse L. Lasky Jr. remembered, "found Hedy as nearly fulfilled as she would ever be. Admired, adored, worshiped by all of us who worked with her."[14]

When it came to wooden acting, she was outdone by Mature, who seemed to have no sense of his character (the scene in which he wrestles with the fat, moth-eaten lion is excruciatingly lethargic). As the image of DeMille's dream of a "dark-eyed temptress . . . her beauty, her love and her greed on display," Hedy was, however, perfect.[15] From her first scene, popping plum stones at her sister Semadar (Angela Lansbury) and Samson, there is something feline in her mien that bodes ill for those who cross her path. Her prey, her ever-tautening body intimates, will be the beautiful, moody, and slightly effeminate Samson (after all, this is a man whose power resides in his hair). "Will you tame me, Samson?" she thrills, clinging to his back as they ride out in his chariot to face down the lion. When Samson chooses her sister Semadar over her, Delilah is swift to seek vengeance. Hers is, as Miriam (Olive Deering) charges, a "treacherous beauty." In a film with few pretensions to realism, Hedy's limited acting range was of little consequence; any dramatic effect called for she achieved by widening her eyes or shrugging her shoulders and pouting. Occasionally, she trailed a languid hand carelessly around her male prey of the moment. As the Saran, Sanders is characteristically sardonic, and the scenes between him and his old lover are loaded with understanding. Dangling jewels before her as she reclines on a divan, Saran acquiesces companionably to her request that Samson be horribly tortured.

There was too, in her on-screen relationship with the biblical strongman, a hint of sadomasochism that her costumes, offset by jeweled belts and clunky ankle bracelets, did nothing to diminish: "He's magnificent, even in chains," she gasps as she watches her blinded lover grinding the millstone. But her finest line remains her triumphant, "No man leaves Delilah!" when she shears the hero's hair in a fit of jealous rage.

Hedy had contracted to participate in publicity for the film but, as its release approached, she refused. Only after intervention by DeMille and an exchange of terse telegrams did she consent to one interview, with Edwin Schallert of the *Los Angeles Times* in January 1950.

Responses to DeMille's heroine were predictable: "Hedy Lamarr's Delilah would be more at home in a Yorkville bar than in a high-toned Philistine residence. All in all, this film does not enhance the glory of De Mille or his Associate [God]; its splendors are purely in the camp division."[16] Most famously, Groucho Marx allegedly quipped that it was the "First picture I've ever seen where the man's tits are bigger than the woman's." Nothing the critics said mattered—*Samson and Delilah* was a massive hit. It was the top moneymaker of 1950, earning $11 million for Paramount.[17] In addition to its Academy Award for costume design, it won another for art direction (color), and it kick-started the flood of biblical epics in the 1950s. After a decade of lackluster films, it returned Hedy to big box office and commercial favor. Once again, she was seen on magazine covers, the now-familiar beauty of her face undimmed, even if her figure was slightly matronly. Equally important, her advertising career was reignited. For Lucky Strikes cigarettes, she posed in the peacock gown, crooning, "a good cigarette is like a good movie—always enjoyable." She became the face for Lux Toilet Soap, again posing in her costume from *Samson and Delilah*, with the advertisement inviting the reader to link the whiteness of her skin with the quality of the soap. She also promoted Max Factor makeup, once again in the exotic headgear from DeMille's epic.

Hedy might also have passed into film history in yet another way— Billy Wilder had used a clip of DeMille shooting *Samson and Delilah* in Norma Desmond's doomed visit to the studio in *Sunset Boulevard* (1950). In addition to including DeMille, Wilder had wanted Hedy to appear as herself being directed by DeMille to surrender her chair to Norma. Hedy's asking price was, however, $25,000; Wilder altered his script to have Norma sit in DeMille's chair, from where she angrily pushes away the boom mike when it ruffles the peacock feather in her hat.[18]

As it was, *Samson and Delilah* secured Hedy's cinematic reputation in a way that none of her previous films, save *Ecstasy* and perhaps *Algiers*, had done. Indeed, audiences could remind themselves of the distance she had traveled since her early scandalous performance for Machaty, as the distributors of *Ecstasy* capitalized on its star's return to fame by rereleasing the film.

• • •

As Hedy moved into the 1950s, now age thirty-six, with her career revived, she seemed set to defy silent-star Norma Desmond's fate and those of other former studio-era beauties now stranded by time, tastes, and the end of the studio system. The 1950s would bring the rise of the independent producer, ushering in a new era of affluence and embracing a new notion of sexiness, epitomized by one iconic star, Marilyn Monroe. It was going to be hard to stay on top.

14

Acapulco

BY THE SPRING OF 1950, Hedy was enjoying the comforts of financial security. She had proven herself professionally and could indulge her interests. If she had never learned to love Hollywood, she had grown used to
West Coast sunshine; most of all she enjoyed swimming and relaxing on
the beach. She headed to the Naples Beach Club in Florida, but she was
determined to appear in another role for DeMille, who was rumored
to be working on another epic, a "circus picture" (*The Greatest Show on
Earth*, 1952). Never much of a letter writer, she assaulted the director with
a steady flow of telegrams.

In the summer she holidayed in East Hampton. She took painting
classes from Franz Bueb and, still flush with money, invested in art, purchasing paintings that included Grandma Moses's *The Homecoming* and
works by Pierre Bonnard, Maurice Utrillo, Modigliani, and Camille Bom-
bois. The burgeoning collection suggests something of a preference for
naïve art, which was currently in vogue. "Every time I work hard I give
myself a present," she said firmly.[1]

Would she be able to continue working hard? Most important for her
career, she turned to television, where she made a startling impact as a
game and quiz-show contestant. Her shows in the 1950s included appearances on the *Ed Sullivan Show,* the *Colgate Comedy Hour,* the *All Star Revue,*
Shower of Stars, the *George Gobel Show,* and the *Merv Griffin Show.* Taking
their cue from the old radio shows, the TV shows had stars appear as
themselves or act out scenarios inspired by their best-known film roles.[2]

Hedy's first television appearance was as a last-minute replacement for
Gloria Swanson on the *Ed Sullivan Show,* in September 1950. Her costar
was Pat O'Brien, who proved himself well adapted to the new entertain-

176

ment medium. "O'Brien justified his booking," *Variety* considered. "Miss Lamarr made no such attempt. Apparently all she was hired to do was look pretty, and she's extremely capable in that department."[3]

Indeed, Hedy's television appearances are notable for her look of bemusement. She often seems hardly able to believe what she is doing, settling for standing still as the action revolves around her. Part of the problem lay in the shows' various scripts. In Donald O'Connor's *Colgate Comedy Hour* of 1952, the host had to duel for the beautiful lady, leaving Hedy with nothing to do but look decorative. Apparently, the show's writers were unable to recall or imagine the strong women she had played in her 1940s heyday or to comprehend that she had any talent for comedy. More successful was the madcap *Colgate Comedy Hour* later in 1952 (28 December), where a manic Ben Blue enacted an extended parody of wartime spy thrillers. Hedy's role was to play off her parts in *The Conspirators* and *Comrade X* as an outrageously over-the-top Mata Hari figure. This she did with something approaching gusto.

Nor did her filmmaking dry up in the 1950s. In 1950, for instance, she earned $138,059.36.[4] Having turned down the role of Elizabeth Taylor's mother in Vincente Minnelli's *Father of the Bride* (1950), she appeared in *A Lady without Passport* in 1950, a part for which she was paid $90,000. The film was one of a number released in the 1950s dramatizing the situation of illegal immigrants crossing the border into the United States. MGM tied itself in knots as it attempted to accommodate the conflicting perspectives of various audiences as well as the official perspective on immigration. Hedy was to play a down-on-her-luck Cuban refugee who is just looking for "a home, respect, freedom, and neighbors who want the same thing." If that was found by escaping to America, then the film had to emphasize that not all beautiful Cuban women would enjoy the same entitlement. So, in a play on the audience's knowledge of the star's offscreen life and persona, Hedy's Marianne Loriss became a Viennese-born beauty who had (inexplicably) washed up in Cuba. In common with her earlier roles, she had to validate and complicate a foreigner's desire to become an American, and she was expected less to carry the narrative than to appear as a sideshow to the main action.

To shoot the film, MGM hired film noir director Joseph H. Lewis. After the release of *Gun Crazy* in 1949, Lewis saw his reputation as a maker of classy-but-cheap B movies soar. In many ways, his Hollywood career and output most resemble Ulmer's; he was an intensely visual director with a preference for moody thrillers and Westerns. A *Lady without Passport* was his first contract film for MGM, and he later rued his decision to join the studio.

Mayer's original proposal was that Lewis make a documentary about "a poor immigrant in Cuba struggling to come into this country [the United States], and to make it with the Immigration Department: no actors, done with all portable equipment. I was fascinated by this idea and pretty soon I was greatly involved."[5] Suddenly, he found his project changing before his eyes with nothing he could do about it. He knew he ought to quit, he said, but was so struck with the idea of a contract from the studio (a dream that began when he was a boy) that he persisted with the film.

The script was one matter, his leading lady another: "I finally accepted the thing and I was sorry from the moment I stepped on the stage. Hedy Lamarr was disgraceful, absolutely disgraceful." As Lewis recalled it, Hedy refused to take his direction. For one scene, he asked her to walk from the background to the foreground; she refused, proposing instead that they take for granted that she has walked to the position and that she start the scene in the foreground. The two argued until Lewis lost his temper. "I said: 'Get the hell off this stage!' I picked her up by the ass and by the back of her neck and I threw her. I said: 'Get the hell out of here! We don't want you anymore.'" The most disconcerting aspect of this anecdote is Hedy's alleged response: "She came up to me and put her arms around me in front of the whole set and said: 'Oh, isn't he vunderful! Oh, you are vunderful, what a powerful man, I'm in love with you! Oh, now vere do you want me to go? I'll do anything you say, anything!'"[6]

"I'm not proud of that film," Lewis later told Peter Bogdanovich. "But it proves one thing: that I'm capable of making a stinker."[7] It also proves how Hedy was still mocked as a foreigner in Hollywood—the comic rendition of her Germanic consonants in Lewis's unpleasant anecdote underlines this. Nor does its tone of disgust suggest a collaborative working relationship—Hedy meant not only foreignness but also an overheated (read foreign) sexuality that both threatened and titillated her director.

Hedy's troubled role in the film was exacerbated by a weak script; in one sequence, she casually reveals that she is a survivor of Buchenwald, rather as if she were remarking on a bad holiday experience. Watching her perform, there is little evidence that she knew what was expected of her, and one can imagine that her differences with her director made matters worse. Viewers know what she is meant to represent—yet another rootless émigrée who must throw herself on the many mercies of the bountiful United States to find a safe haven. Her wooden performance militates against this sort of easy propaganda; perhaps this was the best she could do, or perhaps, at a deeper level, her performance reflected her own ambivalence about assimilating to American culture.

In other respects, *A Lady without Passport* is easily recognizable as a Joseph H. Lewis picture, notably in the swamp sequences toward the end, which recall the setting of *Gun Crazy*. Nor is it quite the stinker that its director described. Cuba was one of several Latin American settings favored by noir directors and Lewis makes the best of its steamy locales, notably in a sequence where an INS agent (John Hodiak) walks into a café where a local dancer (Nita Bieber) is performing to Latin music; as he enters, the camera switches to a low-angled position that looks up at the dancer from floor level. Later, in an almost casual shot, one sees the dance continue in the background, the moving figure now throwing vast shadows against a wall.

If the film's reputation is undergoing something of a revival, the critics were little moved on its release:

> This latest attempt at melodramatizing the shady characters who try to outwit the U.S. Immigration Service is not very well cast, acted, directed, or screen-written. The main drawback is an unbelievable script. The situations are neither novel or interesting . . . Hedy's camera beauty is never shown to full advantage. For one thing she is badly gowned; for another, her diction is not always clear.[8]

The word around Hollywood was that Hedy was difficult; she needed direction but resisted what she saw as interference. Her films were always hit or miss but at least her beauty could once have been relied on to sufficiently dazzle reviewers and audiences into overlooking her stilted acting. Now in her late thirties, she was, in Hollywood's eyes, aging. Her repeated refusals to tour and promote her films didn't help.

Sensing that her choices were shrinking and long without a studio contract, Hedy accepted the lead opposite Ray Milland in *Copper Canyon* (John Farrow, 1950). The decision resulted in a film that no one liked, least of all Hedy: "We were all miscast . . . All through the picture everyone complained of hardships and I complained most of all."[9]

The plot, taken from a script by Jonathan Latimer, is at best flimsy. The cardsharp and possibly former Confederate officer Johnny Carter (Ray Milland) is asked by his local Southern mining community for protection against a band of rebel-haters led by the deputy, Lane Travis (Macdonald Carey). Hedy's part, as the sharp-talking adventuress with a quick hand at cards who mysteriously rides into town, was evidently inspired by Marlene Dietrich's turn in *Destry Rides Again* (George Marshall, 1939). Just whose side she is on is never made clear and arguably her inexpressive performance heightens the film's mystery. In reality, she gives audiences little opportunity to engage with her character and seems, yet again, to be moving directionless through the film. She briefly comes to life when she slaps Milland across the face, but their lovemaking is decidedly flat. She does, however, look magnificent in Edith Head's period costumes, whether a full-bodied off-the-shoulder turquoise gown or a demure black top with the vivid red bow hanging down her front. Technicolor undoubtedly became her.

Evidently, director John Farrow found little of Marlene Dietrich in his female lead and the film appears thrown together, as if all concerned had conceded failure before it even made the final edit. The shoot lasted from 14 April to early June 1949 and the film premiered in October 1950.

Hedy responded to her career's downward spiral by turning increasingly to psychoanalysis and her interviews reflected its influence; in particular, she began to view her relationship with her father as having adversely affected her in later life:

Something must have gone wrong in my very earliest infancy. Either my parents did not really love me, perhaps because they had wanted a boy, or to me it seemed they did not love me because they put me so much in the care of servants. Maybe they were so careful trying not to spoil me that they overdid it. However it was, I did not feel that I was loved and I was miserably unhappy from as long back as I can remember. As early as the age of three, I was so hurt because someone hit me that I ran away. I suppose that I was looking for the love that I never could find . . . Even as a child I sensed that people adored my beauty, but they did not adore *me*. It may be that I felt that they envied my beauty and I showed my resentment and was therefore not treated too well. I know only that always I felt abused in spite of all my trying to be kind and pleasing. The best example of this was my own father. He was an enormous man, six feet four inches tall and 15 [actually 18] years older than my mother. One day I put on a pretty new hair ribbon which I thought would please him, but it seems he hated bows and he got very angry. I ran like mad and he chased me and hit me. I could never forget this. Usually he was so quiet.[10]

Scripts were still arriving, mainly from the indefatigable Paul Kohner but Hedy knew her age worked against her: "I was getting along in my thirties. In the industry, these were the suicide years. So many actresses attempted suicide as they approached forty. Why? I suppose for many reasons. Speaking for myself, I was beginning to get tired. Really physically tired. The emotional strain, plus the hours and the pressures, were taking their toll."[11] Clutching at straws, she accepted a part from Bob Hope in *My Favorite Spy* (Norman Z. McLeod, 1951), although alternate sources of income were looking increasingly attractive: "I resolved to do *My Favorite Spy,* and then concentrate on finding a husband and one good picture."[12]

According to Hedy, Bob Hope was mostly concerned with how far he could push the boundaries of sexual explicitness, both on-screen and in the accompanying publicity materials. In fact, Hope needed Hedy as much as she needed him, and Hedy was to be one of a number of glamorous female stars (later screen partners included Madeleine Carroll and Eva Marie-Saint) appropriated by Hope to convince audiences of his sex appeal. The casting of Hedy was also an in-joke aimed at his fans, who were familiar with Hope's long-running gags about his passion for the star and her failure to reciprocate his feelings.

The film is a hokey spy farce organized around Hope's dual performance as the burlesque artist Peanuts White and his double, the international criminal Eric Augustine. With its Tangier setting, several Casbah chase sequences, fortune-telling gypsy, glamorous nightclub, and casting of the substantially built actor Francis L. Sullivan in the role of the menacing gang boss Karl Brubaker, audiences were evidently intended to recall *Casablanca, Algiers,* and other exotic wartime thrillers.

Hedy was the glamorous agent Lily Dalbray—"All women are dangerous—she's all woman!" punned Peanuts/Augustine. With the kind of lazy casting the film acquired from television, Hedy was forced to play yet another Mata-Hari comic figure. Herein lay the crux of the film's dilemma—how can one take the romance seriously when the film itself is a spoof? In Hollywood's creative lull that constituted much of the 1950s, actors like Hedy Lamarr could no longer convincingly play the type of wartime roles that had so gripped American audiences; those audiences were now comfortably ensconced in their homes enjoying the new delights of television. Filmmakers sought only to remind their viewers of what they had once enjoyed while playing the characters for laughs the second time around. Although Hedy is leaden in the film's opening, she demonstrates a good-spiritedness in the finale by joining in the comic mayhem that sees her and Hope escape, disguised as firemen, from the villains. The sequence concludes with her driving the fire engine at top speed as Hope clings to the ladder for dear life. "If I saw this on television, I'd never believe it," Hope quips, winking furiously at the camera.

Hedy might have hoped that her association with Hope would energize her career, but she was unlucky in his choice of star vehicle. Nor was Hope allegedly too pleased when it became apparent that his costar was better at comedy than he had imagined; he had the final sequences of *My Favorite Spy* re-edited so that he would be the funnier of the two. If anything could be learned from this debacle, it was that there was little place in Hollywood for its prewar sirens, unless they were happy to parody themselves—and they needed better material than this. Once again, Hedy refused to tour and promote the film, which was released before Christmas 1951. She planned to retire from acting, she announced to a now cynical and increasingly negative press corps, who reported:

> Hedy's outburst came just about the time that the word seeped in from Europe that her flame, director Anatole Litvak, was about to marry the German-born blonde charmer, Hildegarde Neff. Hollywood went ha-ha, but nobody was surprised when the Casbah lovely started talking about giving up her movie career for good. Hedy's let that pearl of information drop before—right in the ears of a couple of millionaires.[13]

How quickly the celebrity press turned on a performer whose reputation was on the skids! American culture is geared toward the celebration of success; step off the ladder and you're fair game. As a foreigner, someone who had several failed marriages, and most of all, someone whose career was looking shaky, Hedy found herself lashed by the tongues of once-fawning columnists, eager to curry favor with their readers. There was more to come.

She longed for a word from her favorite director: "DEAR C.B. HAVE JUST BEEN DRIVING A FIRE TRUCK, DRIVING A CHARIOT WOULD BE DELIGHTFUL CHANGE YOUR EVER LOVING DELILAH OF TROY" read one cable to Cecil B. DeMille.[14] DeMille remained silent.

It was time to find a new husband. He turned out to be Edward (Teddy) Stauffer. Stauffer was a friend of John Loder's and had met Hedy back in 1944, when she and Loder were just married. A colorful character, Stauffer was born in Switzerland in 1909, and made his name playing jazz and swing, as a member of the "Original Teddies-Band" in Germany. His music found little favor with the German authorities, and he moved on to Hollywood. When problems arose with his residence papers, Stauffer skipped to Mexico, but not before falling in with the Hollywood set, where, with his tall frame and blond hair, he was a popular figure. In Acapulco, he found work managing the Casablanca Hotel, and attracted some publicity when he became embroiled in a dispute in which a local fisherman shot at him five times in the hotel lobby. Before he met Hedy, Stauffer was rumored to be on the verge of marrying Rita Hayworth, whom he had escorted around Europe following her divorce from Orson Welles. His first, brief marriage was to Faith Domergue; she in turn had previously been romantically linked with Howard Hughes.

In 1949, Stauffer opened his first nightclub, La Perla, in Acapulco. La Perla was no ordinary venue. It was built, according to Stauffer's design, in rings around the La Quebrada cliff face. Each ring was one table wide, allowing guests to sip their cocktails (notably the Coco Loco, a mixture of tequila and coconut cream), sample the steaks that Stauffer had flown in from Mexico City, or try his own house recipe, Swiss enchiladas. At 10:30 and 12:30, after darkness had fallen, a drum roll announced the evening's entertainment. A seminaked diver, holding aloft a flaming torch, made his way down the cliff face. To applause from diners, he then tossed his torch into the sea, swam to the opposite shore, climbed the sheer cliff face, paused for more applause, knelt and prayed in the candlelit chapel, and walked to the cliff's edge. Lit now only by a circle of flames, he dove off the cliff deep into the Pacific waters.[15]

By 1950, La Perla had, in Stauffer's words, "really started rolling."[16] Out of the blue, he received a phone call from Hedy. She was in Acapulco, she said, "being 'hounded by some man who owned razor blades' who insisted on marrying her."[17] Stauffer offered her sanctuary in La Perla and the two fell in love. A visit to an Indian fortune-teller who promised them wealth and happiness sealed the relationship. Stauffer then bought two rings, one for him and one for Hedy: "in this manner we became married—unofficially."[18]

Hedy left Acapulco in May and shortly after her departure, her psychiatrist (presumably Dr. Philip Solomon) stayed at La Perla. He interrogated Stauffer thoroughly and the tall Swiss was to find out that Hedy was paying this man a dollar an hour to watch and observe him. In July 1951, according to his account, Stauffer went to Los Angeles to enjoy a break at the Beverly Hills Hotel. There he came across Hedy talking to an elderly woman. "She [Hedy] came over instantly and called back to the lady, 'Mother, this is Teddy from Acapulco. I hope you like him, because I'm going to marry him tonight.'"[19] She was as good as her word.

In fact, these events took place in June (the marriage was held on 11 June 1951, in the home of Superior Court judge Stanley Mosk). The newlyweds and Hedy's children honeymooned together in Carmel before settling down in Acapulco.

Hedy had decided to divest herself of paraphernalia from her Hollywood past. A week after the star's wedding to Stauffer, auctioneer Arthur B. Goode received a surprise phone call from Hedy, announcing that she wanted to sell all her goods: "I mean *all*." Even her aspirin bottles and toothbrush went under the hammer. She had been guided in this decision, she notified the press, by the advice of her favorite astrologer. Another reporter was told that she wanted to bury the past and start over with her new husband. The list of personal possessions for sale included four wedding rings (one wide wedding ring had been cut in two). She also put up a gold children's ring engraved "J.M." (presumably John Markey/ Loder's). As the auctioneers sifted through everything from old underwear to Modiglianis, they were on the point of throwing away an old coffee tin, when they heard it rattle. It was full of a shining mass of bracelets, lockets, necklaces, and earrings. "Only a woman would use a coffee can as a safety-deposit vault and then forget about it," sighed Goode.[20]

The day of the auction, a crowd, in which women outnumbered men by ten to one, gathered to catch a glimpse of the star's belongings. When they saw a signed photograph from DeMille to Hedy that was inscribed, "To Delilah, A contented New Year to you," a woman in a blue print dress sniffed: "Why wouldn't she be contented? Look at all that money she's getting!" Another woman said, "If that's all it takes to make her contented, this sale ought to make her very happy." The sale netted $58,000. As the reporter from the *Saturday Evening Post* commented, "it wasn't necessary to be a psychologist to sense that it gave some of those who waited a feeling of superiority to think that they could pick up the debris of a glamorous movie star's life at bargain prices—if they wanted to."[21]

Hedy's motivation to clinch an official vow of matrimony was, according to Stauffer, only to avoid criticisms of immorality. She might have lived with him by herself, but not with her four- and five-year-old children in tow. Stauffer called Acapulco and asked his second-in-command to ready a room for him and his new bride. "'But, Señor Teddy, it is filled to the roof with baskets of champagne,' said he. 'You'll have no place to sleep.' I told Hedy. 'Tell him we'll sleep on top of the baskets,' she laughed."[22]

Hedy dreamed of a simple life, of starting over in Acapulco. Her Hollywood baggage had been disposed of—literally and in her imagination. She and Teddy would run La Perla together and she would never need to deal with the machinery of stardom again.

Life with Stauffer in Acapulco did indeed begin well and Hedy briefly contented herself with acting the role of nightclub hostess. By August, however, her unofficial position was souring and she reportedly snubbed Ava Gardner and Frank Sinatra when they were at the club. The urbane Stauffer quickly organized for an early morning torch-diving display for the two lovers. "Acapulco life was just too primitive for Hedy, and unfortunately the children didn't adapt to the climate, and the change in food made them repeatedly ill," Stauffer remembered.[23]

They decided to send the children to school in San Francisco, although Hedy wasn't happy with that. They came to visit during holidays, but each time they drank the tap water and became ill. Hedy responded by sequestering herself from her former friends and colleagues. Paul Kohner, for one, found that it was impossible to reach her by telephone and had to resort to telegrams in his ongoing attempt to interest her in roles. His proposed version of a Mata Hari story to be shot in Rome and for which he believed she would receive $75,000 in cash fell on deaf ears.[24]

Hedy had been developing other plans and they did not include life in Rome, or in Acapulco.

She was determined to try one more shot at film production. By October 1951, the new Mrs. Stauffer was back in Hollywood, looking to make deals. For several months, Stauffer flew out to Los Angeles on weekends or Hedy traveled to Acapulco. Hedy and he spent long hours on the telephone.

She returned to Acapulco in January 1952, but now it was with an eye toward exploiting her new address as a production base. Rumors were leaked to the press about a project involving Hedy and independent producer Victor Pahlen.[25] At first, they planned to shoot a TV series entitled "The Great Loves of History" in Mexico. At this stage, thirty-six half-hour shows were planned with Hedy playing a series of beautiful women from history. The scripts were to be written by Salka Viertel and Æneas MacKenzie, with Edgar Ulmer set to direct.

All this and family life too was becoming overwhelming and in February 1952, Hedy once again moved into the Beverly Hills Hotel, her favorite haunt when she was in town, and started looking into local boarding schools for her children. By now Jamsie was nearly thirteen, Denise would soon be six, and Tony was five. She entrusted Paul Kohner with the task of finding a suitable educational establishment. Kohner found Chadwick School (a boarding and day school) in Palo Verdes. But there was, he suggested, a problem, "Most schools do not take children as young as 5 as they believe such youngsters should be with mother or nurse."[26] Hedy was apparently undeterred. Chadwick would accept her small children as well as Jamsie, she insisted.

Not surprisingly, Jamsie seems to have been a troubled child, prone to outbursts of anxiety. Still that doesn't adequately explain or excuse what happened next. Looking back on those years:

> I got in trouble in Chadwick and they told me I couldn't go there any more. But there was a teacher [there] by the name of Ingrid Gray (she was also German, Kleppern was her maiden name). She said I could live with her and her husband and go there daytime and not stay at night and since all my friends were there and everybody I knew, I agreed and my mother was disenchanted with that and she didn't want anything more to do with me. She was just angry.[27]

Hedy threw him out of the house. "The last I saw of my mother as a child would have been when I was about in fifth grade. I tried to write to her, but the letters were returned. Effectively she said, 'You're no longer my son. Good-bye.'"[28] Abandoned by his family, James Loder moved in with Ingrid and Edward Ray Gray at Redondo Beach until he was eighteen and then joined the Air Force (hence the birth certificate requirement). Afterward, he joined the Omaha City Police and was back in the news in 1969, when he was charged with the manslaughter of a fourteen-year-old African American girl during Omaha's race riots in June of that year. The judge found him not guilty, further inflaming feelings, particularly in the (now-demolished) Logan Fontanelle projects. Throughout these long years, James never again saw his adoptive mother or siblings.

We only have James Loder's account to go on; curiously Chadwick School has no record of his attendance there. Yet, it is hard to dismiss his experience. Paul Kohner's letters to Hedy from this time are evidence of her, even to his Hollywood eyes, disquieting selfishness when it came to her children, who often seemed to function as props in press photographs of "happy family life" before, one may imagine, being dispatched to the care of nannies. Grandmother Trude Kiesler did involve herself somewhat in their lives but her own parenting was equally chilly. Hedy's background in interwar Vienna did not lend itself to modern-day concepts of parenting, nor did it prepare her for the challenge of combining single motherhood and a career. Even with a charitable heart, however, it is impossible to excuse her treatment of Jamsie (how much more vulnerable the adoptive child was), in particular, but also of her own birth children.

Next to go was Teddy Stauffer. Hedy and he began divorce proceedings in March 1952, after Hedy testified that he had hit her on several occasions. The court hearing provided an early insight into the increasingly unreal atmosphere that circulated around Hedy's later, more frequent court appearances. She prepared by releasing press information as to how she would plead. When she entered the courtroom on 17 March 1952, the actress was surprised to see an array of journalists poised to follow the proceedings. Why should they be there, she wished to know, when they already knew what she was going to say. The judge ought to get rid of them. Superior Court judge Thurmond Clarke had to remind the plaintiff that this was a public hearing and he had no authority to turn anyone out. In fact, the judge was already familiar with the glamorous figure in front of him, having presided over her divorce from John Loder. None too happy with this edict, Hedy began her testimony by adhering to the prepared script. "I moved to Mexico with all intentions of staying there," she affirmed. "It was quite a big change for me. Now I am very disappointed to have to come to this decision. But as charming as Mr. Stauffer can be to his patrons and the people he likes to impress, to be a good husband is something else again."

At each hesitation, she was prompted by her attorney, William G. Israel, who had advised the court, somewhat surprisingly, that she was not seeking alimony and would pay her own legal fees. "There have been weeks," Hedy continued, "when Mr. Stauffer wouldn't say a kind word or do a kind deed and I was sort of on my own. He wouldn't take any responsibility of any sort and at times he would hit me. Last New Year's Eve he went too far." At this, Hedy suddenly appeared to forget her lines and the judge now had to prompt her as well as her attorney.

"Did he hit you on many occasions?" Israel asked.

"Yes, he did."

"This all upset you and made you unhappy?" Judge Clark offered helpfully.

"It did."

Realizing that this was going to go no further, Israel swiftly called Hedy's chauffeur, Marvin Neal, to the stand. Neal testified that he had seen Stauffer hit Hedy in the face and knock her against the door following an altercation.[29]

In *Ecstasy and Me,* Hedy is vague about her marriage to Stauffer, blaming its breakdown on the weather in Acapulco. She and the children were, she wrote, happy to return to Hollywood.

15

Houston, Texas

IN EARLY 1952, Hedy announced that her production company intended to produce *Queen Esther and the King of Egypt* (a series of films for television) to be filmed in Britain, with Edgar Ulmer slated to direct. She had purchased the rights to the story for $25,000. But as negotiations spilled over into 1953, the project fell through.

Then a new source of funding arrived, in the shape of an extremely wealthy prospective husband, Texan oil magnate W. Howard Lee. The two met at Houston's Pin Oak Horse Show in June 1952. Hedy then headed for Rome and the relationship cooled; instead, it was rumored that she had set her sights on Giovanni Agnelli, heir to the Fiat fortune. According to one report, she and Agnelli holidayed together in the south of France. One day, Hedy decided to swim out to take a closer look at a magnificent yacht anchored in the bay. It turned out to be owned by Fritz Mandl; she swam away, apparently without seeing her former husband.[1] Lee, on the other hand, seemed a more promising candidate for marriage and appeared happy to invest in the project, or in a future with Hedy. In fact, Lee only lent Hedy the money ($125,575); later, when they were divorcing, he claimed it back.

By now, the TV proposal had been whittled down to a three-episode feature film about three famous beauties—Helen of Troy, Genevieve of Brabant, and the Empress Josephine—to be shot in Rome in 1953. According to Arianné Cipes, in an interview with Tag Gallagher published after Hedy's death: "Dad [Ulmer] was originally going to do the entire trilogy. The film was originally financed by Del Duca, the magazine magnate in Italy, but during the filming Hedy Lamarr married the Texan Howard Lee and had him buy out Cino Del Duca, and now Dad had to contend with Lamarr as producer. It was the only time he ever walked on a film . . . She still owns the film and has reedited it over and over again."[2]

Ulmer brought his wife, Shirley, on board to work on the script for the trilogy. Even before the cameras rolled, trouble was brewing. In 1953 Victor Pahlen was brought in as coproducer with Hedy. As Pahlen put the last touches on his production, including coping with the late arrival of Hedy, Warner Bros. announced that they would be making their own Helen of Troy film to star either Virginia Mayo or Hedy Lamarr. Pahlen, himself no stranger to Hollywood maneuvering, summoned the press to make it clear that the only Helen of Troy show on the road was his and he had secured Hedy.

Titled variously *The Face That Launched a Thousand Ships* (in Britain), *L'amante di Paride* and *L'Eterna Femmina* (in Italy), *La manzana de la discordia* (in Spain), and *The Loves of Three Queens* (in the United States), the project was characterized by the kind of high melodrama that now seemed an inevitable element in Hedy's public engagements. According to her own account, she had difficulty gaining the respect from cast and crew that she needed to produce a fine film; she also ran out of money and had to ask Lee for more funding.[3]

One young actor in the film was John Fraser, who would become well known in British films and television. In his autobiography, he remembers the shoot in vivid detail. Hedy arrived accompanied by her assistant, Frankie Dawson, and her psychiatrist. The latter was evidently unable to get to the cause of the star's free-associating monologues, which were, to Fraser at least, quite baffling. "I miss them so much," he remembers Hedy telling the set, "but I never see their father. Where is it now? Tucson, or some such dump. If he ever sells, I get half. I have my lawyer working on it, sure, in one big silver frame, so I don't have to shuffle them like cards. You think it's expensive? Not for that district. I couldn't ask her. She'd be lost without Buzz. But he's no good for, with all that Schlitzbergen business. I'm supposed—they told me I had costume approval!" Her voice rising, she focused momentarily on her costume: "How can they stick me in that ball gown! I need scarlet! Or lilac to go with my eyes." She threatened to walk off the set. Fraser foolishly intervened and later discovered that she tried to have him removed from the film. Failing to achieve this, she refused to talk to him and all their communications were channeled through Edgar Ulmer, then the director. That relationship, Fraser, writes, was "bitter and hate-filled and spectacularly stormy."[4]

In Fraser's scene with the star, Ulmer and Hedy wound up at logger-heads. Ulmer flew into a temper and threatened to shoot the scene with a double. Hedy, who in this scene was cradling Fraser's head to her breast, let go of his head, and "firmly putting one hand on the collar of her dress, with one savage wrench, she ripped the priceless garment from the neck to the navel. She then walked off the set for a week."[5]

Soon after, Ulmer quit and stormed off the set; Marc Allégret took over direction. Little was lost or gained by this change.[6] The film verges on a Monty Pythonesque parody of the historical epic, with Hedy constantly center stage. Depending on which version you watch, a plot device has Hedy appear as a languid beauty in Romani's traveling show, whose impresario stages an episode from history every evening. The camera segues from the traveling show's cheap stage setting to an equally tawdry film set.

In the first episode, Hedy makes a startling Genevieve of Brabant, appearing in long, golden curls. Wrongly sentenced to death for adultery, she flees into the woods when her guards take pity on her and let her escape. There she gives birth to a son and is eventually reunited with his father. In the second episode, her character Josephine is now a brunette. This time she is unjustly cast aside because she has borne Napoleon (Gerard Oury) no children. In the final sequence, she plays Helen of Troy, fleeing Menelaus (Robert Beatty) for Paris (Massimo Serato), and in so doing causing the outbreak of the Trojan War. The unifying theme of these sequences is the notion that beauty is a burden to which the bearer will inevitably be sacrificed.

"What else has it brought me, save sorrow!" Hedy/Helen declaims. A lament that was to become an oft-repeated mantra, not least in *Ecstasy and Me*, drives the film in a repetitive loop that neither its many writers, directors, nor even Nino Rota's score could prevent. Most of all, Hedy's languid, passive performances decelerated the pace. She was unaccustomed to carrying a film, particularly when she was so actively and punishingly participating in its production. It was, in a way that could not have been said of *The Strange Woman* or *Dishonored Lady*, a vanity project from which no one escaped with glory.

As *L'Amante di Paride*, the film was shown briefly in Italy, where it was distributed by Republic Pictures. This version was attributed solely to Marc Allégret and contained only the Helen of Troy episode. Hedy claimed that she was unable to find a distributor for her production outside of Italy. In fact, it did play in Spain and Britain, but in different versions than the eventual U.S. release; the British version ran at seventy-three minutes, the Spanish ninety-seven minutes, and the American ninety minutes.

As the published synopses attest, different edits produced different structures. In one, the focus is on the story of Helen of Troy, which is told at a wedding banquet as a warning that goes unheeded. In another, a woman tries to decide which of the three famous beauties she ought to dress up as for a costume ball. In the most often seen U.S. television version, an admirer comments on the playing of the roles by an actress named Liala (Hedy), whom he hopes will leave the traveling troupe and run off with him.

Later Hedy's two lawyers sued her for unpaid fees of $15,500 from the making of the film; though she counter-claimed that it was never properly finished.[7] Certainly, it made no money.

On 10 April 1953, Hedy took her oath of allegiance to the United States. The event received heightened press coverage when one of the Marine Corps guards fainted on the parade ground. On 23 December 1953, she married W. Howard Lee at a civil ceremony at the Queens County Courthouse in New York. "I married him," she later said, "through a combination of love and need."[8] Before the marriage, she consulted with her old friend Paul Henreid, who remembers his surprise at the turn the discussion took:

"I have this millionaire Texan who says he loves me and wants to marry me. What should I do, Paul?"

"Why ask me?" I laughed. "If you love him, Hedy, marry him."

"Oh yes, love—well, I thought I'd have my lawyer draw up a marriage contract."

"What do you mean by a marriage contract?" I asked in bewilderment.

"Why, a contract that stipulates exactly how much money I'll get if he divorces me."

I stared at her, not believing what I'd heard, then I said, "I've had no experience with marriage contracts, Hedy, so I can't give you any advice. I've heard that rich people make them here, but why they get married at all is more than I can understand."

"I think I'm right," she said after a moment's reflection. "I'll get him to sign it or tell him I won't marry him!"[9]

She married in some secrecy, with just her longtime friend, the agent Robert Lantz and his wife, as witnesses, and the couple then left for Los Angeles with, it was reported, Tony and Denise. No mention was made of Jamsie. Lee's family claimed to be astonished by the news of the wedding.[10]

The newlyweds returned briefly to Rome, where Hedy planned to shoot a second film, but it was never started. Back in Texas, Lee signed a two-year lease on an $85,000 Mediterranean-style house on 3239 Del Monte, in River Oaks, Houston. Hedy's new home was palatial, with a high-ceilinged entrance hall, a large drawing room with a wood-burning fireplace, and a large dining room dominated by a vast chandelier. There were four bedrooms, maids, cooks, and everything Hedy desired.

In *Ecstasy and Me,* she writes that she was happy. Having decided to give up her acting career, she idled away her time in the American way, spending quantities of her new husband's money on their house, adding wings that doubled its size and hiring shifts of interior decorators. Why not?—"Yes it did cost a lot of money, but Howard had a lot of money, and was always making more."[11] In fact, although lavish spending seems to have been the hallmark of their marriage, since the house was leased, it is unlikely that she oversaw major additions.

The press soon reported rifts between the couple. In a bizarre interlude that occurred in 1955, Hedy announced that $50,000 worth of her jewelry had been stolen. To establish the whereabouts of the missing gems, the entire household, including Lee and his new wife, was subjected to lie detector tests, but no new information was revealed. Three weeks later, they mysteriously reappeared resting on a sewing-room shelf. A policeman who had searched that shelf a few days before said firmly that they had not been there when he was looking.[12]

Still the marriage was to last longer than many predicted. Hedy and Lee traveled together, and in August 1955 she made her first visit to Vienna since she had left her home. "I cried like a schoolgirl when I arrived here," she said.[13] She visited old friends and acquaintances, though she must have been shocked at the changes to her beloved city. Although its architecture was surprisingly intact, the old way of life had vanished; most notably its Jewish influence. Following the Anschluß, two-thirds of Vienna's Jews had been expelled and more than 65,000 were murdered in concentration camps.[14]

For most of the populace of 1950s Vienna, the arrival of Hedy Lamarr meant little or nothing. Undoubtedly, for the group of teenagers preparing for training at Vienna's rowing club on a beautiful summer's day, the appearance of a huge open-topped American automobile was enough to catch their eyes. At that time, there were still few cars in Vienna, let alone American models. A chauffeur, cap in hand, stepped out and opened the door to an elegantly dressed woman on the arm of an older man. "It's Hedy Lamarr," one of the senior club members whispered. "That meant nothing to me," Anton Haslinger, one of those teenagers remembered in correspondence. "Years later I realized what a star was visiting the club."[15] In fact, Hedy's father had been a keen rower and had helped the club secure credit to make renovations in the prewar period. Sadly, little remained of his intervention as it had fallen victim to Allied bombing.[16] Hedy and Lee also attended the Salzburg Festival, but on a return trip after one of the shows, their driver fell asleep and the car overturned, causing Hedy a back injury from which she was slow to recover.

Back home in Texas, she devoted herself to worthy causes, including entertaining veterans at a local Texas hospital and appearing in two plays at the University of Houston. The children spent their summers in camp; Hedy painted large abstract canvases that took up considerable wall space.

In November 1957, she and Lee established a business partnership to build a hotel in the ski resort town of Aspen, Colorado. The hotel would be called the Villa Lamarr and initially Hedy threw herself into its design. The finished result was a little bit of home—a Tyrolean Swiss Alps–style building that enjoyed temporary curiosity value in the resort. It never made money.

Soon Hedy tired of life in Houston, just as she had in Acapulco. As much as she derided Hollywood and all it stood for, she couldn't bear to leave it. Her return to acting was in *The Story of Mankind,* one of 1957's less-than-illustrious productions. Directed by Irwin Allen, the film was financed by Warner Bros. and produced by Allen's independent company, Cambridge Productions. Hedy had maintained her own production company, Lamarr Productions, and received a check for $5,000 for her services.[17]

If the film was of minor financial benefit, it only added to her career troubles. In *The Story of Mankind*, two angels in heaven discuss the startling news that man has just invented a super bomb, which if detonated, would bring an end to all mankind. The angels, who are represented as stars in the sky, report their finding to a High Tribunal, which is called into session to decide whether to allow the bomb to explode and destroy civilization or to prevent the bomb from exploding and allow the world to survive.

Defending mankind and his achievement is the Spirit of Man played by Ronald Colman; his adversary, the Devil, is played by Vincent Price. The Judge (Cedric Hardwicke) tells the Spirit of Man and the Devil that they may visit earth to present as evidence any event that occurred during any period of time.

It is in these flashbacks to earth that the story of mankind unfolds. With twenty-five above-title cast names and a further twenty-four appearing below the title, the film was as much as anything else a showpiece for its fading stars. It was to be the last joint-screen appearance of the Marx Brothers, with Harpo Marx playing Sir Isaac Newton, Groucho as Peter Minuet, and Chico as the monk who advised Columbus. Even Groucho's daughter, Melinda, had one of numerous minor roles as an early Christian child. Many of the sequences depicting historical events were taken from old Warner Bros. and 20th Century Fox films, including *King Richard and the Crusaders* (1954) and *The Adventures of Robin Hood* (1938) among others. Hedy played Joan of Arc against a background of clips from the 1950 Victor Fleming production, *Joan of Arc*. With her pageboy haircut and 1950s turtleneck outfit, she appeared to have little or no idea what was expected of her. Not being able to supply the kind of offhand hammy performance of so many of her fellow thespians, she settled on some wan sword-waving before gracefully acceding to being burned at the stake, an apparently painless procedure.

The reviews were dire:

It is impossible to guess why "The Story of Mankind" was filmed. At times the aim would seem to be a kind of exercise in fundamentalist doctrine; at others a lesson in courtroom procedure, and at others a plea for turning H-Bombs into radioactive plowshares . . . If there is humor in this anecdotal and sparse survey of history, only rarely can one suppose it was intentional.[18]

Hedy settled into the Beverly Hills Hotel for the duration of the shoot and devoted her spare time to finding a distributor for *The Loves of Three Women*.

Also in 1957, Hedy acted in what would be her last film, *The Female Animal*, directed by Harry Keller and released in 1958. In the tradition of aging stars (or what Hollywood considered to be aging stars), Hedy plays Vanessa Windsor, a glamorous-but-faded actress who has succeeded the hard way. She has an emotionally disturbed adopted daughter (played by Jane Powell) with whom she competes for the attention of a young movie extra, Chris Farley (George Nader). A further wrinkle in this tale of female jealousy and desire enters with Jan Sterling as Lily Frayne, a wealthy screen siren, who also has her eye on Farley.

"How exciting for you, my angel," Lily remarks to Vanessa, with an appreciative eye to Farley's bodybuilder frame. "He's a little rude but so virile." She has further advice for her friend, who has boasted that the young stud also holds down a job at the studio: "My dear, that's a mistake. Never let him have a career. That's one thing I've realized about men in Hollywood, success goes to their little heads . . . Keep them sharecropping."

Hedy's agreed fee for the shoot was $8,333 per week for a total of $50,000.[19] Albert Zugsmith, the film's producer, had *Sunset Boulevard* in mind as they launched the project, but neither director nor cast was able to re-create Wilder's masterpiece. Hedy's on-set behavior won her no friends; she snapped at production crew and reportedly behaved "like the pampered spoiled movie queens of the old days."[20] Denise and Tony were allegedly meant to play one scene with her (they didn't) and eyebrows were raised when Hedy sent a car and chauffeur all the way to Houston to collect them. Howard Lee was reportedly too busy to attend.

The star's bad behavior may well have been exacerbated by the new shooting schedules and economies of the post–Studio era production regime. A visitor to the set found Hedy dazed by the speed of Keller's shoot: "A few years ago," she said, "this would have taken three days to film. Even in television, you are allowed an ample period of rehearsal. But, here, we are shooting set-up after set-up and, without even much continuity."[21]

On another occasion, the star of the popular TV show *The Range Rider*, Jock Mahoney, swung by the set, prompting Hedy to fly into a rage and have him barred. He never discovered why. After Hedy's conduct with Eunice Field, the Hollywood columnist, the producers had to request that reporter Harold Heffernan hold a column mentioning her until after the film's release.[22]

Ironically, Hedy's insecurities fed into her role, lending to her performance just the right air of uncertainty to form a low-key but fitting conclusion to her acting career. Once again, she plays a predatory beauty who is led by her sexual desires. The coincidence of her adopted child turning on her and of a traumatic mother-daughter relationship in the plot may have added to her identification with the role of Vanessa. As Vanessa realizes that her love for Farley is misguided, if sincerely felt, she seems to waver and lose her self-assurance. By the end of the film, Hedy's Vanessa is as bereft as were Gloria Swanson's Norma Desmond in *Sunset Boulevard* and Bette Davis's Margo Channing in *All about Eve* (1950). If Hollywood had wished to send a message to the ever-insecure Hedy about the effects of aging, here it was.

In a further irony, the film was released as the A movie to Zugsmith's other production, the now second-billed and radically altered Orson Welles film *Touch of Evil* (1958). The critics were unimpressed with *The Female Animal*: "Aside from the frank discussions of sex, the picture hasn't much to offer," concluded the *New York Herald Tribune*.[23]

With her movie career over (even if she didn't know it), Hedy was forced to rely on television to remind casting agents that she still had a professional life. The outcome was less than inspiring and it is surprising that she continued to headline television shows until the late 1960s. It is less surprising that she was deeply ungracious about her new career opportunity, remarking that "I'm just an old-fashioned housewife who has to do these TV things not to get into a rut." She no longer wished, she said, to continue to appear as a Mata Hari type.[24] The latter comment was clearly a dig at her casting in *Shower of Stars*, which aired on CBS in March

1957. In the show, she once again enacted her foreign spy routine, this time in a number with Jack Benny shot against the background of a Lisbon café. Audiences were left wondering if she was there to do anything other than plug *Love of Three Queens*, which she mentioned at every opportunity. That October on the *George Gobel Show*, Hedy was cast as the owner of the Chi Chi Poodle Beauty Parlor and reprised her recent film roles by playing all the beautiful women in history in a dream sequence where Gobel fantasizes that he has married each one in turn. She was also required to sing a song that *Variety* tartly dismissed as "so off-key it might have been used to comedy advantage rather than played straight."[25]

Also in 1957, Hedy starred opposite Paul Richards in the Zane Grey Theater half-hour television drama *Proud Woman*, directed by Louis King. Choosing Hedy's lustrous native persona rather than her sophisticated European one, the scriptwriters had her play a Spanish-American ranchero in the old West. In a precredit sequence, Hedy appears wielding a whip, which she swirls suggestively as she evicts the cowboys from the ranch.

The premise of the show, Dick Powell explains to his TV audience, is to illustrate the Spanish influence on the West. This materializes in the form of Hedy astride her horse, asserting: "I do a man's job and I ride wherever my work takes me." She is, viewers learn, Consuela, daughter of a local ranch owner who is confined to his wheelchair, leaving her in charge.

Her tough words are leavened by her feminine buttoned cardigan and ribbon headband; somewhat incongruously for the alleged time period, her eyes are conspicuously highlighted with dark up-sweeping liner. She knows what she wants—inviting the lone rider Frayne (Richards) home. Of course, a romance develops between the two, with Frayne clear on the terms of engagement: "Like your father said, you could use a good solid hand." To remind audiences of what they most admired about the star, viewers watch Consuela as she tries on gowns and jewelry in preparation for dinner. Only in the finale does she once more wield a weapon, but now the payoff comes as she succumbs to Frayne's masculine charms and allows him to carry her off to marriage.

If the Hollywood films that made Hedy's name glamorized its stars and imbued them with an aura of inaccessibility, television concentrated on the opposite effect. Now stars were guests in their spectators' living rooms; celebrities were no longer presented as remote images but ordinary folk just out to have some fun. Some of the guest stars adapted well to this new attempt at democratization; Hedy didn't.

Her remoteness was clear to the audience's surrogates, those members of the public who played in quiz shows alongside the stars. In the 1964 episode of *Celebrity Game Show* in which she appeared with Cliff Arquette, Walter Brennan, Ed Byrnes, Joseph Cotton, Betty Hutton, and Eartha Kitt, the stars were asked a question and the panelists had to guess if the stars had voted yes or no. Questions ranged from "Do plain women make better wives than beautiful women?" and "Should a married man be forced to wear a wedding ring?" to "Do you object to the Hollywood custom of calling everyone 'darling,' 'sweetheart' or 'honey'?" In contrast to the more crowd-pleasing guests, Hedy looked preoccupied during much of the show, and appeared so indifferent that the panelists hesitated to nominate her as the star whose answer they were most confident of guessing. In the first round, she was the last to be questioned and this pattern continued, as the game progressed, with little variance. Indeed, there is something deeply discomforting about watching her attempting to be "ordinary," joining in charades, for instance, in Pat Harrington Jr.'s *Stump the Stars* of 1962, where it takes her a while simply to understand the game.

There is no doubt that from the late 1950s, Hedy was becoming increasingly distracted. She herself ascribed this to a feeling of disorientation that being an émigrée still caused her: "It's difficult to live without roots. But my roots are in Austria! My second home is in California and to have made this change to Texas under most awkward circumstances . . . Some day I want to get a house and boat and live on a lake near Salzburg." Interviewers found their task challenging: "Miss Lamarr, who now has short, dark red hair, is difficult to interview because her conversation tablehops from one subject to the next. That makes her delightfully charming in a European way. But it makes an interview sound like two radios playing at once."[26] In 1957, she was due to appear in Arnold Laven's *Slaughter on Tenth Avenue* but her cameo was edited from the final version.

Marrying J. Howard Lee had promised Hedy financial security but the urge to work pulled her back to the entertainment world. It's doubtful if the marriage ever had a chance. Lee, like Fritz Mandl, liked the idea of marrying glamour; she regarded the marriage as a contract, with benefits to be exploited. They separated in August 1958 and she moved back to Los Angeles, to her home at 614 North Beverly Drive.

The divorce case was once again marked by bitter fighting and an exchange of personal insults. Hedy was now evidently becoming more and more unstable. Claims of stolen goods peppered her conversations and she telephoned DeMille's assistant claiming that the photo he had inscribed to her ("To Hedy Lamarr—for the artistry and magic of Delilah—and for the good work of a good girl") had been stolen and she would like him to send her another.[27] The divorce trial was repeatedly delayed. First, Lee filed suit on the grounds of cruelty; Hedy responded with a countersuit denying his allegations. Then Hedy fired her lawyers. When the case eventually moved to an initial hearing, she sent her movie stand-in, Sylvia Hollis, to appear in her place.

Lee was determined that Hedy should not receive anything near the amount of property and income that she sought (if she had signed a prenuptial agreement, as she told Paul Henreid, there was no mention in court of such a document). In April 1959, the courts awarded her $3,000 a month alimony, which was half of what she wanted. At the same time, it emerged that she had investments in dormant film companies that were unlikely to produce returns and that she was paying $850 a month to lease a house in Beverly Hills that was unoccupied and unfurnished.[28]

As she would often to do from this time forward, Hedy retreated into a self-punishing poverty in which she refused to pay her bills and reduced the family (minus James Loder) to eating TV dinners and staying indoors. Her only occupation was painting. In February 1960, she filed a petition claiming that Lee was behind on his payments.

In the end it was Lee who pursued the divorce and, to the judge's annoyance, Hedy refused to travel to Texas for the court case. In her absence, Lee testified that she had slugged him and called him ugly names. She had been profligate with his money, he insisted, spending almost half a million dollars on living expenses during their marriage. By the time the divorce was finalized and a settlement reached, she had incurred about $73,000 in bills. Under the settlement, Hedy was to receive an interest in 103 oil wells, which would bring her around $3,600 per month, sufficient cash to pay her debts, and another $50,000 in cash.

In reality, much of the money went to her legal fees, which were staggering.[29]

As she looked back on her life and career, she found new reasons to blame her parents for what she felt had gone wrong with her life. In one interview, she mentioned that her father had hit her in the face to express his displeasure at her seeing a boy. She then blamed her parents for consenting to her casting in *Ecstasy* and claimed that fear of her father pushed her into agreeing to the nude sequence. She also said her parents forced her to marry Mandl: "Once she gave up her career and Fritz Mandl moved her to a cavernous, lonely castle in the Black Forest, Hedy learned things about the indisputable father symbol she had taken as her husband," according to a report. "She ran home to her parents. She begged to be taken in but the Keislers [sic], the proud new in-laws of one of Austria's mightiest industrialists, sent her back." Whether through design or carelessness, the interview also described Hedy as a devoted mother to her son James (by Markey) and her son and daughter Tony and Denise (by Loder).[30]

Shortly afterward, Lee married Gene Tierney, who had played, among other high profile roles, the lead in *Laura*, which Hedy had turned down. Hedy continued to live in the rented house at 614 North Beverly Drive. Ironically, Hedy and Gene Tierney were to compete for another role, that of Frieda Winter in *Youngblood Hawke*, which was casting in 1963. The project was one of the last gasps in Jack Warner's production career and had attracted Delmer Daves to direct and Warren Beatty to play the lead, a young author who uses his good looks to exploit older, influential women. Later the central male part went to James Franciscus.

Along with Hedy and Gene Tierney, Bette Davis also sought the role of Frieda Winter. But Warner informed her that the film had already been released with Geneviève Page in the coveted lead. An odd feature of Jack Warner's correspondence with Hedy is that her letter is dated 5 February 1963 and addressed from 1802 North Angelo Drive, Beverly Hills. She opens it with an apology: "Sorry I never had a chance to see you even though I've lived across the street for two years." Yet Warner's reply, dated 14 February, was returned to him with the notification, "Moved. Left no address."[31]

Maybe her mind was already on her next marriage. On 4 March 1963, Hedy married her sixth and final husband, the lawyer Lewis

Boies Jr. At forty-two, he was five years younger than his wife. Boies had worked as part of her legal team on her dispute with Lee and, according to Gene Ringgold, "was such a tower of strength that Hedy, continuing to follow the teachings of childhood, married him."[32]

The marriage took place on notice that was, even by Hedy's standards, short. Although they had been dating for about a year, they turned up abruptly at the home of one of Boies's legal partners, L. Kenneth Say, with a gold ring, and announced that they wanted to get married. Say was friendly with the county clerk and was able to persuade him to produce a marriage license. Another friend, Superior Court judge Joseph L. Joy, arrived at Say's home and performed the rite an hour later. The guests and witnesses were Say's wife Elza and stepdaughter, Cissy; and the judge's wife and son. "I happened to have a bottle of champagne around and we split that and talked for about half an hour," Say said. "Then they left."[33]

In the same month, Hedy posted a dozen abstract paintings for sale at Marymount, a Catholic girls school in Palos Verdes, California. She said that her approach to painting consisted of getting into a pair of Capri pants and pouring paint from can to canvas, losing herself in her art. Asked how she could bear to part with the finished result, Hedy answered with her usual pragmatism, "I'm attached to it, but not that much. I'll sell everything."[34]

From May 1964, Hedy was seeing psychiatrist Dr. Henry Hamilton two or three times a week. Whether her sessions on the couch prompted her decision to split up or whether the marriage had always been a mistake, on 10 May 1965, she sued Boies for divorce, claiming extreme cruelty, specifically that he had threatened her with a baseball bat and a bottle of vodka. She also claimed that she did not have the funds to pay her court costs. She was awarded $1,250 alimony a month for two years, one half of Boies's gross income over $15,000 for the same period, and a half interest in his machine-manufacturing company.

Always a worry, her financial insecurities increasingly preyed on her mind. No job, no husband, no future, no money. Although she did eventually succumb to plastic surgery, it was not reaping its rewards and her other ventures (most notably her paintings) yielded little or no financial return.

When Gene Ringgold interviewed her for an article in 1965, she said she was keeping up with current trends by continually raising her price

HEDY LAMARR

for a starring role. Recently, she had demanded $650,000 per picture plus a percentage of the profits.[35] Whether any such offers were actually coming in could only be a matter of speculation. Publishing her memoir was, as she told Ringgold and others at that time, a safer bet as a money-maker. This goal became a full-time preoccupation.

16

A Filthy, Nauseating Story

THE EVENTUAL PUBLICATION of Hedy's long-planned autobiography, *Ecstasy and Me,* devolved into the first in a series of court cases involving the star. Hedy's encounters with American courts were many and legendary. It is hard to know just why she resorted to litigation so frequently: was she driven by a faith in the fairness of the courts or was she unable to negotiate conflict without third-party intervention?

Undoubtedly, her high-handed approach to settling debts—not paying invoices—resulted in numerous court appearances. Several of these were for outstanding bills in the thousands of dollars. On the odd occasion—such as when her friend Lois Ross thought she was stepping into the washroom in Hedy's house but instead found herself falling down a steep staircase to the cellar—Hedy was the defendant. In this latter instance, Lois Ross lost her case.

Hedy's disregard for the law was as remarkable as her frequent recourse to it. To take one example among many, after her divorce from Boies, Hedy entered a court battle with the Arrowhead Savings and Loan Association over the ownership of her home at 9550 Hidden Valley Road in Coldwater Canyon. The Association alleged that she had received a $65,000 loan for the property but had never completed the purchase. In other words, she was living in a house for which she had received a loan but that she had never bought.

In *Ecstasy and Me,* Hedy recalls a conversation with Cecil B. DeMille. Asked what her favorite scenes through the years had been, she answered diplomatically that she most preferred the love scene in *Samson and Delilah.* "Then I told him the truth. I told him I thought several of my appearances in court contributed most to my satisfaction . . . Everyone acts all the time. I was my most natural and most convincing in court."[1] It's no wonder that, in later life, her favorite TV show was *Judge Judy.*

More publicity would result from her dealings with the publishers of *Ecstasy and Me*. When in 1939 Nathaniel West asked his publisher, the wit Bennett Cerf, about the sales for his latest book, *The Day of the Locust*, Cerf informed his protégé that in the last two weeks, they had sold exactly twenty-two copies. "By God," Cerf declared, "if I ever publish another Hollywood book, it will have to be *My 39 Ways of Making Love* by Hedy Lamarr."[2]

Ecstasy and Me would have pleased Cerf, as indeed would its book's publication history. The latter weaves in and out of another of Hedy's brushes with the law, and an equally notorious one: the first of the star's shoplifting charges. These events, taken together, mark the point where Hedy's reputation shifted from one reflecting a lingering respect and even sympathy for her declining career, to one where she became an object of accumulating disbelief that bordered on ridicule. These events also indicate that her mental balance, which was always delicate, was tipping in the wrong direction.

The sequence of Hedy's court appearances are as follows: In 1965, Hedy signed a $200,000 contract with Bartholemew House, a subsidiary of the Bartell Media Corporation, to publish her autobiography. Bartholemew hired two ghostwriters, Leo Guild and Cy Rice, for the project. Hedy recorded fifty hours of interviews with Rice, and Guild wrote the book using the interviews. In fact, as early as January 1959, Hedy told the press that she was writing her autobiography, to be called *Ecstasy and Me*.

In late 1965, Hedy was becoming increasingly thin and nervous. Anxious about her finances, she was hoping the autobiography would bring in the money she needed. She worried that she would lose her home and there would be nowhere for her family to stay when they visited. The prospect of making her first film in twelve years (*Picture Mommy Dead*) was adding to her stress. These anxieties filtered into her writing:

I have to pause at this critical phase of my private life and career which took place fifteen years ago. Today, I am a woman over fifty with no money for the next meal, and children that I am unable to help.

I recently suffered the extreme indignity of being "exposed" by a reporter. Thus my children, friends, and former fans were treated to a feature story about an old "dishwater blonde" has-been, pushed around by a sheriff's deputy; a woman who had *lived* in Salzburg

Castle . . . who couldn't get a job in *The Sound of Music* which was filmed there; a Beverly Hills goddess who is ashamed to walk on Sunset Boulevard, and plans to quit the United States entirely, if she can find anyplace else where she is still wanted.

Such is my inspiration for getting back to the narrative of 1940, the decade when I was something of a "goddess," at that.[3]

Alarmed about his mother's well-being, Tony Loder moved out of his UCLA dorm and in with her. The house he moved into showed serious neglect, causing it to stand out for all the wrong reasons in its salubrious neighborhood. Some of its windows were broken and no curtains hung from them. The swimming pool was half built, and plants and other rubbish floated in the muddy rainwater that partially filled it. Hedy's 1956 Lincoln Continental was parked outside and someone had pasted the letters H.L. in Blue Chip trading stamps on its dashboard.

She also took up with Marvin Paige, the casting director at ABC-TV, a soft-spoken man in his mid-thirties, who seems to have been happy simply to adore the star. It was Paige who persuaded her to go on the TV show *Shindig,* along with the Dave Clark Five in October 1965, and Paige who mediated between her and Burt Gordon, the producer of the forthcoming *Picture Mommy Dead,* an exercise in cheap horror. Paige, uniquely, had been able to give Hedy back her confidence. She was to return to the big screen.

In 1966, as her comeback loomed, Hedy was charged with shoplifting. An undignified event that reflected well on nobody, it began on January 27 with the actress feeling unwell and dizzy. The previous night, she had watched *The Pawnbroker* (1964), Sidney Lumet's Holocaust drama, on television and found the film and the memories of the war that it sparked deeply upsetting. *The Pawnbroker* was the first major American film to explore what it meant to escape the Holocaust. Its central character, Sol Nazerman (Rod Steiger), has witnessed his wife being forced into prostitution in the camps as well as the deportation of their two children. Nazerman has come to live in New York but has lost his ability to feel emotion. Hedy was increasingly feeling alienated from American culture herself and, as she grew older, she found herself torn between two cultures: one that had nurtured her and one that had given her the opportunity to reinvent herself, but both of which had rejected her.

HEDY LAMARR

On the afternoon of the 27th, she visited her physician, who gave her a vitamin shot. Driving away, she swerved on the road and was pulled over by a policeman who accused her of drunk driving, though she was able to reassure him that she did not drink. She hadn't eaten all day by the time she drove to the May Company department store. There she went shopping with her manager, Earl Mills. Mills left her in the store, apparently unaware that she was dropping item after item into her shopping bag, and went to fetch the car. According to Hedy's account, she had expected him to pay for the goods and had signed a blank check for him to use. Later, Mills made it clear through his attorney that he knew nothing of the shoplifting.

Leaving the store, Hedy was picked up by a female store detective, Helen McGarry, who had recognized the actress and followed her around the store as she helped herself to the goods, including a knitted suit, some panties, cheap makeup, and eight birthday cards. The value of the items totaled $86. When McGarry stopped Hedy outside the store, the actress said that she wanted to sit down. McGarry led her back into the store. "I'll pay for these things and that will settle everything," Hedy assured the night service manager, Howard W. Palmer, adding that she had already been allowed to do this by Magnin's and Neiman-Marcus. McGarry, however, was certain she had seen Hedy shoplift before and May's called the police. Two policemen were dispatched to the store and one of them, James Flowerre, asked Hedy if she were still acting. "Yes, and this is what these are for," she replied. She asked the other officer, William A. Welch, why she was being arrested. On hearing the explanation, she commented, "Other stores let me do it."

The actress was taken to the Sybil Brand Institute (the women's jail) and shortly before 2 a.m. she was released, after a $500 bail bond was paid on her behalf. Marvin Paige was waiting at the door to meet her. He took her back to her house and they rehearsed her lines for *Picture Mommy Dead;* she was word-perfect.

The next day, while eating at the upscale Bistro Restaurant, Hedy was pulled before news cameras for a swiftly arranged press conference. At her side were her lawyer, Arthur G. Lawrence, and the press agent for *Picture Mommy Dead*. Looking dazed, the fifty-one-year-old faced the cameras from the podium. "Did you steal the items?" "Are you broke?" The questions came hard and fast from the fifty or so gathered journalists. Although she had arrived neatly dressed, with her hair freshly styled,

Hedy soon began to appear confused. Asked about the shopping bag, she mumbled, "I had the shoes, yes, so I must have had the shopping bag," and talked about visiting the store to buy shoes and being approached by "some woman," presumably the store detective. She started rooting in her handbag and pulled out two checks. These she said totaled $14,000. "Why would I steal if I had $14,000?" Hedy demanded. At this point, the press agent broke in and the reason for the press conference became clearer to some, who began to suspect that it had been stage-managed to promote the new film. The strange nature of the event increased when, in answer to a question, Hedy told the group that the coat she was wearing had been purchased from the same May's store. "I like it very much," she added.

"Are you under the care of a psychiatrist?" one reporter asked her. "No, but you should be," she replied. By now, the press was beginning to feel more than a twinge of pity for the confused figure before them. "Are you feeling well these days?" a TV reporter asked her more gently. "Yes," she said. "You know my son is six feet four." Mercifully, her attorney now intervened. "My client has paid you the courtesy of meeting you here," he announced as the press agent tried to slip in another plug for the forth-coming film. "Now we will leave." Hedy rose, quickly, awkwardly, and then, falling back on her acting instincts, pulled herself together and strode out of the room. As she left, a middle-aged fan standing outside the restaurant turned on the reporters. "Why don't you leave her alone?" she demanded. "Let her be a star."[4]

"This unfortunate happening will make no difference in our plans," announced *Picture Mommy Dead*'s producer/director, Bert Gordon. "I'm behind her 100 percent." Soon after, they replaced Hedy with Martha Hyer. Hedy gave the press confused responses to this news, alternating between comments such as, "I couldn't have cared less . . . I was just a mechanical instrument to be used," to "I was doing everything they wanted me to do . . . I posed for stills . . . I went to a press conference. I tried my best . . . I would have liked to have done it." Then she announced that she was retiring to write her memoir.[5]

On 2 February, when a Beverly Hills psychiatrist examined her, he found Hedy to be suffering from stress and to be confused about recent events. Most of all, she seemed unwilling to engage with reality.

Meanwhile, her few remaining Hollywood friends rallied behind her. Mary Pickford telegrammed the May Company on her behalf, begging Tom May, whom she knew, to consider that the actress was undergoing psychiatric treatment and adding that surely she had been punished enough by the loss of *Picture Mommy Dead*. Marvin Paige later said he was certain that the whole event had been engineered by Hedy's "so-called agent" to garner publicity for her return to the screen, which, if true, was a strategy that backfired.[6]

The court case opened under Municipal Judge Eric Auerbach on 19 April 1966. Attracted by press coverage of the event, crowds stood outside the Los Angeles Municipal Court as Hedy entered, wearing a beige suit and an elegant straw hat. She signed autographs and moved indoors accompanied by her attorney, Jordan Wank. A jury of seven women and five men listened in fascination over the next six days as the case was outlined. Wank stated that he would argue that his client suffered a mental lapse due to nervous strain; later, however, he focused more on Hedy's intention, which he claimed was to pay for the goods. Someone in her position shopped differently than the rest of us, he explained to the jurors. For added effect, he claimed that McGarry and Palmer were out to get his client and invoked a phrase that would resonate with her history: "These are Gestapo tactics." The young Departmental City Attorney, Ira K. Reiner, however, told the courtroom that Hedy had in fact removed the items deliberately and by stealth, which prompted a previously impassive Hedy to slam her kid-gloved hand angrily down on the table.

Tony Loder testified on his mother's behalf. "She was worried because she was not as beautiful as she once was," he told the Los Angeles Municipal Court. "She didn't think she looked very good. She had a tooth infection. Her jaw was swelled the size of a golf ball." Two psychiatrists for the defense, including Dr. Hamilton, also testified that Hedy was so confused that she did not know what she was doing when she lifted the goods. She was, they testified, distressed at the end of her recent marriage and the threat to her property; and she was ill.

Elegantly dressed on each day of her court appearance, Hedy responded to questions with a combination of guilelessness and outrage. "I have never experienced anything like that before," she told the jury, referring to the events around the case. "I have always been forgetful but I was more so at this time. I had so much on my mind." Later a ripple of laughter ran through the courtroom when, asked by her attorney why she had included in her items a pair of baby-blue stretch slippers, she responded, "I wanted them to keep my feet warm." The police, she said, had been very nice. "I have never been to jail before," she told the room. "It was so fascinating since I'm writing a book." Asked what the book was about, she replied, "My life." Would she tell all? "Yes."

During the case, two more May Company employees testified that they had spotted Hedy shoplifting in November and December 1965, though the actress denied that she had stolen the clothes they named and the evidence was removed as being prejudicial.

After the six-day trial, the jury retired for five hours of deliberation. Midway through, they were deadlocked and returned to ask the judge to repeat his instructions. At 5:28 pm, they returned to pronounce a verdict of "not guilty." The forty-five spectators in the court burst into applause for which they were duly reprimanded by the bailiff. Guided to the box by Jordan Wank, Hedy shook each of the jury members' hands, saying either "Thank-you, very much" or "I knew I would get fair treatment." She then kissed Wank, her manager, and actor Bob Osborne, who had been at her side during the trial. Next she held an impromptu press conference and signed autographs in the court. City Attorney Roger Arnebergh was not pleased with the outcome. Noting that he was not commenting on any particular case, he fulminated that:

> In the performance of my duties as city attorney, it has always been my policy to treat all persons equally under the law. It is not my view that people who are, or have been, famous are entitled to special privileges, privileges which include placing them above the law. Neither is it my belief that financial reverses grant a license to steal. Fortunately most juries agree with me. Otherwise I could not in good conscience continue to prosecute the ordinary person for similar violations of the law. If the famous are to be immune from the law, then in fairness the law should not be enforced against the ordinary individual.[7]

Hedy responded by lodging a claim against May and company for false arrest, assault and battery, false imprisonment, and malicious prosecution.[8]

Ira Reiner had been particularly solicitous toward the Hollywood star. During the trial, when the jurors were out to lunch, he walked into the jury assembly room and found her lying flat on the table, resting. Not wanting to disturb her, he quickly walked out. After the trial, about half the jurors approached him and said they knew she was guilty, but it was clear to them he didn't want them to convict her. "That was the last time I was Mr. Nice Guy in the courtroom," Reiner said years later, at the end of a stellar career.[9]

On May 11, as the court case came to an end, *Ecstasy* was rereleased in Los Angeles at the Cinema Theater, this time with the scant dialogue dubbed in English. One may speculate whether this was an opportunistic move, prompted by Hedy's return to the headlines, or pure coincidence.

In July 1966, Earl Mills announced that Hedy would be appearing in a new film, *Circle,* which would start shooting in October or November in Washington, D.C. Nothing more was heard of it. Her next film appearance was by default. In 1966, Andy Warhol's disciple Ronald Tavel shot the sixty-six-minute feature titled variously *Hedy* or *Lives and Loves of Hedy Lamarr* or *Hedy Goes Shopping.* In it, the transvestite Mario Montez enacts scenes from the life of its subject, including the shoplifting arrest and her plastic surgery (he said that he fully empathized with Hedy). The soundtrack was supplied by Lou Reed and John Cale. An instant hit on the college circuit, the film shocked older viewers with its free interpretation of the star's life as well as its bricolage aesthetic. For instance, in the background of one shot, viewers see the backstage crew moving scenery for the next shot; no attempt is made to render the settings realistic, and the cast simply moves from one corner of the Factory to another to film. In the opening scenes, Hedy/Montez is preparing to go under the knife in order to return to the fourteen-year-old girl she believes herself to be. As she rambles on about how beautiful she is, the surgeon (played by Tavel) declares, "I'll give you the face of an eighty-year old hag!" Next she goes shopping, where she is arrested by another Warhol protégée, Mary Woronov. Following this, she briefly returns home to an apartment filled with stolen goods before heading to court, singing "I am Pretty" and "Young at Heart" while her husbands dance around her. In court, she is tried by the judge (Tavel again) and her jury (the same people who just appeared as her husbands). If the project sounds a tad unsympathetic, not to say downright exploitative, toward its subject, Mario Montez performs Hedy with a detachment that declares, for the star, the show will go on. Thus he/she doggedly goes about her day, primping for the camera and posing at every opportunity, no matter how rudely or disrespectfully she is treated.

In September 1966, Hedy was back in court, this time on her own volition, and once again in a case marked by its unseemly nature. Now she was trying to halt the publication of her autobiography. Suing Bartholemew House for $9.6 million, she claimed the book was "false, scandalous and vulgar." Isaac Pacht, attorney for the publishers, gave those in the courtroom a taste of what was in the book:

> "We are dealing with the experiences, mostly sexual, of a woman out of pictures for fifteen years. She was in the doldrums as far as the picture business is concerned, and she was desperate to revive her name in the public mind. The only thing she had to sell was her sex life.

> "This woman has been married to six men," he continued. "She discarded six of these husbands. But you and I are not interested in that."

> "Do you think this is a filthy book?" Judge Nutter enquired of Pacht.

> "The language was not very elevating," came the reply, "but sex was the theme of this woman's life."[10]

Conceding that Hedy had recorded fifteen hours of interviews with Cy Rice, Hedy's attorney, Leo Burgard argued that the material had been substantially altered by ghostwriter Leo Guild. Many salacious scenes had been added to the manuscript and the book now went "far beyond the bounds of reality and propriety."

"In some parts," Burgard informed the judge, "I was shocked, if not nauseated, and thought it was a filthy thing."[11]

Pacht hit back with the comment that Burgard's client's reputation for morality, integrity, and honesty could not be damaged as it was already notoriously bad. Although Burgard claimed that Hedy had only received $30,000 for the publication, Pacht said that she had been paid $80,000 and had shopped for a Bentley automobile as well. He also said that Hedy had approved the manuscript in writing, initialing her name on every page.

Superior Court judge Ralph H. Nutter agreed with all concerned, adding that the autobiography was, "filthy, nauseating and designed to exploit the worst instincts of human beings." However, he could find no grounds to halt its publication.[12] The case was settled out of court and the offending sections of the book remained in place.

Still, the legal ramifications of *Ecstasy and Me* rumbled on. In February 1967, Hollywood journalist Gene Ringgold sued Hedy, Leo Guild, and Bartholemew House, claiming that large portions of the book had been lifted directly from an article he had written in the July 1965 issue of *Screen Facts* magazine. Indeed, both article and book shared much of the same material, but these facts were already in the public domain in other press reports. Ringgold's useful article contains none of the mildly pornographic details that so offended many of the book's readers, nor its pop-psychology insights.

The lawsuits continued when, in May 1967, Cy Rice and Leo Guild sued the Macfadden-Bartell Corp. and Hedy over the book for unpaid royalties. Hedy's manager Earl Mills then sued Hedy for $300,000, claiming that she had agreed to pay him 10 percent of the royalties. He also said he was owed $3,000 for securing the book contract and that he had lent her $750, which she had not paid him back.[13]

By late 1967 *Ecstasy and Me* was reaching number one in the *New York Times* best-seller list, despite or because of its largely derisive reviews. Hedy moved to capitalize on its success by announcing the launch of a new perfume, called, unsurprisingly, Ecstasy. A notice was placed in the newspapers looking for distributors who would pay from $1,500 to $10,000 for the privilege of access to the product. Nothing seems to have come of the venture, although later an Ecstasy perfume was indeed branded and produced.

On 19 February 1969, Hedy filed a $21 million suit against the publishers, the writers, her literary agent, one lawyer, and one psychiatrist claiming that in December 1965, they had conspired to "fraudulently reap untold profits by knowingly and willfully causing the publication of a book falsely and maliciously alleged by defendants to be an autobiography."[14] She claimed that what the ghostwriters had produced was largely untrue; the book was, she stated, "deliberately written as an obscene, shocking, scandalous, naughty, wanton, fleshy, sensual, lecherous, lustful and scarlet version" of her life. The Court of Appeals in Albany dismissed the case, ruling that it lacked jurisdiction because Hedy's lawyers had not proved that the actions leading to the publication of the book occurred in New York State. In June 1966, Bartholemew House sold its rights to Fawcett Publications for a $200,000 advance against royalties.[15]

Just why Hedy went to such lengths to claw back her own publication is not clear. She may simply have been after greater publicity or a higher royalty deal; or she may have had genuine reservations about *Ecstasy and Me*'s dubious qualities. So what of the book and its supposed inaccuracies and lewdness?

Ecstasy and Me contains two introductions. The first is by a psychologist, Philip Lambert, who suggests that the book was written as a form of therapy that would be as beneficial for the "guilt-ridden" reader as for Hedy herself. At the same time, he seems to favor Hedy's self-diagnosis as oversexed and, in a thoroughly 1960s manner, represents this as taking a stand against contemporary culture's moral restrictions. "Her admitted talent for quick and joyful orgasm," he wrote, "indicates an uncomplicated natural sex response. Her curious search for new love-play settings and her candid delight in unexpected sexual episodes place her in a position of psychological unassailability."[16] The second introduction again suggests some kind of mental illness, this time induced by Hollywood's unreasonable demands on its actresses.

In 1972, when Christopher Young interviewed Hedy for his book *The Films of Hedy Lamarr,* he found that she didn't recall much of her early work. The "factual" content of *Ecstasy and Me* reflects this and most of the information in it could be found in press cuttings. Thus, the detail in Hedy's memoir is largely correct, as are dates of her marriages, her children's births, and so on. Hedy's comments on her films, one may assume, are genuine and the tone of voice seems to be hers—detached, rueful, and caught between acknowledging her brief success and dismissing the industry that created it. As a commentary on her professional life, her autobiography is, then, of value. The sudden lurches in register, outbreaks of self-pity, mildly titillating reminiscences, particularly of lesbian encounters and masochistic sex games, the tendency to speak of herself in the third-person all ring true, if not in fact, then in tone.

She was certainly, by the late 1960s, verging on delusional and had a tendency in interviews to speak in a disjointed fashion that left journalists feeling more than slightly disconnected themselves. Whether there was any accuracy to the sexual reminiscences is another matter. Hollywood gossip does not seem to have registered her lesbian relationships; that is, unless one takes the book by Devra Hill and Jody Babydol Gibson seriously. That she did have multiple sexual encounters, many of them with her leading men, is the stuff of innumerable Hollywood histories, not all, by any means, referenced here and many inspired by wishful thinking. Unquestionably, Hedy loved to have sex with men, and that was, in part, how she defined herself. It would be simplistic, however, simply to describe her as a nymphomaniac. Underlying the more coherent parts of *Ecstasy and Me* is a tension in Hedy's identity: how she saw herself and how the public saw her. Writing in 1952, journalist Dorothy Kilgallan commented: "The truth about Hedy is this: There are two of her. One is the siren she appears to be, the other is the unremarkable, prosaic, humorless Viennese girl that she is. In her adventures with men, her personality has never managed to live up to the excitement of her façade."[17]

The course of Hedy's life was, she acknowledges in *Ecstasy and Me*, dictated by her extraordinary beauty. Its icy qualities drew men to her, and they grew angry when they found themselves unable to crack her glacial surface. Yet, she needed their admiration to confirm her identity, and she confirmed their admiration by having sex with them. To return to George Sanders, who termed himself a "professional cad," and who appreciated beauty in women, as you might appreciate a work of art:

To many a beautiful woman her beauty is a religion, a vocation, a profession, and her life's work. To her, men are merely accessories which, if carefully chosen, enhance her beauty.

They act as a sort of mirror—which is why they are indispensable to her. In their faces she sees herself. Their desire is a reflection of her desirability. Their interest in her conversation is a reflection of her wit. Their love is a reflection of her endearing nature. As she sweeps through life, she will glance at men so that she may see mirrored in their faces all the virtues she believes she possesses.[18]

"Never stay too long, anywhere, with anyone—that is my slogan," Hedy told Gladys Hall.[19] It seems to have been a slogan that she adhered to well into her old age. Men were accessories to Hedy Lamarr, and they seldom lasted beyond their immediate usefulness to her. Her marriages broke down because her husbands ignored her, she said, or hit her. They probably broke down because of a profound mutual misunderstanding of the consequences of marrying an image, and the discovery that behind that image stood a damaged, brilliant, contradictory, and frustrated woman. They ended because Hedy had already moved on.

She was also deeply traumatized by her loss of country and its fate under the Nazis. Stefan Zweig, who also grew up as a Jew in Vienna, expressed it this way: "I must acknowledge with dismay that for a long time past I have not belonged to the people of my country any more than I belong to the English or the Americans. To the former [Zweig's hosts in exile] I have never become wholly linked. My feeling is that the world in which I grew up and the world of today, and the world between the two, are entirely separate worlds . . . All the bridges between our today and our yesterday and our yesterdays have been burnt."[20] Zweig committed suicide not long after writing this. Hedy also found herself increasingly estranged from her old world and from her adopted country, without an identity or a place where she felt at home. Her only security had been her beauty and that she was losing.

It's too late now to uncouple *Ecstasy and Me* from the myth of Hedy Lamarr. So many subsequent accounts of her life have drawn from its often-breathless prose that it has become "the official story." Nor are there any strong grounds for separating Hedy from its writing, even if it omits much of her life, from her Jewishness and its consequences to her part in the invention of Spread Spectrum technology.

By the late 1960s, as the public attention surrounding Hedy's autobiography and various lawsuits seemed to be waning, Hedy found herself once again on her own. Still estranged, her son James Loder was in Milwaukee. Denise had married Robert Colton, a pitcher in the Pittsburgh Pirate chain, on 10 July 1965; Marvin Neal (cousin to Patricia Neal) gave the bride away and Tony Loder, who was now trying his hand on Broadway, served as best man. Hedy moved into an apartment in Beverly Glen, a modest, three-roomed affair, with only "H. L." next to "Room 106" to identify its occupant. In fact, the lawsuits had only just begun.

In August 1967, Hedy, now fifty-two, accused a forty-year old man, Donald Blyth, a business-machine repairman for Los Angeles city schools, of raping her at gunpoint. She had known and dated him for six months, she told the court. Blyth insisted that she had accepted his advances. Blyth's personal interests emerged in the court as, at best, macabre. He liked to keep "people" in jars, Hedy told the judge. "I don't know why she was shocked, no one else is," Blyth responded. "I have a five-month-old baby and a fetus that I got from a hospital in the east; a mummy, and also a unicorn."[21]

The next day, Hedy dropped the case, announcing that for her physical and mental well-being, she did not wish to pursue it. Blyth, in turn, sued her for $1 million for "loss of reputation" and other damages. He told the court that he had introduced a number of girls to Hedy and she had grown jealous. He was awarded $15,000.

In October 1968, Hedy left California and went to live in an apartment in New York. After she left, her old friend Gloria Geale supervised a four-day auction of the star's goods. As with her 1951 auction, the sale took place at Arthur Goode's gallery and in the hot Los Angeles sun, prospective purchasers and curious fans queued to preview the wares. "When does the clothing go on sale?" a woman standing at the door asked. "What size are the dresses?"

"Ten and twelve, I think," answered Geale.

"What size are the shoes?"[22]

Others sniggered over the seller's reputation. One, on hearing that she had moved to New York quipped, "Now, she's Macy's worry."

Interestingly, the inventory for this sale included what the auctioneer termed "a rare collection of 18th and 19th century Judaica"; rare indeed, in that it suggested that Hedy retained some interest in her religious heritage. The listing of these items occasioned a heated discussion in the crowd, with one couple arguing that she was a convert to Judaism and another countering that she was not Jewish and these items did not belong to her. The journalist sent by the *Los Angeles Times* asked Louie Wass, father-in-law of Arthur Goode, to settle the dispute. "She's not Jewish," Wass told him. "The collection belongs to a friend of hers." In any event,

Christ figures rubbed shoulders with Passover plates, and the journalist counted sixteen mattresses.

Despite the suggestive sales patter (a loveseat went under the hammer with the words, "I can tell you how it was made and who was made on it"), it was the second auction of personal affairs, mostly lingerie, that attracted the seamier set. "A lot of these clothes are being bought by men who don't have wives or secondhand stores," someone whispered, "every morning these creeps will get up and stroke the dresses." Another man handed over $23 for a bundle of items: "My wife read Lamarr's book, you know, *Ecstasy and Me,* and she wants the clothes because she thinks maybe Hedy wore this or that in bed. It's, you know, sultry, sexy."

In the end, the sale raised over $300,000.[23] This was not enough for Hedy; in October 1969, she tried to extract more money from the richest of her ex-husbands, W. Howard Lee. Claiming that he had not fully disclosed the value of his community property, she filed suit in Houston, Texas, for a further $26 million.

Surprisingly, Hedy was able to resume her television career in the late 1960s. In September 1966, she appeared on *Bob Hope Presents,* alongside seventeen of Hope's other famous costars (including Lucille Ball, Dorothy Lamour, and Joan Fontaine). In June 1969, she was a guest on the *Dick Cavett Show.* This was followed by appearances on the *David Frost Show* (August 1969), and two appearances on the *Merv Griffin Show,* in August 1969 and June 1970, which were her last.

She had moved to New York, she told a journalist, to concentrate on her legal claims.[24] This she did: In 1971, at fifty-seven, her air-conditioning failed and Hedy called a repairman. Subsequently, she claimed the repairman raped her and he was arrested. He then brought a case of false arrest against her and she failed to turn up in court. In her absence, she was found guilty and ordered to pay a fine of $15,000. In 1972, she was sued by the State of California for unpaid back taxes.

At the same time, it was apparent her tendency to free-associate verbally, a style of thinking out loud that erupted on occasion in *Ecstasy and Me,* was increasingly undermining her ability to communicate rationally:

> I looked into a cat's eyes once. The cat went to sleep. A lady said, "You have higher powers." The lady said so, too. I'm Lourdes, let's face it. I have a power that can bring things about. I'm a little person suing a big company, but I'm going to win because I know I'm right.

A man held a gun against my head one time in bed. Another man tried to push me out of a 22-story window. Yesterday, a girl said, "Do you mind if I say I'm your cousin?" I want to be independent. When I win, we will all get on that yacht. We will say, "Where to?" Portofino . . . St. Jean de Luz . . . Ha![25]

17

Final Years

In 1972, Hedy took a room at the Blackstone Hotel, where she spent the next three years. "To live in a hotel," she said, "means that I don't live here. It's like a bridge. It means I'm finally away from California, where we made fine films. That was the Golden Years. They've gone; that doesn't exist any more . . . But I would like to go back, to Europe, to Vienna, because my heart is there."[1] She liked staying up watching old films, often her own, on television and sleeping late in the morning, fortifying herself with vitamin pills and the occasional steak tartar. Never much of a drinker, she seldom touched alcohol and never smoked.

Her next move was to a small apartment on 57th Street. As she withdrew further and further to a world peopled with occasional visits from gay men and the odd friend from the old days, so newspaper reports of her lifestyle became increasingly prurient, to the point of punishing, as if she were somehow at fault for failing to live up to her impossible screen image, for growing old so visibly, for flaunting her poverty.

She sued the newspapers, as many and as often as she was able. In 1974, she filed a $10 million invasion of privacy lawsuit in Manhattan Supreme Court charging Warner Bros. and Mel Brooks with exploiting her name without permission in *Blazing Saddles*. One of the film's characters is called Hedley Lamarr. She settled out of court for $1,000. "I apologized for almost using her name . . . I don't think she got the joke," Brooks muses on the DVD release. Apparently, however, it eluded her attention that Frank Loesser created a character named Hedy LaRue in his musical, *How to Succeed in Business Without Really Trying*.[2]

Although it was now twenty years since her last film, Hedy did not surrender. She continued to have plastic surgery on her face and body and continued to work on scripts that would ensure her return to the screen. In 1974, *Variety* reported that the screenplay Hedy had been working on for the last three years with actor-writer Christopher Taaj was now completed. The title role was to be a composite of the "late Montgomery Clift, Judy Garland, Marilyn Monroe, James Dean and a still-living personality."[3]

The occasional journalist managed to track down the star. One, Bob Edison, asked her if there were any words she lived by. Her response was to quote a poem by Pushkin that Reginald Gardiner once taught her:

Thus, wicked fate has ruled forever
That fools for happiness be fit
While those who happen to be clever
Must always suffer woe from wit.[4]

Others continued to battle with disentangling her free-associating responses to questions. Most were shown the door.

In 1975, news had filtered out that Hedy was going blind; by the end of her life she was legally blind. In June 1975, however, she had her cataracts removed and regained her vision. Her ophthalmologist, Dr. Charles Kelman, later related that she had intimated that payment in kind might be in the cards.[5] Energized by her return to sight, she announced that she would open boutiques in New York and London to carry a line of clothing and jewelry under the Lamarr label.

On 3 February 1977, her mother, who had been living with Tony Loder in Glendale, Los Angeles, died. Rumors had always circulated that Hedy had little time for her mother and they do not seem to have been close.

Her vision again deteriorated and in the late 1970s, she moved to a Renoir Arms apartment in the east 70s. According to filmmaker and Hollywood chronicler Kenneth Anger, it was a "respectable looking apartment house until you went into her apartment and it looked like a slum . . . She was nearly blind at the time and she didn't see how dirty it was and she wouldn't let any maid come in to clean it." Not surprisingly, Anger noted that, "she wasn't part of the party scene. She was like a recluse, she was in this strange private world of her apartment. She wouldn't go out much."[6] Descriptions of her slumlike lifestyle seeped out to an ever prurient press, and in June 1978 the *National Enquirer* ran a typically nasty story describing her as "old and ugly" and a "pathetic recluse," who "lives in an unkempt one-room apartment." She sued them.[7]

Undaunted, Hedy continued to work her way through court cases, including one in 1980 where she filed a $3 million libel suit claiming that she had been defamed in a story and photograph of a two-headed goat named Hedy Lamarr.

Then, in July 1981, Hedy received implanted lenses and once more her sight dramatically improved. Suddenly and briefly, she found herself injected with energy and dropped her reclusive lifestyle. She picked up again with her old friends, although no one could now fail to notice that the years of plastic surgery were taking their toll and her face had long lost its beauty. Still, she announced that she would be returning to acting. At the same time, Tony Loder was reported to be down on his luck and forced to sell some of his mother's furs to support his family of three small children.[8] It seems too that, at this time, he traveled to England to attempt a reunion with his father but John Loder was uninterested, as it appears he always had been, in developing a relationship with his son. In the end, Hedy's return to the screen was indirect—as the inspiration for the replicant Rachel in Ridley Scott's 1982 release *Blade Runner*.

In the early eighties, she entered a new relationship, with the colorful Barnard (Barnie) Sackett. Sackett was no stranger to notoriety; during the war he had worked for the American Forces Network (AFN). After he was discharged in 1946, he penned his own satirical soap opera, *Rough in the E.T.,* which questioned the reasons for the continuation of military activities and other issues including the detention of Japanese Americans and the privileges held by top brass. The authorities took badly to this scion of Germantown's indiscretions and he found himself persona non grata for many decades after.

He followed *Rough in the E.T.* with a showbiz career that included more writing for radio, acting as personal manager to Sylvia Syms, and running the Playhouse in the Park in Philadelphia. Part of Sackett's claim to fame also rests on the number of celebrity lovers he enjoyed. Outside of Hedy, they apparently included Bette Davis and Corrine Calvet, and his friendships included Mae West and Orson Welles. He was briefly married in the 1970s, when he lived in Germantown. By the time he and Hedy moved into a penthouse in New York's salubrious Gramercy Park, his filmmaking days—primarily as a producer of exploitation pictures— were over. A small role in the 1965 cult lesbian fantasy thriller *Bad Girls*

Go to Hell (Doris Wishman) had not led to bigger parts and Sackett was planning a comeback with his new lover. "It was really Hedy who convinced me that I was wasting my time and my talent on a lot of crap," Sackett told an interviewer. "She says I have a lot of nervous creative energy." Their project had the working title of *Sugar, Sex and Savages*. In the same interview, Hedy appeared "swinging in from the bedroom in her Da-Glo minishift and go-go boots doing what appeared to be a hybrid of hula and hopscotch." Questioned as to what she was doing, she replied: "It is called the Frog. . . . I am not too bad for a grandmother, am I?"[9] Both shared a sense of exclusion from the Hollywood in-crowd and for a while it looked like another marriage might be in the wings.

Hedy took to holidaying in the Caribbean, and it was on a beach in Aruba that Arlene Roxbury was startled to fall into a conversation with a tall sixty-six-year-old with a foreign accent and a bright pink bikini. Roxbury became Hedy's confidante and was to see her or chat with her on the phone every day, often four or five times, to the end of Hedy's life. The Roxburys had a house on Long Island with a pool, and when they returned from the Caribbean, they invited Hedy, knowing that she loved to swim. She said, "That would be delightful. I would love it." As Roxbury remembered:

> I had a separate bedroom for her. She had her own privacy. She loved to watch television. One night, we were sitting in the room watching television and her movie came on, *White Cargo*. She loved to lay on the floor, on her stomach and just watch like that. As we were watching the movie, which was in black and white, she was telling us which color the dress was, little tidbits about the movie she played in. That was interesting watching her on the TV screen and seeing her laying on the floor watching herself and explaining all of this to us.[10]

For the next seven or eight years, Hedy continued to spend a month or more in Aruba, taking a room in a hotel and forming the occasional friendship. She loved the warm water and the sun. Never as broke as she liked to make out, by now she received a small pension from the Screen Actors Guild and her day-to-day costs were modest. Of her Hollywood friendships, few remained, though she and Ann Southern stayed in touch.

Back in New York, the relationship with Barnie Sackett ended but she and Taaj kept in contact. Both never gave up, and in 1985, Taaj was performing numbers that they had jointly penned, including "Alone in the City" and "Who Knows What I'll Find Tonight" in a Manhattan night club.

Hedy would regularly sail out of her small Manhattan apartment onto the streets of New York dressed in jeans, with a handkerchief covering her now platinum blonde hair. Dining in less-than-glamorous eateries, she would respond to the odd passerby who thought they recognized her, with "Hedy? My name is Mimsy."[11]

In the late 1980s, Hedy moved to Altamonte Springs, a retirement community in Florida. She loved the warmth and sun and the proximity to the water. Neighbors passing by late at night would glimpse her swimming in the pool. Most didn't know who she was.

In August 1991 she was once again arrested for shoplifting goods (including eye drops and a laxative) to the value of $21.48 from a drugstore in Altamonte Springs. She told her neighbor Peter Giglio that she had gone shopping on the arm of a transvestite friend, and he took some cosmetics and put them in her handbag without her knowing it. As soon as she left the store, the alarm went off and the police were called.[12] Locally, it was well known that the retired star was light-fingered.

Finally, too, the package of jewels and valuables that she had taken with her from her life with Fritz Mandl, her security, vanished; this time, the paper bag was not to return.

In these last years, she was closer to her family than she had been before, or at least to Tony and Denise Loder and her grandson Tim (James's son), who had moved to Florida. Later, however, when they reflected on their childhood, Tony and Denise were less sure about their relationship with their mother; "She should have never been a mother," according to Denise. Tony agreed, "She enjoyed being a film star. I don't think she enjoyed being a mother."

"We were shipped off to summer camp in the summer and boarding schools in winter," Denise further remembered.

"I grew up in fear," Tony continued. "I was afraid to wake her up, afraid to say the wrong thing because she took a swing at you and smacked you in the face as hard as she could."

"Our Mom was really hard on both of us," Denise said. "There was a huge void where there should have been nurturing. There was always the mixed emotions; as much as I loved talking to her, I dreaded talking to her as well. I was just missing my Mom so much, I would take my allowance and buy Hedy Lamarr paper dolls and look at the doll and look at my Mommy and cry and cry and cry so much that the paper clothes would get all wrinkled 'cos they would get all wet all the time. She was often on set making a film and the paper doll couldn't sing Austrian lullabies."[13]

According to James Loder, whose son Tim tracked down her address, James and his "adoptive" mother reached some kind of reconciliation. They talked on the phone from time to time; in her case, an activity that could last for hours. In 1995, James traveled from Nebraska to visit his mother: "she reminded me of what I could have had and I just feel . . . that I made my own way. I'm not a rich man but I have enough." They talked and played some games, but "she did remind me that I made my choice."[14] Later Denise and Tony said in court that James and Hedy had nothing to do with each other.

A home movie from 1996 shows Hedy with her hair now dyed cerise, posing on her sofa. Her face has fallen from the falsely elevated cheekbones, the skin is gathering around oddly pouting lips, and the neck is pulled this way and that, but she seems game for the camera. She points out images of herself, and then takes a Delilah-moment back on the sofa. In another sudden movement, she is laying out on her bed, rolling in her blanket, as if it were a silk sheet. She models an Austrian hat, shows off her photographs of Tony and Denise, and then strikes a mock pose for "Mr. DeMille."[15] Still the occasional press photographer made their way to Florida. On 5 November 1996, the *National Enquirer* again covered her decline, publishing a photo of the star wearing a scarf and sunglasses, her skin puckered and lined, with a headline that suggested sympathy but was really an invitation for readers to feast on a narrative of fallen beauty.

It was in the 1990s too that Hedy's reputation as a forgotten inventor began to grow. In the early 1980s, Robert Price, an electrical engineer in Lexington, Massachusetts, unsuccessfully tried to persuade Congress to award Hedy a Medal of Honor. Now, suddenly, it seemed like every official scientific organization wanted to recognize her. She received, in short succession, the Millstar award from Lockheed, the Bulbie Gnass Spirit of Achievement Award, the Electronic Frontier Foundation (EFF) Award, the Chariot Award of the Inventors Club of America, and the Viktor Kaplan Medal from Austria. David Hughes had long lobbied for her and Antheil's recognition as scientists and it was he who was behind the EFF's decision to recognize their achievement in 1997. "Even today," he wrote in his citation:

> 44 years after this young woman, not operating out of a research or university center, grasped and articulated the novel technical ideas underlying spread spectrum, and which she pursued to the point of a formal US Patent, the offering of these ideas to the public, very few, even technically savvy Americans understand today how, and why spread spectrum works, or its significance in providing a revolutionary form of high speed, quite secure, non-interfering (shared spectrum) data communications.[16]

Tony Loder accepted the award from the EFF on his mother's behalf and played a message that she had taped to the audience. She acknowledged them for honoring her; of her invention she said, "I hope it will do you good as well. I feel good about it and it was not done in vain."[17]

He also accepted the Victor Kaplan Medal (Austria's most prestigious scientific honor for an inventor) on Hedy's behalf in October 1998. This recognition had been organized by Peter Sint, who came across Hedy's name in an *Economist* article and vaguely remembered her image from old black-and-white films on television: "I supposed it would be useful if her country of origin gave her some recognition too," Sint said. "Actually she wanted to come to fetch the prize but she was already too ill."[18]

To coincide with her eighty-fifth birthday, an exhibition called Hommage à Hedy Lamarr, with photographs, film clips, and other memorabilia, toured Austria. Her birthday, 9 November, is now celebrated as Inventor's Day in Europe. Since 2006, Austria has awarded an annual Hedy Lamarr Prize for special achievement by women in Communications Technology. Still, it seems that recognition of her professional achievements, onstage or off, was slow arriving in the country she spoke of so warmly and so sadly, so often.

Most recently, Hedy has become something of an icon for women inventors and, somewhat ironically, given her reputation, a model for promoting scientific discoveries to young people. These publications include populist histories of scientific invention such as Steve Silverman's *Einstein's Refrigerator* (2001) as well as at least two comic books: Jim Ottaviani's *Dignifying Science* (chapter illustrated by Carla Speed McNeil, 2003) and Trina Robbins's *Hedy Lamarr and a Secret Communication System* (illustrated by Cynthia Martina and Anne Timmons, 2007). All draw closely on *Ecstasy and Me,* relating with some relish the narrative of Hedy's early marriage to Mandl, the filming of *Ecstasy,* the encounter with George Antheil, the failure of the military authorities to capitalize on the patent, and (with the exception of *Dignifying Science*) her belated recognition by the Academy.

If her dreams of a return to the screen were now past, Hedy's fondness for invention remained with her until the end. In her last years, she worked on "a functionable, disposable accordian [sic] type attachment for and on any size Kleenex box" as the solution for used paper tissues.[19] She had a proposal for a new kind of traffic stoplight and some modifications to the design of the Concorde. There were plans for a device to aid movement-impaired people to get in and out of the bath, a fluorescent dog collar, and a skin-tautening technique based on the principle of the accordion. To the end of her days, she could perform devastatingly complex card tricks.

Still, the litigation continued. In 1998, she sued Corel Software Company for illegally using her image in their publicity and was awarded $5 million; compensation, one might say, in however roundabout a fashion, for her neglected career as an inventor. She in turn invested in shares on the stock market. In the same year, the Calgary-based technology company, Wi-LAN bought 49 percent of her interest in the frequency-hopping patent in return for shares in the company and the right to use her name in publicity. This money left her, contrary to rumor, a relatively wealthy woman.

Aside from the inventions and the litigation, the midnight swimming and an addiction to daytime TV, Hedy passed her last years dreaming of writing a new version of her autobiography, one that would tell the real story of her life. Her own, intensely complex relationship with the land of her birth occupied her thoughts as much as did her career in Hollywood, both of which now seemed to belong to a past that was almost inconceivably remote but which had made her who she was. Those who knew her in those last years remembered a woman who was as feisty as she was difficult, her mind still alert and open to new ideas; her memories tinged with bitterness, but little regret.

She was still making new friends (although few met with her face to face) and liked to reminisce with them about her days in Hollywood. One such friendship was with an engineer named Don Nardone from Agoura Hills in California. When he was appointed liaison for one of the technology awards, he called Hedy up to tell her the news. An instant bond formed between the two. For the rest of Hedy's life, they spoke daily on the phone, usually around 10 p.m., their topics ranging from art to music to the stock market.

In October 1999, financially secure at last, Hedy moved again, this time to a three-bedroom house at 968 Wesson Drive in Casselberry, just north of Orlando, Florida. The move, her housekeeper Robin Petts recalled, was traumatic, with the reclusive star hiding behind scarves as she was bundled into her car, "and when we got her there, we pulled her into the garage, because she didn't want anybody to know she was there."[20]

Hedy settled in slowly, only beginning to feel comfortable when she had made over the property to look like her old apartment. The Florida house was gradually transformed into a circa 1920s Viennese home. The once-vanilla walls were repainted a deep burgundy, mixed with greens and golds. She moved in her favored white brocade French provincial sofa and hung a large gold-framed mirror over it. The room was filled with candles, plants, and pictures of her children and grandchildren. She had a selection of photographs of herself, which were displayed on the walls, alongside autographed pictures of James Stewart and Clark Gable. In the dining room, she hung a crystal chandelier. The house had a swimming pool, and at night, just as she had so long ago in Venice, she liked to slip out for a swim. On other evenings, she would sit outdoors, listening to the fountain, which she always kept running. During the day, when she wasn't watching television, she slept; when she did venture out into the daylight, mainly to check her mailbox and often leaning on a cane, she refused to return her neighbors' waves. Her beauty,

HEDY LAMARR

she knew, was gone, and she feared people's responses to her looks. From now on, her only contact with the outside world was to be with a select group of trusted friends, none of whom knew her when she was "the most beautiful woman in the world."

In Casselberry, the most enduring, and demanding, of these friendships was with police lieutenant Chuck Stansel and his family. Stansel had been contacted by an organization that wanted to pay tribute to Hedy for her wartime work. Stansel replied that he'd try to get a message to her. When he called on Hedy, she received him warmly, asking him if he'd like an autographed poster. He thanked her and left her his card, in case she ever needed anything. A week later, she needed a carton of cranberry juice. The friendship was sealed. The family became regular guests at her home and helped her to shop for groceries, visiting her at least twice a week. She was, Stansel remembered, an imperious charge, right up until her death. She would ring him up and demand to be taken to the dentist, or that he come by and fix the coffee machine, or simply buy her cranberry juice. "She ordered the most beautiful clothes from Nordstrom and Talbots and Neiman Marcus," Stansel's wife, Edie remembered. "Always two of everything or even more."[21] A favored outing was to purchase a milk shake from the drive thru.

"To me from the first time I met her she was someone special," Stansel said. "She was a person who needed some help at the time (while she was stuck here on her island) and who later became a good friend to me and my family."[22] Still, she was happiest at home. She loved watching *Judge Judy* and became so excited when *Who Wants to Be a Millionaire* came on that she phoned her friends and called out the answers to them.

Another long-distance friendship was with the celebrated pianist and conductor Michael Tilson Thomas, the music director of the San Francisco Symphony, whom she adored. She had seen his *Keeping Score* program on PBS and admired his ambition to make classical music more accessible. He, in turn, had seen *Ecstasy*, which he considered an "abstract complex movie" and recognized that its star was coming from "a very sophisticated European artsy place." The two exchanged autographed photos and talked often on the phone, always late at night. They discussed, according to Tilson Thomas, "cultural goings-on," and he found she had "a wonderfully amused sophisticated arch quality in the way she spoke about things, a wry fatalistic attitude to civilization." She told him that her life could be condensed into two statements:

"(A) How delighted men were to see how beautiful I was, and (B) How horrified to learn how intelligent I am."[23]

She had a tremendous sense of curiosity about things she didn't know about, he recalled. Interestingly, since he didn't know Hedy was Jewish, Tilson Thomas likened his conversations with her to those he remembered having with his grandmother, Bessie Thomashefsky, who along with her husband, Boris, was a pioneer of the American Yiddish theater. Hedy and Tilson Thomas never met; although he offered to visit, she always turned him down.[24] Indeed, no one knew she was Jewish and to the end of her days, Hedy kept this part of her identity secret.

Hedy's secretary, Canadian Madeleine Merrill, also would become much more than an employee. She and Hedy spoke together in French and Hedy was impressed that Merrill was a Scorpio too. One evening, Merrill was watching television at home when *Ziegfeld Girl* came on. She rushed to the phone, "Hedy, quick! *Ziegfeld Girl* is on television, and you're walking down the steps."[25] On cue, Hedy began to sing the songs from the film, remembering every word, and then described each detail of her dress, which she recalled was pale blue; Lana Turner's had been pink, and Judy Garland's red. On another occasion, when Merrill was at her house, Hedy suddenly decided to treat her confidante to a re-creation of her role in *White Cargo:* the thin octogenarian transformed once more into a dancing, lissome Tondelayo.

Surprise calls from old friends were now far from welcome, and Hedy was suspicious of visitors, many of whom she accused of stealing from her. Sometimes, she seemed confused; on other days she was quite clear. One day, she phoned Merrill. "I want you to call Ted Turner."

"Ted who?"

"You know, Turner Classic Movies," Hedy responded impatiently. "Tell him that somebody stole my movies, and I would like to have them replaced."

Merrill could do no less. Within days, a box of tapes arrived with a note from a Turner staff member commiserating with her for her misfortune and saying that they had replaced all the films they could. That November, they contacted her again to say that they were planning to honor her eighty-fifth birthday by screening a selection of her films.[26]

On their last Sunday together, ten days before Hedy's death, the Canadian remembered that after a leisurely breakfast, the two settled down to watch an old movie on television. The film was *Moulin Rouge,* John Huston's 1952 biopic of French artist Henri de Toulouse-Lautrec. Hedy pointed to Jose Ferrer, who starred in the leading role. "I'm the one who suggested Joe for that role," she told Merrill. As the day grew late, Merrill recognized Hedy's signs of tiredness and said she would leave. Hedy walked her to the door and presented herself for an embrace, as was her wont. This time, Merrill was surprised to find her embrace returned. "Then she said, 'Thank-you, Sweetie,' an endearment she had never used before."[27]

In 1999, Hedy had granted one last interview, to *Vanity Fair* as part of their "Proust Questionnaire" series. Her state of mind was, she said, "terrific." She most enjoyed playing poker and her greatest achievement was "having been a parent." The greatest love of her life was her father; her greatest time of happiness, between her marriages; and her motto, "Do not take things too seriously." Her favorite authors were Khalil Gibran and Tennessee Williams, and her favorite literary figure, Bart Simpson. Michael Tilson Thomas was the greatest living individual. She told her interviewer that she would most like to die after sex.[28]

In the end, on 19 January 2000, Hedy Lamarr died alone in her bed watching TV, an eye-mask on her forehead. This was the way that Chuck Stansel found her the next day; soon enough media reporters, many who knew little about the Viennese star or her films, were on their way to Casselberry. For most of the neighbors, this was the first they knew that they had had a famous movie star living in their midst.

Denise Loder picked out her mother's burial outfit carefully, selecting tailored khaki trousers, a white shirt, and dark blazer topped off with a velvet riding hat. She placed the star's favorite pair of pink sunglasses on her face. Madeleine Merrill made her up carefully, and tucked her hair behind her ears, just the way she liked to wear it. After a small, private funeral with just a dozen mourners, including Denise, Tony, Hedy's stockbroker, and a representative from Austria, the actress was cremated. Tony read Kipling's "If." Back at her home, Hedy's children opened a bottle of Dom Perignon champagne, which Hedy had bought to see in the new millennium but had never opened, and lifted their glasses in a toast to "Mrs. Hedelweiss." It was a nickname she had given herself—a hybrid of her name and the edelweiss flower. Tony Loder promised he would scatter his mother's ashes in the Viennese woods.

Although she had long claimed to be destitute, Hedy left behind an estate valued at $3 million. Much of this money was the result of her final tilt at the legal system, particularly her successful case against Corel. She left a bequest to Chuck Stansel of $83,000. Another beneficiary was Don Nardone. Arlene Roxbury and Madeleine Merrill also received $83,000. She bequeathed her stamp collection to her eleven-year-old grandson. The residue went to Denise ($1.2 million) and Tony Loder ($1.8 million). Her executor was her friend, Arlene Roxbury.

Even after her death the litigation did not end; Hedy had omitted James Loder, now a security guard in Omaha, Nebraska, from her legacy and he sued the estate. As well as claiming that his mother had been of unsound mind and unduly influenced by some of the beneficiaries of the estate, James Loder also, through his lawyer, now officially announced that he was Hedy Lamarr's natural son. The judge was unimpressed by Loder's argument that Hedy had only mentioned two children in her will. The estate offered James Loder around $20,000 to drop his claim, but he declined. Tony and Denise also disputed James Loder's claim that he and Hedy had been reconciled. They had invited him to the funeral, they said, but he had not come.[29] In the end, James Loder settled for $50,000.

In the summer of 2005, Denise and Tony scattered their mother's ashes, appropriately filmed, at "Am Himmel," in the Vienna woods.[30] It would be neat to end at this point, noting only that at last Hedy Kiesler had come home. In fact, her story was to take one more twist. It subsequently emerged that Tony and Denise Loder had only scattered half the ashes; the other half lay in a plastic bag in a cutting room belonging to the production company, Mischief Films, who had organized the scattering of the ashes. Apparently Tony Loder had wanted the second set of ashes to be interred in the Zentralfriedhof, the principal graveyard in Vienna, in the special section called the Ehrengräb, where composers, writers, artists, and politicians are buried. However, he was not prepared to cover the cost, which was estimated at around €10,000. The Vienna City Council stated that it could not pay for the memorial though it would maintain the grave. When Hans Dichand, the publisher of the tabloid newspaper *Kronen Zeitung,* offered to cover the cost of the monument, Loder was not amused. He did not wish for his mother's final resting place to be funded by a newspaper that published pictures of naked women, he announced. In the end, Andreas Mailath-Pokorny, City Councillor for the Arts in Vienna, ordained that the city should pay for the memorial. He further announced that a public space in Vienna would be named after Hedy Lamarr and the "Hedy Lamarr Weg" was created.

At the time of this writing, however, there is no Ehrengräb bearing the name Hedy Lamarr in Vienna's Zentralfriedhof. Hedy Kiesler is still waiting to come home.

Appendix: Lichtwitz Family Tree

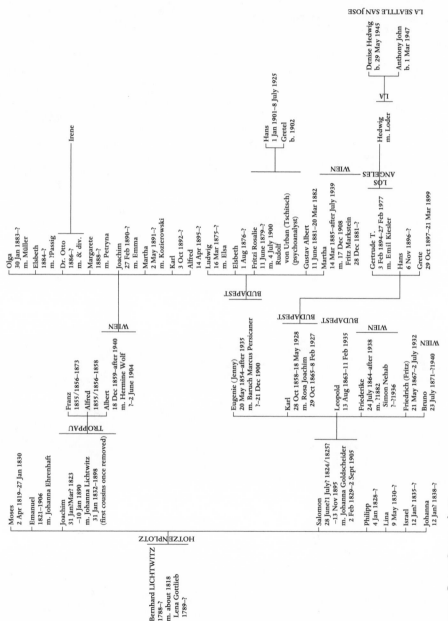

SOURCE: Georg Gaugusch, Vienna

Filmography

Gold on the Streets / Geld auf der Straße (1930)
Director, Georg Jacoby; producer, Nicolas Deutsch; written by Rudolph Österreicher, Friedrich Raff, and Julius Urgiss.

Storm in a Water Glass / Die Blumenfrau von Lindenau / Sturm im Wasserglas (1931)
Director, Georg Jacoby; producers, Herman Fellner and Josef Somlo; written by Bruno Frank, Felix Salten, Walter Schlee, and Walter Wassermann.

The Trunks of Mr. O. F. / Die Koffer des Herrn O. F. (1931)
Director, Alexis Granowsky; producers, Mark Asarow and Hans Conradi; written by Alexis Granowsky, Hans Hömberg, and Léo Lania (also with Peter Lorre).

We Don't Need Money / Fun and Finance / Man Braucht Kein Geld (1932)
Director, Carl Boese; producer, Arnold Pressburger; written by Károly Nóti and Hans Wilhelm.

Ecstasy / Ekstase (1933)
Director, Gustav Machaty; producers, Moriz Grunhut and Frantisek Horký; written by Gustav Machaty.

Algiers (1938)
Director, John Cromwell; producer, Walter Wanger; written by John Howard Lawson.

Lady of the Tropics (1939)
Director, Jack Conway; producer, Sam Zimbalist; written by Ben Hecht.

I Take This Woman (1940)
Director, W. S. van Dyke; producers, [not credited] Bernard Hyman, Louis B. Mayer, and Lawrence Weingarten; written by James Kevin McGuinness.

SOURCES: The Internet Movie Database (IMDB.com [accessed 10 July 2009]); Film Index International (http://fii.chadwyck.co.uk/home [accessed 10 July 2009]).

Boom Town (1940)
Director, Jack Conway; producer, Sam Zimbalist; written by John Lee Mahin.

Comrade X (1940)
Director, King Vidor; producers, Gottfried Reinhardt and King Vidor; written by Ben Hecht and Charles Lederer.

Come Live with Me (1941)
Director, Clarence Brown; producer, Clarence Brown; written by Patterson McNutt.

Ziegfeld Girl (1941)
Directors, Robert Z. Leonard and Busby Berkeley; producer, Pandro S. Berman; written by Marguerite Robbins and Sonya Levien.

H.M. Pulham, Esq. (1941)
Director, King Vidor; producer, [uncredited] King Vidor; written by Elizabeth Hill and King Vidor.

Tortilla Flat (1942)
Director, Victor Fleming; producer, Sam Zimbalist; written by John Lee Mahin and Benjamin Glazer.

Crossroads (1942)
Director, Jack Conway; producer, Edwin Knopf; written by Guy Trosper.

White Cargo (1942)
Director, Richard Thorpe; producer, Victor Saville; written by Leon Gordon.

The Heavenly Body (1944)
Director, Alexander Hall; producer, Arthur Hornblow Jr.; written by Michael Arlen and Walter Reisch.

The Conspirators (1944)
Director, Jean Negulesco; producer, Jack Chertok; written by Vladimir Pozner and Leo Rosten.

Experiment Perilous (1944)
Director, Jacques Tourneur; producer, Warren Duff; written by Warren Duff.

Her Highness and the Bellboy (1945)
Director, Richard Thorpe; producer, Joe Pasternak; written by Richard Connell and Gladys Lehman.

The Strange Woman (1946)
Director, Edgar Ulmer; producers, Hedy Lamarr, Jack Chertok, Eugen Schüfftan, and Hunt Stromberg; written by Herb Meadow, Hunt Stromberg, and Edgar G. Ulmer.

Dishonored Lady (1947)
Director, Robert Stevenson: producers, Jack Chertok and Hunt Stromberg; written by Edmund H. North.

Let's Live a Little (1948)
Director, Robert Wallace; producers, Robert Cummings and Eugene Frenke; written by Howard Irving Young, Edmund Hartmann, Albert J. Cohen, and Jack Harvey.

Samson and Delilah (1949)
Director, Cecil B. deMille; producer, Cecil B. deMille; written by Jesse L. Lasky Jr. and Fredric M. Frank.

A Lady Without Passport (1950)
Director, Joseph H. Lewis; producer, Samuel Marx; written by Cyril Hume.

Copper Canyon (1950)
Director, John Farrow; producer, Mel Epstein; written by Jonathan Latimer.

My Favorite Spy (1951)
Director, Norman Z. McLeod; producer, Paul Jones; written by Edmund L. Hartman and Jack Sher.

L'Amanti di Paradi/Loves of Three Queens/L'eterna Femmina (1954)
Directors, Edgar Ulmer and Marc Allégret; producers, Victor Pahlen and Hedy Lamarr; written by Æneas MacKenzie.

The Story of Mankind (1957)
Director, Irwin Allen; producer, Irwin Allen; written by Irwin Allen and Charles Bennett.

The Female Animal (1958)
Director, Harry Keller; producer, Albert Zugsmith; written by Albert Zugsmith.

Notes

INTRODUCTION

1. Zyda, 1973.
2. Schallert, 1950.
3. Gabor, 1992, 67.
4. Sanders, 1992, 102–3.
5. Basinger, 1993, 166.
6. Barthes, 1993, 57.
7. Negra, 2001, 103–35.
8. Horak, 2001, 34, 37.

1: A CHILDHOOD IN DÖBLING

1. *Creditanstalt Bankverien* was the largest of the Austrian banking houses; the bank was to fall on hard times in the 1920s as a result of the postwar economic depression.
2. Rogin, 1996, 66.
3. For more on the Film Guild Cinema, see Guzman, 2005.
4. Lania, 1942, 28.
5. Joseph, "Hedy's Here!"
6. Kiesler, "Hedl in Hollywood."
7. Ibid.
8. Joseph, "Hedy's Here!"
9. Proctor, "Play Truth or Consequences with Hedy Lamarr."
10. "Hedy Lamarr Writes on the Curse of Beauty," 1951.
11. Dubini and Obermaier, 2006.
12. Lamarr, 1967.

13. Kiesler, "Hedl in Hollywood."

14. Ibid.

15. Lamarr, 1941.

16. Young, 1978, 13.

2: THE MOST BEAUTIFUL GIRL IN THE WORLD

1. Lamarr told this to a reporter in a 1937 interview. Professor Arndt was almost certainly the actor, Ernst Arndt (born in Germany in 1861), who was active in film and theater in Vienna during these years. He took a part in *Leise Flehen Meine Lieder* directed by Willi Forst, in 1933 (see Chapter Four). Arndt died in Treblinka extermination camp, probably in 1942 ("Hedy Kiesler soll Jean-Harlow-Rollen übernehmen," 1937, 2).

2. Lamarr, 1967, 7.

3. Elsaesser, 2000, 332.

4. The film opened in Berlin a month later on 21 April.

5. "Großer Heiterkeitserfolg," 1931; "Sturm im Wasserglass," 1931, 11.

6. "Die Blumenfrau von Lindenau," 1931.

7. *Die Bühne*, March 1931, 6.

8. Reinhardt, 1979. Fans of Carol Reed's *The Third Man* (1949) will remember that it was in the Theater in der Josefstadt that Holly Martins (Joseph Cotton) goes backstage to meet Harry Lime's (Orson Welles) girl, Anna (Alida Valli).

9. "Eine junge Wienerin debutiert bei Reinhardt," 1931, 5.

10. Weller, 1939.

11. Antel, 2001, 14–15; Sinclair, 1987, 21; Dubini and Obermaier, 2006.

12. Friedrich, 1974, 7–8.

13. Ibid.

14. Lania, 1942, 243.

15. Ibid.

16. Adler 1980, 40.

17. Lania, 1942, 244.

18. Ibid.

19. *Lichtbildbühne*, 1931.

20. *Kinematograph*, 4 December 1931.

21. "Die Koffer des Herrn O.F.," 1931.

22. *Film Kurier*, 24 February 1932.

23. *Variety,* 22 December 1931, 21.

24. Lania, 1942, 244.

25. "Die Koffer des Herrn O.F.," 1932.

26. Ibid., 6.

27. *Kinematograph,* 6 February 1932.

28. *Lichtbildbühne,* 5 February 1932.

29. *Variety,* 6 February 1932.

30. *Kinematograph,* 6 February 1932.

31. *Der Film,* 6 February 1932.

32. "Man Braucht Kein Geld," 1932.

33. "Wir brauchen kein Geld," 1931, 6.

3: ECSTASY

1. For a detailed analysis of Machaty's career, see Cargnelli, 2005.

2. *"Extase* in Schönbrunn," 1932, 10.

3. Ibid.

4. Garncarz, 2001.

5. Miller, 1945, 65, 66–67, 70, 75.

6. Lamarr, 1967, 21.

7. Ibid., 22.

8. Dubini and Obermaier, 2006.

9. Jan Stallich quoted in Horak, 2001, 32.

10. Dubini and Obermaier, 2006.

11. Ibid., 23.

12. *"Extase* in Schönbrunn," 1932, 10.

13. "Filmarbeit in Schönbrunn," 1932, 12.

14. "Hedi [sic] Kiesler will nicht nackt austreten," 1933, 6.

15. Jung, 2001, 95.

16. Ross, 2005, 20.

17. Loacker, 2001, 36; Garncarz, 2001, 161.

18. "Krawalle in Ufa-Tonkino," 1933, 12; Rollet, 1933, 7; *Wiener Allgemeine Zeitung,* 21 February 1933, 5; "Filmschund 'Ekstase,'" 1933, 12.

19. "Krawalle in Ufa-Tonkino," 1933, 12.

20. Rollet, 1933, 7.

21. Jung, 2001, 84–93.

22. Harmon, 1937.

23. Hediger, 2005.

24. National Legion of Decency, 1936.

25. Stein, 1936, 15.

26. *Hollywood Spectator,* 1 August 1936, 6.

27. Breen, 1937.

28. Cummins, 1937.

29. Harmon, 1937.

30. Herczif may be a misspelling of Geza Herczeg's name in the PCA files—
Herczeg was a Reinhardt alumnus of Hungarian-German origin who
enjoyed a successful career in exile in Hollywood; my thanks to Chris
Horak for alerting me to this.

31. White and deBra, 1950.

32. Breen, 1937.

33. Cargnelli, 2005, 209–11; Jung, 2001, 84–92.

34. Kael, 1993, 212.

4: FRITZ MANDL

1. *"Extase* in Schönbrunn," 1932, 10.

2. von Dassanowsky, 2006.

3. Author interview with Martha Eggerth, 28 April 2009.

4. Ibid.

5. Luise Rainer had been the first choice to replace Paula, but she was
working in Berlin (*Wiener Allgemeine Zeitung,* 6 January 1933, 5).

6. *Wiener Allgemeine Zeitung,* 7 February 1933.

7. "Wieder eine neue Sissy: Hedy Kiesler," 1933.

8. Newton, 1986; Arnbom, 2002.

9. *Time,* 16 April 1945.

10. Lamarr, 1967, 16; Bock, 1991, 136–37.

11. Arnbom, 2002, 37–38.

12. *Wiener Allgemeine Zeitung,* 28 February 1933, 1–2.

13. *Wiener Allgemeine Zeitung,* 17 May 1933, 3.

14. "I Have Lived by Hedy Lamarr as Told to Marian Rhea," 1939.

15. Lamarr, 1967, 17.

16. Liepmann, 1939.

17. *Los Angeles Times,* 11 January 1940.

18. Ibid.

19. Dubini and Obermaier, 2006.

20. "I Have Lived," 1939.

21. Lamarr, 1967, 19.

22. Ibid., 17.

23. *Wiener Sonn- und Montags Zeitung,* 27 February 1933, 1.

24. Oxaal, Pollak, and Botz, 1987, 161–62.

25. Liepmann, 1939, 83.

26. Bono, 2001.

27. Ibid., 121–22.

28. Ibid., 134.

29. "I Have Lived," 1939.

30. *Daily News,* 19 September 1937.

31. Lamarr, 1967, 27.

32. Puppe Mandl, correspondence with author, 18 March 2009.

33. Young, 1978, 20.

34. Arnbom, 2002, 45.

35. *Daily News,* 19 September 1937.

36. Ibid.

37. Arnbom, 2002, 45.

38. *Time,* 24 November 1947; *The Daily Sketch,* 12 October 1953.

5: The Most Beautiful Woman in the World

1. Remarque, 1998, 276.

2. Tims, 2003, 92–93.

3. Swindell, 1983, 113.

4. Lamarr, 1967, 30, 31 (emphasis in original).

5. Higham, 1994, 2.

6. Schulberg, 1981, 484–85.

7. Preminger, 1977, 49–50.

8. Lamarr, 1967, 33.

9. Goluboff, "Musical Prodigies" (online), 14, 33–34.

10. Lamarr, 1967, 34.

11. Goluboff, "Musical Prodigies."

12. McGilligan, 1991, 222.

13. Ibid.

14. Eyman, 2005, 252–53.

15. Crowther, 1957, 250.

16. "Hedy Kiesler soll Jean-Harlow-Rollen übernehmen," 1937, 2.

17. Troyan, 1999, 102.

18. Eyman, 2005, 316.

19. Kohner, 1977, 111.

20. Dubini and Obermaier, 2006.

21. McGilligan, 1997, 392.

22. Klapdor, 1991, 115.

6: To the Casbah!

1. Lamarr, 1967, 47.

2. Swindell, 1983, 114.

3. *Algiers,* 18 February 1938.

4. Bernstein, 1994, 143.

5. *Algiers,* 18 February 1938.

6. Swindell, 1983, 119.

7. Ibid., 114–15.

8. Lamarr, 1967, 50.

9. "Insanely beautiful," according to Pauline Kael (1993, 14).

10. *Time,* 25 July 1938.

11. Howe, 1969.

12. Kobal, 1991, 144.

13. Gladys Hall Collection, 1938.

14. *Los Angeles Times,* 14 July 1938.

15. Hopper, 1938. Interestingly, at this point, the official narrative of Hedy's marriage to Mandl was not yet fully established; a letter from John LeRoy Johnston, head of publicity, states that she and Mandl separated "over religious differences" (*Algiers,* 18 February 1938).

16. Kellow, 2004, 222–23.

17. Fuller, 2002, 92.

18. "As I See Me," 1941.

7: This Dame Is Exotic

1. Lamarr, 1967, 53.
2. Welles, Bogdanovich, and Rosenabum, 1998, 1–2.
3. Swindell, 1969, 148.
4. von Sternberg, 1987, 277.
5. Lamarr, 1967, 63.
6. Markey, March 1939.
7. Uncredited, undated press clipping from private collection.
8. Summers and Swan, 2001; Dubini and Obermaier, 2006.
9. Summers and Swan, 2001, 184.
10. Ibid.
11. Swindell, 1969, 148–49.
12. Lamarr, 1967, 56.
13. Interestingly, the song was composed by Phil Ohman and predates the similar Cole Porter composition.
14. "Lady of the Tropics," *Daily Variety*, 1939.
15. "Lady of the Tropics," *Photoplay*, 1939.
16. Edison, 1971.
17. McClelland, 1992, 240.
18. West, 2001.
19. *Motion Picture Daily*, 30 January 1940.
20. Lamarr, 1967, 54.
21. *Los Angeles Times*, 30 August 1940.
22. Kotsilibas-Davis and Loy, 1987, 190.
23. *Los Angeles Times*, 28 September 1940.
24. Ibid.
25. Lamarr, 1967, 72–79.
26. Parsons, 1940, 82.
27. Spicer, 2002, 28.
28. Harris, 2002, 223.
29. Summers and Swan, 2001, 162.
30. Lamarr, 1967, 79.
31. *New York Times*, 6 September 1940.
32. *Time*, 26 August 1940.
33. Edison, 1971.

34. Lamarr, 1941, 10.

35. "There's Hope for Hedy," 1941.

36. *Variety*, 11 December 1940.

37. Cornell, 1941–1942, 3.

38. "Come Live with Me," 1941.

8: THE SIREN OF THE PICTURE SHOW

1. Lamarr, 1967, 88.

2. Santon, 1998, 593.

3. Dyer, 2004, 80–86.

4. Ibid., 137–91.

5. Edison, 1971.

6. Richard Thorpe, correspondence with author, 30 May 2009.

7. Wald, 1941.

8. Harmetz, 1993, 48.

9. Lamarr, 1967, 91–92.

10. Marquand, 1941.

11. *New York Times*, 7 September 1941.

12. *Pictorial Review*, 14 September 1941.

13. Marquand, 1959, 50.

14. Ibid., 218.

15. Bell, 1979, 282–83.

16. Basinger, 1993, 244.

17. Vidor, 1972, 52.

18. Ibid., 53.

19. *Hollywood Reporter*, 13 November 1941.

20. Bell, 1979, 287.

21. *New York Times*, 5 November 1941.

22. Kiesler, "Hedl in Hollywood."

23. Lamarr, 1941, 6.

24. *New York Times*, 24 May 1942.

25. Aumont, 1977, 72.

26. Ibid., 75–76.

27. Ibid., 76.

28. Lamarr, 1967, 173.

29. *Hollywood Reporter,* Constance McCormick Collection.

9: THE RATHER UNFEMININE OCCUPATION OF INVENTOR

1. Lamarr, 1967, 93.
2. Uncredited newspaper clipping, Constance McCormick Collection.
3. Breuer, 2001, 184.
4. Hecht, 1943, 38.
5. Braun, 1997, 10–16.
6. Whitesitt, 1983.
7. Hecht, 1965, 155.
8. Antheil, 1945, 255.
9. Antheil, n.d.
10. Antheil, 1945, 255.
11. Ibid., 257.
12. *New York Times,* 1 October 1941.
13. *Los Angeles Times,* 11 October 1941.
14. Antheil, n.d.
15. Antheil, 1942.
16. Elyse Singer and Mauro Piccinini, correspondence with author, 18–17 October 2008.
17. *Time* described the Fourth Symphony as "vulgar, raucous, unabashedly sentimental, as enjoyable as a baseball game or a day at Coney Island" (28 February 1944).
18. Granger, 2007, 72. Another of Antheil's friends was the Viennese dancer Tilly Losch. He introduced her to Hedy and they seem to have hit it off, both enjoying the easygoing atmosphere of dinner at the Antheils' latest home.
19. Antheil, 1945.
20. Antheil, 1945, 258.
21. Mock, 2005, 16.

10: ENTER: LODER

1. Edison, 1974, 353.
2. Cukor and Long, 2001, 56.

3. Loder, 1977, 43.

4. Ibid., 130.

5. Steinbeck, 1976, 111.

6. Ibid., 115.

7. Steinbeck, 1973, 111, 115, 117.

8. Ibid., 70.

9. Kael, 1993, 782, 783.

10. *Hollywood Reporter*, 22 April 1942.

11. Lamarr, 1967, 97.

12. *Screen Guide*, n.d.

13. Breen, 1940.

14. Saville and Moseley, 2000, 153–54.

15. Asper, 2002, 492.

16. Lardner, 1942.

17. Loder, 1977, 132.

18. Ibid., 132–33.

19. Lamarr, 1967, 99.

20. Loder, 1977, 133.

21. Ibid., 171.

22. Briggs, 2007, 93–96.

23. Loder, 1977, 133.

24. Remarque, 1998, 382.

25. *Screenland*, n.d.

26. Lamarr, 1967, 102.

11: Exit: Loder

1. Prokosch, 1983, 116.

2. Negulesco, 1984, 121–22.

3. Ibid., 122.

4. Lamarr, 1967, 107.

5. Henreid, 1984, 161.

6. Lamarr, 1967, 103.

7. Henreid, 1984, 160.

8. *The Conspirators* file.

9. Zweig, 1987, 310.

10. *Hollywood Reporter,* 31 October 1944.

11. Prokosch, 1944.

12. Henreid, 1984, 163–64.

13. Kafka, 2002, 111.

14. Lamarr, 1967, 101–2.

15. Delahanty, 1944; Fujiwara, 1998, 112–22.

16. Lamarr, 1967, 102.

17. Allyson and Leighton, 1982, 44.

18. "Thorpe Does Well with Lean Script," 1945.

19. Lamarr, 1967, 104.

20. Dubini and Obermaier, 2006.

21. Lamarr, 1967, 111.

22. Ibid., 112.

23. Loder, 1977, 138.

24. Loder, 1947.

25. Hopper, 1947.

26. *Los Angeles Times,* 13 July 1947.

12: INDEPENDENCE

1. Eyman, 2005, 339.

2. Lamarr, 1967, 194.

3. The film version was directed by John Stahl in 1945 and starred Gene Tierney.

4. Interview with Shirley Castle. Supplementary material on DVD release of *The Strange Woman.* Edgar G. Ulmer Archive.

5. Peter Bogdanovich, "Interview with Ulmer," in Flynn and McCarthy, 1975, 405.

6. Grissemann, 2003, 238.

7. Weaver, 2001, 235.

8. Vanderbeets, 1991, 144–45.

9. Shirley Castle interview, *Strange Woman.*

10. Gallagher, 2001; Shirley Castle interview.

11. Edgar G. Ulmer File.

12. Lamarr, 1967, 116–17.

13. Moullet and Tavernier, 1961, 14.

14. *New York Times,* 24 February 1947.

15. *Variety*, 1 January 1946.

16. *Time*, 28 October 1946.

17. IMDb, accessed 7 July 2009.

18. Parsons, "The Strange Case of Hedy Lamarr."

19. Summers and Swann, 2001, 186.

20. Breen, 1944.

21. Breen, 25 April 1945.

22. Breen, 11 June 1945.

23. *Los Angeles Herald Examiner*, n.d.

24. Lamarr, 1967, 121.

25. As one reviewer noted, the three acts were almost like three individual stories (Grant, 1947).

26. "Dishonored Lady," 1947. The *Hollywood Reporter* (28 October 1946) tipped her for an Academy Award nomination for *Strange Woman*.

27. *Hollywood Reporter*, 28 October 1946.

28. *New Yorker*, 7 June 1947.

29. Balio, 1976, 203.

30. Edgar Bergen Collection.

31. Letter from Ilse Lahn (Paul Kohner Agency) to Hedy Lamarr, 18 April 1946. Deutsche Kinemathek–Museum für Film und Fernsehen. Nachlassarchiv, 4.3–88/14–6 (1/1).

32. "Laughs Missing in Last Part of Film," 1948.

13: No Man Leaves Delilah!

1. Lamarr, 1967, 137.

2. Wilcoxon, 1991, 162.

3. DeMille papers.

4. Wilcoxon, 1991, 164. In fact, Ian Keith only played a minor role.

5. Contract, CBDM papers.

6. Lamarr, 1967, 140.

7. Head and Castro, 1983, 81.

8. Head and Ardmore, 1960, 99.

9. Ibid.

10. Lasky Jr., 1973, 220–21.

11. Gabor, 1992, 66.

12. Ibid., 67.

13. McClelland, 1992, 130.

14. Lasky Jr., 1973, 221.

15. Birchard, 2004, 336.

16. Kael, 1993, 652.

17. Steinberg, 1981, 434.

18. Lally, 1996, 192–93.

14: Acapulco

1. *Los Angeles Herald Examiner,* 21 June 1950.

2. See also Negra, 2002.

3. *Variety,* 20 September 1950.

4. We know the figure down to the last cent as it later became the subject of a court battle with the Internal Revenue Service.

5. Bogdanovich, 1997, 680.

6. Nevins, 1998, 40–41.

7. Bogdanovich, 1997, 681.

8. *Hollywood Citizen News,* 15 September 1950.

9. Lamarr, 1967, 153.

10. "Hedy Lamarr Writes on the Curse of Beauty," 1951.

11. Ibid., 155.

12. Ibid., 156.

13. Undated, uncredited press clipping, private collection.

14. DeMille papers.

15. Alisau, 2002.

16. Stauffer, 1976, 26.

17. Ibid.

18. Ibid.

19. Ibid.

20. Martin, 1951.

21. Ibid.

22. Stauffer, 1976, 265.

23. Ibid., 266. He also, interestingly, mentions only two children, Tony and Denise, and it seems that James was already out of the picture by 1951.

24. Letter from Paul Kohner to Hedy Lamarr, 15 October 1951.

25. Allegedly one of the prototypes for Vincente Minnelli's satire on Hollywood, *The Bad and the Beautiful* (1952).

26. Letter from Paul Kohner to Hedy Lamarr, 19 February 1952.

27. Dubini and Obermaier, 2006.

28. Summers and Swan, 2001, 185.

29. *Los Angeles Times*, 18 March 1952.

15: Houston, Texas

1. Frazer, 22 December 1953.

2. Gallagher, 2001.

3. Lamarr, 1967, 211.

4. Fraser, 2004, 103–6.

5. Ibid.

6. Although Ulmer scholars believe that he deserves credit for the film in its entirety given his participation in the pre-production process (Krohn, 2002, 161–62).

7. *Los Angeles Herald Examiner*, 18 September 1962.

8. *Los Angeles Times*, 23 April 1960.

9. Henreid, 1984, 164.

10. Frazer, 24 December 1953.

11. Lamarr, 1967, 212.

12. Kaplan, 1955.

13. *Los Angeles Times*, 20 August 1955.

14. Häupl.

15. Anton Haslinger, correspondence with the author, 24 August 2009.

16. Florian Seebolm and Rainer Rigele, correspondence with author, 22 August 2009.

17. Lamarr, n.d.

18. *New York Herald Tribune*, 9 November 1957.

19. Universal Collection.

20. *Pasadena Examiner*, 30 June 1957.

21. Uncredited clipping, Universal Collection, USC Library.

22. Jack Diamond, 5 June 1957, Inter-Office Communication to George Lait.

23. *New York Herald Tribune*, 21 January 1958.

24. Mosby, 1957.

25. *Daily Variety*, 28 October 1957.

26. Mosby, 1957.

27. DeMille papers.

28. *Los Angeles Times,* 16 April 1959.

29. *Los Angeles Times,* 23 April 1960.

30. Unsourced clipping, 1961.

31. *Youngblood Hawke* file.

32. Ringgold, 1965, 44.

33. *Los Angeles Times,* 6 March 1963.

34. *Newsweek,* 18 March 1963.

35. Ringgold, 1965, 45–46.

16: A Filthy, Nauseating Story

1. Lamarr, 1967, 144–45.

2. Gehman, 1950, xi.

3. Lamarr, 1967, 72.

4. Bart, 1966; Bascombe, n.d.; Berman, 1966.

5. Berman, 1966.

6. Dubini and Obermaier, 2006.

7. *Los Angeles Times,* 21–28 April and 13 May 1966.

8. Ibid.

9. Rasmussen, 2002.

10. *Los Angeles Times,* 27 September 1966.

11. Ibid.

12. Ibid.

13. *Hollywood Citizen News,* 21 September 1967.

14. *New York Times,* 18 February 1969.

15. "Hedy Lamarr Book Planned," 1966.

16. Lamarr, 1967.

17. *American Weekly,* 3 February 1952.

18. Sanders, 1992, 103.

19. *Motion Picture,* 16 November 1941.

20. Zweig, 1987, 6.

21. *Los Angeles Herald Examiner,* 22 August 1967.

22. Sutherland, 1968, 3.

23. Prelutsky, 1968.

24. Birmingham, 1970.

25. Ibid.

17: Final Years

1. Dubini and Obermaier, 2006.
2. The production would later be made into a film of the same name directed by David Swift in 1967.
3. *Variety,* 25 September 1974.
4. Edison, 1974, 366.
5. Summers and Swan, 2001, 161–62.
6. Dubini and Obermaier, 2006.
7. "Labeled 'Old,' 'Recluse,' Hedy Lamarr Sues," 1979.
8. Bacon, 1980.
9. Fonzi, "Hedy and Who?"
10. Dubini and Obermaier, 2006.
11. *Los Angeles Herald Examiner,* 6 October 1985.
12. Dubini and Obermaier, 2006.
13. Misch, 2004.
14. Dubini and Obermaier, 2006.
15. Misch, 2004.
16. Brem and Ligthart, 1999, 79.
17. Colonel Hughes, audio clip emailed to the author, 18 August 2009.
18. Peter Sint, email with the author, 30 March 2009.
19. Dubini and Obermaier, 2006.
20. Ibid.
21. Summers and Swan, 2001, 186.
22. Chuck Stansel, email to the author, 4 September 2009.
23. Dubini and Obermaier, 2006. ORF interview, supplementary material on DVD release.
24. Interview with Michael Tilson Thomas, 19 June 2009.
25. Bloodsworth, 2000.
26. Ibid.
27. Ibid.
28. *Vanity Fair,* April 1999, 414.
29. Stutzman, 2000.
30. Misch, 2004.

Bibliography

Allyson, J., and Frances Spatz Leighton. 1982. *June Allyson*. New York: Putnam.

Antel, F. 2001. *Verdreht, Verliebt, mein Leben*. Vienna: Amalthea.

Antheil, G. 1945. *Bad Boy of Music*. London; New York: Hurst and Blackett.

Arnbom, M.-T. 2002. *Friedmann, Gutmann, Lieben, Mandl und Strakosch*. Wien: Böhlau.

Asper, Helmut G. 2002. *"Etwas Besseres als den Tod—": Filmexil in Hollywood; Porträts, Filme, Dokumente*. Arte Edition. Marburg: Schüren.

Aumont, J.-P. 1977. *Sun and Shadow*. New York: Norton.

Balio, T. 1976. *United Artists: The Company Built by Stars*. London; Madison: University of Wisconsin Press.

Barthes, R. 1993. *Mythologies*. London: Vintage.

Basinger, J. 1993. *A Woman's View: How Hollywood Spoke to Women, 1930–1960*. London: Chatto & Windus.

Bell, M. 1979. *Marquand: An American Life*. Boston: Little, Brown.

Bernstein, M. 1994. *Walter Wanger: Hollywood Independent*. Berkeley; Los Angeles; London: University of California Press.

Berry, S. 2000. *Screen Style*. Minneapolis: University of Minnesota Press.

Birchard, R. S. 2004. *Cecil B. DeMille's Hollywood*. Lexington: University Press of Kentucky.

Bock, H.-M. 1991. *Joe May: Regisseur und Produzent*. Munich: Text und Kritik, 125–50.

Bogdanovich, P. 1997. *Who the Devil Made It*. New York: Ballantine.

Bono, F. 2001. "Extase am Lido: Chronik eines Skandals." In *Extase*, ed. A. Loacker. Vienna: Filmarchiv Austria, 115–45.

Brem, R., and T. Ligthart, eds. 1999. *Hommage à Hedy Lamarr*. Vienna: Edition Selene.

Breuer, W. B. 2001. *Deceptions of World War II*. New York: Wiley.

Briggs, C. 2007. *Cordially Yours, Ann Sothern*. Albany, N.Y.: Bear Manor Media.

Cargnelli, C. 2005. *Gustav Machaty: Ein Filmregisseur Zwischen Prag und Hollywood*. Vienna: Synema.

Crowther, B. 1957. *The Lion's Share: The Story of an Entertainment Empire*. New York: Dutton.

Cukor, G., and R. E. Long. 2001. *George Cukor: Interviews.* Jackson: University Press of Mississippi.

Davidson, B. 1987. *Spencer Tracy: Tragic Idol.* London: Sidgwick and Jackson.

Dyer, R. 2004. *Heavenly Bodies.* London; New York: Routledge.

Eisner, L. 1969. *The Haunted Screen.* Norwich: Jarrold and Sons.

Elsaesser, T. 2000. *Weimar Cinema and After.* New York; London: Routledge.

Essoe, G., and L. Raymond. 1970. *DeMille: The Man and His Pictures.* South Brunswick: A. S. Barnes.

Eyman, S. 2005. *Lion of Hollywood: The Life and Legend of Louis B. Mayer.* London: Robson.

Flynn, C., and Todd McCarthy. 1975. *Kings of the Bs.* New York: Dutton.

Fraser, J. 2004. *Close Up: An Actor Telling Tales.* London: Oberon Books.

Friedrich, O. 1974. *Before the Deluge: A Portrait of Berlin in the 1920s.* London: Joseph.

Fujiwara, C. 1998. *Jacques Tourneur: The Cinema of Nightfall.* Jefferson, N.C.: McFarland.

Fuller, S., with Christa Fuller and Jerome Rudes. 2002. *A Third Face: My Tale of Writing, Fighting, and Filmmaking.* New York: Alfred A Knopf.

Gabor, Z. Z. 1992. *One Lifetime Is Not Enough.* London: Headline.

Garncarz, J. 2001. "Ekstase ohne Ende: Variationen eines Films." In *Ekstase,* ed. A. Loacker. Vienna: Filmarchiv Austria, 147–90.

Gehman, R. B. 1950. "Introduction." *The Day of the Locust* by N. West. New York: New Directions.

Granger, F., with R. Calhoun. 2007. *Include Me Out.* New York: St. Martin's.

Grissemann, S. 2003. *Mann im Schatten. Der Filmemacher Edgar G. Ulmer.* Vienna: Paul Zsolnay Verlag.

Harmetz, A. 1993. *Round Up the Usual Suspects: The Making of Casablanca— Bogart, Bergman, and World War II.* London: Weidenfeld & Nicholson.

Harris, W. 2002. *Clark Gable: A Biography.* London: Aurum Press.

Head, E., and J. K. Ardmore. 1960. *The Dress Doctor.* Kingswood: World's Work.

Head, E., and P. Castro. 1983. *Edith Head's Hollywood.* New York: Penguin.

Hecht, B. 1965. *Letters from Bohemia.* London: Hammond.

Hediger, V. 2005. "Film History, Copyright Industries and the Problem of Reconstruction." In *Cinephilia, Movies, Love and Memory,* ed. M. de Valck and M. Hagener. Amsterdam: Amsterdam University Press, 135–53.

Henreid, P., with Julius Fast. 1984. *Ladies Man.* New York: St. Martin's.

Higham, C. 1994. *Merchant of Dreams: Louis B. Mayer, M.G.M., and the Secret Hollywood.* London: Pan Books.

The Internet Movie Database (IMDb). www.imdb.com.

Jung, U. 2001. "Am Ende überwiegt der falsche Mythos, Zur Rezeption von Ekstase." In *Ekstase,* ed. A. Loacker. Vienna: Filmarchiv Austria, 71–113.

Kael, P. 1993. *5001 Nights at the Movies.* New York; London: Marion Boyars.

Kafka, H. 2002. *Hollywood Calling.* Hamburg: ConferencePoint Verlag.

Kellow, B. 2004. *The Bennetts*. Lexington: University Press of Kentucky.

Klapdor, H. 1991. "'A Man Who Has Learned His Lesson': Joe May im amerikanischen Exil." In *Joe May Regisseur und Produzent*, ed. H.-M. Bock and C. Lenssen. Munich: Text Und Kritik, 115–24.

Kobal, J. 1991. *People Will Talk*. London: Aurum.

Kohner, F. 1977. *The Magician of Sunset Boulevard*. Palos Verdes; San Francisco; New York: Morgan.

Körte, P. 2000. *Hedy Lamarr: Die Stumme Sirene*. Munich: Belleville Verlag.

Kotsilibas-Davis, J., and Myrna Loy. 1987. *Being and Becoming*. London: Bloomsbury.

Krohn, B. 2002. "Le Cineaste nu." In *Edgar G. Ulmer: Le Bandit Démasqué*, ed. Charles Tatum Jr. Amiens: Yellow Now, 149–73.

Lally, Kevin. 1996. *Wilder Times*. New York: Holt.

Lamarr, H. 1967 [1966]. *Ecstasy and Me*. Greenwich: Fawcett.

Landis, D. N. 2007. *Dressed: A Century of Hollywood Costume Design*. New York: HarperCollins.

Lania, L. 1942. *Today We Are Brothers: The Biography of a Generation*. London: Houghton Mifflin.

Lasky Jr., L. L. 1973. *Whatever Happened to Hollywood?* London: New York: Allen.

Loacker, A. 2001. "Gustav Machatý in Österreich." *Extase*, ed. A. Loacker. Vienna: Filmarchiv Austria, 25–50.

Loder, J. 1977. *Hollywood Hussar*. London: Howard Baker.

Marquand, J. P. 1959. *H. M. Pulham, Esquire*. London: Collins.

McClelland, D. 1992. *Forties Film Talk*. Jefferson, N.C.; London: McFarland.

McGilligan, P. 1997. *Fritz Lang*. London: Faber & Faber.

McGilligan, P., ed. 1991. *Backstory 2: Interviews with Screenwriters of the 1940s and 1950s*. Berkeley; Los Angeles; London: University of California Press.

Miller, H. 1945. "Reflections on *Extase*." In *The Cosmological Eye*. London: Editions Poetry, 65–75.

Mock, D. 2005. *The Qualcomm Equation*. New York: AMACOM.

Moseley, R. 2000. *Evergreen: Victor Saville in His Own Words*. Carbondale: Southern Illinois University Press.

Negra, D. 2001. *Off-White Hollywood*. New York; London: Routledge.

Negra, D. 2002. "Re-Made for Television: Hedy Lamarr's Post-War Textuality." In *Small Screens, Big Ideas*, ed. J. Thumin. London; New York: I. B. Tauris, 105–17.

Negulesco, J. 1984. *Things I Did . . . and Things I Think I Did*. New York: Linden Press, Simon & Schuster.

Nevins, F. M. 1998. *Joseph H. Lewis*. Lanham, Md.; London: Scarecrow.

Ottaviani, J. 2003. Hedy Lamarr. *Dignifying Science*. Ann Arbor, Mich.: G-T Labs, 13–36.

Oxaal, I., Michael Pollak, and Gerhard Botz, eds. 1987. *Jews, Antisemitism and Culture in Vienna*. London; New York: Routledge and Kegan Paul.

Preminger, O. 1977. *Preminger: An Autobiography.* New York: Doubleday.

Prokosch, F. 1983. *Voices: A Memoir.* London: Faber and Faber.

Reinhardt, G. 1979. *The Genius: A Memoir of Max Reinhardt.* New York: Alfred A. Knopf.

Remarque, E. M. 1998. *Das unbekannte Werk: Fruhe Prosa, Werke aus dem Nachlass, Briefe und Tagebucher.* Cologne: Kiepenheuer & Witsch.

Robbins, T. 2007. *Hedy Lamarr and a Secret Communication System.* Mankato, Minn.: Capstone Press.

Rogin, M. 1996. *Blackface, White Noise.* Berkeley; Los Angeles; London: University of California Press.

Ross, C. 2005. *Naked Germany.* New York; Oxford: Berg.

Sanders, G. 1992. *Memoirs of a Professional Cad.* London: Scarecrow.

Saville, V., and Roy Moseley. 2000. *Evergreen: Victor Saville in His Own Words.* Carbondale: Southern Illinois University Press.

Schulberg, B. 1981. *Moving Pictures.* Chicago: Ivan R. Dee.

Silverman, S. 2001. *Einstein's Refrigerator.* Kansas City: Andrews McMeel.

Sinclair, A. 1987. *Sam Spiegel: The Man Behind the Pictures.* London: Weidenfeld & Nicolson.

Spicer, C. J. 2002. *Clark Gable, Biography, Filmography, Bibliography.* Jefferson, N.C.; London: McFarland.

Stauffer, T. 1976. *Forever Is a Hell of a Long Time.* Chicago: Henry Regnery.

Steinbeck, J. 1973. *Tortilla Flat.* London: Heinemann Educational.

Steinbeck, J. 1976. *A Life in Letters,* ed. Elaine Steinbeck and Robert Wallsten. Harmondsworth: Penguin.

Steinberg, C. 1981. *Reel Facts.* Harmondsworth: Penguin.

Styan, J. L. 1982. *Max Reinhardt.* Cambridge: Cambridge University Press.

Swindell, L. 1969. *Spencer Tracy: A Biography.* London: Coronet.

Swindell, L. 1983. *Charles Boyer: The Reluctant Lover.* London: Weidenfeld and Nicolson.

Tims, H. 2003. *Erich Maria Remarque: The Last Romantic.* London: Constable and Robinson Ltd.

Troyan, M. 1999. *A Rose for Mrs. Miniver.* Lexington: University Press of Kentucky.

Vanderbeets, R. 1991. *George Sanders: An Exhausted Life.* London: Robson.

Vidor, K. 1972. *King Vidor on Film Making.* New York: McKay.

von Sternberg, J. 1987 [1965]. *Fun in a Chinese Laundry.* London: Columbus Books.

Weaver, T. 2001. *I Was a Monster Movie Maker.* Jefferson, N.C.: McFarland.

Welles, O., Peter Bogdanovich, and Jonathan Rosenabum. 1998. *This Is Orson Welles.* Cambridge, Mass.: Da Capo.

Whitesitt, L. 1983. *The Life and Music of George Antheil: 1900–1959.* Ann Arbor, Mich.: UMI Research Press.

Wilcoxon, H., with Katherine Orrison. 1991. *Lionheart in Hollywood: The Autobiography of Henry Wilcoxon.* Metuchen, N.J.; London: Scarecrow.

Young, C. 1978. *The Films of Hedy Lamarr*. Secausus, N.J.: Citadel Press.

Zweig, S. 1987 [1943]. *The World of Yesterday*, trans. Cedar and Eden Paul. London: Cassell.

Articles

Adler, L. 1980. "Alexis Granovsky and the Jewish State Theatre of Moscow." *The Drama Review* 24 (3): 27–42.

Alisau, P. 2002. "Old Acapulco: This Well-Known Tourist Spot Has a Star-Studded History." *Business Mexico* (1 October).

American Weekly. 3 February 1952.

"As I See Me by Hedy Lamarr as Told to Gladys Hall." 1941. *Motion Picture* (16 November).

Bacon, J. 1980. "Hedy Lamarr's Sad Story." *Los Angeles Herald Examiner* (15 February).

Bart, P. 1966. "Hedy Lamarr After the Fall." *New York Times* (6 February).

Berman, A. 1966. "Hedy Lamarr Fired from Comeback Film." *Los Angeles Times* (4 February).

Berman, A. 1966. "Hedy 'Mystified' over Arrest." *Los Angeles Times* (29 January).

Birmingham, S. 1970. "Would You Believe I Was Once a Famous Star! . . ." *New York Times* (23 August).

Bloodsworth, D. 2000. "A Star's Life." *Orlando Sentinel* (12 March).

"Die Blumenfrau von Lindenau" [review]. 1931. *Lichtbildbühne* (22 April).

Braun, H.-J. 1997. "Advanced Weaponry of the Stars." *Invention and Technology* (Spring): 10–16.

Die Bühne. 1931. nr 299 (March): 6.

"Come Live with Me." 1941. *Variety* (22 January): 16.

Cornell, J. 1941–1942. "Enchanted Wanderer: Excerpt from a Journey Album for Hedy Lamarr." *View* 1(9–10): 3.

Daily News. 19 September 1937.

The Daily Sketch. 12 October 1953.

Daily Variety. 28 October 1957.

Delahanty, T. 1944. "'Experiment Perilous,' But Not to Lamarr." *New York Herald Tribune* (20 August).

"Dishonored Lady" [review]. 1947. *Daily Variety* (21 April).

Edison, B. 1971. "By Hedy Lamarr: Eavesdropped by Bob Edison." *New York Times* (26 September).

Edison, B. 1974. "Interview with Hedy Lamarr." *Films in Review* 25(6): 350–55, 366.

"Eine junge Wienerin debutiert bei Reinhardt." 1931. *Wiener Allgemeine Zeitung* (5 May): 5.

"*Extase* in Schönbrunn." 1932. *Mein Film* 365: 10.

Der Film. 6 February 1932.

"Filmarbeit in Schönbrunn." 1932. *Wiener Allgemeine Zeitung* (16 October): 12.

Film Kurier. 24 February 1932.

"Filmschund 'Ekstase.' " 1933. *Die Neue Zeitung* (19 February): 12.

Frazer, M. 1953. "Hedy Lamarr Marries W. Howard Lee!" *The Houston Press* (22 December): 1–2.

Frazer, M. 1953. "Howard, Hedy at Her Ranch." *The Houston Press* (24 December): 5.

Gallagher, T. 2001. "All Lost in Wonder: Edgar G. Ulmer." *Screening the Past.* http://www.latrobe.edu.au/screeningthepast/firstrelease/fr0301/tgafr12a.htm, accessed 3 December 2001.

Goluboff, Grisha. "Musical Prodigies." http://histclo.com/Act/music/pro/ind/g/pro-gol.html. Accessed 19 March 2009.

Grant, J. D. 1947. "Lamarr in Second United Artists Hit." *Hollywood Reporter* (21 April).

"Großer Heiterkeitserfolg." 1931. *Kinematograph* (23 April).

Guzman, T. 2005. "The Little Theatre Movement: The Institutionalization of the European Art Film in America." *Film History: An International Journal* 17(2–3): 261–84.

Häupl, Michael. "Introduction." *Jewish Vienna Heritage and Mission.* Vienna City Administration: 3.

Hecht, B. 1943. "The Doughboy's Dream." *Collier's* (27 February): 11–23, 37–39.

"Hedi [sic] Kiesler will nicht nackt austreten." 1933. *Wiener Allgemeine Zeitung* (14 February): 6.

"Hedy Kiesler soll Jean-Harlow-Rollen übernehmen." 1937. *Mein Film* nr 617: 2.

"Hedy Lamarr Book Planned." 1966. *New York Times* (29 June).

"Hedy Lamarr Writes on the Curse of Beauty." 5 June 1951. *Look.* Constance McCormick Collection USC Cinema-Television Library.

Hollywood Citizen News. 15 September 1950.

Hollywood Citizen News. 21 September 1967.

Hollywood Reporter. 13 November 1941.

Hollywood Reporter. 22 April 1942.

Hollywood Reporter. 31 October 1944.

Hollywood Reporter. 28 October 1946.

Hollywood Spectator. 1 August 1936, p. 6.

Hopper, Hedda. 1938. "Viennese Gallops Into Favoritism." *Los Angeles Times* (17 July): C1.

Hopper, Hedda. 1947. "Loder-Lamarr Break Reported." *Los Angeles Times* (31 May).

Horak, J. 2001. "High-Class Whore: Hedy Lamarr's Star Image in Hollywood." *CineAction* (55): 31–39.

"I Have Lived by Hedy Lamarr as Told to Marian Rhea." 1939. *Movie Mirror* (January).

Joseph, Robert. n.d. "Hedy's Here!" Uncredited clipping, Billy Rose Theatre Collection, New York Public Library.

Kaplan, M. 1955. "Hedy's Missing Gems Found on a Shelf." *Houston Press* (17 June).

Kinematograph. 4 December 1931.

Kinematograph. 6 February 1932.

"Die Koffer des Herrn O.F." 1931. *Der Film* (5 December).

"Die Koffer des Herrn O.F." 1932. *Wiener Allgemeine Zeitung* (5 June).

"Krawalle in Ufa-Tonkino—Polizeiliche Aktion gegen Ruhestörer." 1933. *Neue Freie Presse* (19 February): 12.

"Labeled 'Old,' 'Recluse,' Hedy Lamarr Sues." 1979. *Los Angeles Times* (11 April).

"Lady of the Tropics." 1939. *Daily Variety* (4 August).

"Lady of the Tropics. 1939. *Photoplay* (October).

Lamarr, H. 1941. "The Story of My Life." *Picturegoer* 7(541): 6–7, 10.

Lardner, D. 1942. "White Cargo." *New Yorker* (28 January).

"Laughs Missing in Last Part of Film." 1948. *Hollywood Reporter* (26 October).

Lichtbildbühne. 3 December 1931.

Lichtbildbühne. 5 February 1932.

Liepmann, H. 1939. "Vienna Farewell." *Photoplay* 53(4): 17, 83.

Los Angeles Herald Examiner. 21 June 1950.

Los Angeles Herald Examiner. 18 September 1962.

Los Angeles Herald Examiner. 22 August 1967.

Los Angeles Herald Examiner. 6 October 1985.

Los Angeles Times. 14 July 1938.

Los Angeles Times. 11 January 1940.

Los Angeles Times. 30 August 1940.

Los Angeles Times. 28 September 1940.

Los Angeles Times. 11 October 1941.

Los Angeles Times. 13 July 1947.

Los Angeles Times. 18 March 1952.

Los Angeles Times. 20 August 1955.

Los Angeles Times. 16 April 1959.

Los Angeles Times. 23 April 1960.

Los Angeles Times. 20 August 1960.

Los Angeles Times. 6 March 1963.

Los Angeles Times. 21–28 April 1966.

Los Angeles Times. 13 May 1966.

Los Angeles Times. 27 September 1966.

"Man Braucht Kein Geld." 1932. *New York Times* (16 November).

Martin, P. 1951. "Hedy Sells Her Past." *Saturday Evening Post* (29 February).

Mosby, A. 1957. "Look What Hedy Lamarr Says about Houston and Married Life!" *Houston Press* (12 March).

Motion Picture. 16 November 1941.

Motion Picture Daily. 30 January 1940.

Moullet, Luc, and Bertrand Tavernier. 1961. "Entretien Avec Edgar G. Ulmer." *Cahiers du Cinéma* 122 (August): 1–16.

National Legion of Decency. 28 December 1936. *Motion Picture Review Digest* 1 (54): 42.

Newsweek. 18 March 1963.

Newton, R. C. 1986. "The Neutralization of Fritz Mandl: Notes on Wartime Journalism, the Arms Trade, and Anglo-American Rivalry in Argentina during World War II." *Hispanic American Historical Review* 66(3): 541–79.

New Yorker. 7 June 1947.

New York Herald Tribune. 9 November 1957.

New York Herald Tribune. 21 January 1958.

New York Times. 26 August 1940.

New York Times. 6 September 1940.

New York Times. 7 September 1941.

New York Times. 1 October 1941.

New York Times. 5 November 1941.

New York Times. 24 May 1942.

New York Times. 24 February 1947.

New York Times. 18 February 1969.

Parsons, Louella. 1940. "My Fight for Jimmy." *Photoplay* (October): 82.

Pasadena Examiner. 30 June 1957.

Pictorial Review. 14 September 1941.

Prelutsky, B. 1968. "Hedy . . . Going, Going, Gone!" *Los Angeles Times* (24 March).

Proctor, Kay. n.d. "Play Truth or Consequences with Hedy Lamarr." *Photoplay*, Billy Rose Collection.

Prokosch, F. 1944. "Is Hollywood Dying." *New Republic* (13 November).

Rasmussen, C. 2002. "Tech Invention, Shoplifting Trial Set Hedy Lamarr Apart." *Los Angeles Times* (10 November).

Ringgold, G. 1965. "Hedy Lamarr." *Screen Facts* (11): 1–48.

Rollet, Edwin. 1933. "Extase." *Wiener Zeitung* (21 February): 7.

Santon, Frederick. 1998. "Ziegfeld Girl." *Movie Collector's World*, p. 593.

Schallert, Edwin. 1950. "Hedy May Play Wire Walker: All's Well with C. B. De Mille." *Los Angeles Times* (22 January).

Stein, Fred. 1936. "New York Spectacle." *The Hollywood Spectator* (23 May): 15.

"Sturm im Wasserglass." 1931. *Mein Film* nr 272: 11.

Stutzman, R. 2000. "Court to Weigh Plea of Lamarr's Estranged Son." *The Orlando Sentinel* (30 October).

Summers, A., and R. Swann. 2001. "The Hidden Life of Hedy Lamarr." *Talk*, pp. 160–62, 184–87.

Sutherland, Henry. 1968. "Auction Crowded as Hedy Lamarr's Effects Go on Sale." *Los Angeles Times* (29 January): 3.

"There's Hope for Hedy." 1941. *Picturegoer* (19 April).

"Thorpe Does Well with Lean Script." 1945. *Hollywood Reporter* (11 July).

Time. 25 July 1938.

Time. 26 August 1940.

Time. 28 February 1944.

Time. 16 April 1945.

Time. 28 October 1946.

Time. 24 November 1947.

Vanity Fair. April 1999, no. 464, p. 414.

Variety. 22 December 1931, p. 21.

Variety. 6 February, 1932.

Variety. 11 December 1940.

Variety. 1 January 1946.

Variety. 20 September 1950.

Variety. 25 September 1974.

von Dassanowsky, R. 2006. "Willi Forst." *Senses of Cinema.* Available at: http://archive.sensesofcinema.com/contents/directors/06/forst.html, accessed 25 June 2009.

Weller, George. 1939. "The Ecstatic Hedy Lamarr." *Ken* 21 (January).

West, Sheldon, 2001. Letter to Magazine. *Talk* (May): 2.

"Wieder eine neue Sissy: Hedy Kiesler." 1933. *Wiener Allgemeine Zeitung* (29 March).

Wiener Allgemeine Zeitung. 6 January 1933, p. 5.

Wiener Allgemeine Zeitung. 7 February 1933.

Wiener Allgemeine Zeitung. 21 February 1933, p. 5.

Wiener Allgemeine Zeitung. 28 February 1933, pp. 1–2.

Wiener Allgemeine Zeitung. 17 May 1933, p. 3.

Wiener Sonn- und Montags Zeitung. 27 February 1933, p. 1.

"Wir brauchen kein Geld." 1931. *Wiener Allgemeine Zeitung* (24 December): 6.

Zyda, Joan. 1973. "Vandalism at Museum." *Los Angeles Times* (27 September): OC1.

Unpublished Theses

Goluboff, B. 1999. "Grisha Goluboff: Memories of a Concert Artist." *Music.* Quebec, Universite de Laval. M. Mus.

Documentaries

Dubini, D., and F. B. Obermaier. 2006. *Hedy Lamarr: Secrets of a Hollywood Star.* Produced by Tre Valli Filmproduktion/Dubini Filmproduktion/Obermaier Filmproduktion/MI Films Inc. Germany, Canada, Switzerland.

Misch, G. 2004. *Calling Hedy Lamarr.* Algemene Vereniging Radio Omroep (AVRO); British Broadcasting Corporation (BBC); Hanfgarn & Ufer Film and TV Produktion; Lone Star Productions; Mischief Films; WDR Cologne; arte Strasbourg. (Academy of Motion Pictures. Austria, Germany, Great Britain.

Library Files

Algiers. 18 February 1938. PCA files, Arts and Sciences (AMPAS).

Antheil, George. n.d. Rough jottings, uncatalogued correspondence, H-N, Box 5, George Antheil Collection, Columbia University Libraries.

Antheil, George. 13 July 1942. Letter to William C. Bullitt, Box 1, George Antheil Collection, Columbia University Libraries.

Antheil, George. 17 November 1945. Letter to Hedy Lamarr, Box 5, George Antheil Collection, Columbia University Libraries.

Bascombe, Laura. n.d. "Hedy Lamarr: The Men Who Made Her Suffer, the Man Who May Save Her." *Modern Screen,* Constance McCormick Collection, USC.

Breen, Joseph. 28 May 1937. Letter to Jewel Productions Company. *Ecstasy* PCA File, AMPAS.

Breen, Joseph. 9 July 1940. Letter to Mr. T. P. Geoghegan. *White Cargo* PCA File, AMPAS.

Breen, Joseph. 28 July 1944. Memo. *Dishonored Lady* PCA file, AMPAS.

Breen, Joseph. 25 April 1945. Letter to Hunt Stromberg. *Dishonored Lady* PCA file, AMPAS.

Breen, Joseph. 11 June 1945. Memo. *Dishonored Lady* PCA file, AMPAS.

The Conspirators file. Warner Bros. archives, USC.

Constance McCormick Collection, USC Cinema-Television Library.

Cummins, Samuel. 15 December 1937. Letter to the Motion Picture Producers and Distributors of America, Inc. *Ecstasy* PCA file, AMPAS.

DeMille, Cecil B. [CBDM] papers. L. Tom Perry Special Collections, Box 621, Harold B. Lee Library, Brigham Young University.

Diamond, Jack. 5 June 1957. Inter-Office Communication to George Lait. Universal Collection, USC Cinema-Television Library.

Edgar Bergen Collection. File 12124. USC Cinema-Television Library.

Edgar G. Ulmer File. AMPAS.

Fonzi, Gaeton. "Hedy and Who?" Hedy Lamarr file, Philadelphia. AMPAS.

Gladys Hall Collection. 12 October 1938. AMPAS.

Harmon, Francis. 21 December 1937. Document submitted to Joseph Breen. *Ecstasy* PCA File, AMPAS.

Hollywood Reporter. n.d. Constance McCormick Collection, USC Cinema-Television Library.

Howe, James Wong. 1969. Recollections. Oral history transcript, interviewed by Alain Silver. YRL Special Collections, UCLA.

Kiesler, Gertrude. n.d. "'Hedl in Hollywood' by Her Mother." Gladys Hall papers, AMPAS.

Lamarr, Hedy. n.d. Miscellaneous files. Warner Bros. Archive, USC Cinema-Television Library.

Lamarr, Hedy. 1961. Clippings, Billy Rose Theatre Collection [Billy Rose], New York Public Library for the Performing Arts.

Los Angeles Herald Examiner. n.d. Constance McCormick Collection, USC Cinema-Television Library.

Loder, John. 17 April 1947. Letter to Hedda Hopper. Hedda Hopper Collection, AMPAS.

Markey, Gene. 8 March 1939. Letter to Hedda Hopper. Hedda Hopper Collection, AMPAS.

Marquand, John P. 18 August 1941. Letter to King Vidor. King Vidor Files, USC Library.

Parsons, Louella. n.d. "The Strange Case of Hedy Lamarr." *Photoplay*. Constance McCormick Collection, USC Cinema-Television Library.

Screen Guide. n.d. Constance McCormick Collection, USC Cinema-Television Library.

Screenland. n.d. Constance McCormick Collection, USC Cinema-Television Library.

Universal Collection. USC Cinema-Television Library.

Unsourced clipping. 1961. Billy Rose Theatre Collection, New York Public Library.

Wald, Jerry. 23 December 1941. Memo to Irene Wald. Casablanca Story File, Warner Bros. Archives, USC.

White, Gordon S., and Arthur deBra. 31 January 1950. Inter-office memo to Sidney Schreiber. *Ecstasy* PCA file, AMPAS.

Wilkerson, W. R. n.d. *The Hollywood Reporter,* Constance McCormick Collection, USC Cinema-Television Library.

Youngblood Hawke file. Warner Bros. archive, USC Cinema-Televison Library.

Index

Cooper, Gary, 65
Copper Canyon, 179–80
Cornell, Joseph, 96–97
Coward, Noel, 30
Crawford, Joan, 5, 74, 100, 113, 161
Cromwell, John, 70–71, 73, 84
Crosby, Bing, 113
Crossroads, 128
Crowther, Bosley, 94
Cuban missile crisis, 2
Cukor, George, 126
Cummings, Robert, 167
Cummins, Samuel, 37–39
Cup of the City of Venice, 55
Curtiz, Michael, 166

Dadaists, 117, 123
Dantine, Helmut, 140
Dark Victory, 141
Daves, Delmer, 201
Davies, Marion, 127, 135
Davis, Bette, 5, 113, 127, 138, 147, 149, 152, 161, 201
Dawson, Frankie, 190
Dead Man's Shoes, 128
death, 231–32
deBra, Arthur, 41
Del Luca, Cino, 189
delusions, 215
DeMille, Cecil B., 3, 39, 140, 169–71, 173–74, 183, 185, 200, 204
Destry Rides Again, 180
de Toth, Andre, 161
Deutsches Theater, 21
de Wolfe, Elsie, 136
Dick Cavett Show, 218
Dietrich, Marlene, 21, 60, 66, 73, 75, 79, 87, 89, 113, 128, 180
Dietz, Howard, 64
Dignifying Science, 227
Dishonored Lady, 161
    message, 164–65
    reviews, 165
    shooting, 162
    story, 163–64
disorientation, 199

divorces
    Edward Stauffer, 187–89
    Fritz Mandl, 56–57
    Gene Markey, 89–91
    J. Howard Lee, 199–201
    John Loder, 149–51
    Lewis Boies Jr., 202
Döblinger Mädchenmittelschule, 12
Döderlein, Alfred, 21
"Doughboy's Dream, The," 114–15
Dow, Richard, 1
dream images, 5
Duel in the Sun, 126
Duff, Warren, 145
Dunne, Irene, 114

Ecstasy, 1, 10, 28, 84, 174, 201, 227, 229. See also *My Life*; *Symphony of Love*
    aesthetic beauty, 32
    as art, 38–39
    audience response, 31, 36
    bathing scenes, 30
    court cases, 40–41
    Fritz Mandl and, 49
    language versions, 30
    lovemaking scene, 33
    marketing, 39
    nude bathing scenes, 30, 32–34, 93
    politics, 32
    premiere, 35
    remake, 41
    reviews, 35–36
    story, 30–32
    success, 43
    underground, 41–42
    in United States, 37–42
    at Venice Film Festival, 54
    Vienna release, 36
Ecstasy and Me (Lamarr), 4, 14, 16, 43, 91, 108, 147, 152, 160, 163, 169, 188, 191, 204–5, 212–16, 218, 227
Eden, Anthony, 103
Edens, Roger, 102
Edgar Bergen/Charlie McCarthy radio show, 107–8, 165–66
Edison, Bob, 87, 221